ON THE VERGE OF THE VERB

AN AUTOBIOGRAPHICAL FICTION
OF PROPHETIC SORTS

Gabriel Meyer

Red Elixir
Rhinebeck, New York

On the Verge of the Verb: An Autobiographical Fiction of Prophetic Sorts © Copyright 2024 by Gabriel Meyer

All rights reserved. No part of this book may be used or reproduced in any manner without the consent of the publisher except for in critical articles or reviews. Contact the publisher for information.

Paperback ISBN 978-1-960090-84-3
eBook ISBN 978-1-960090-85-0

Library of Congress Control Number 2024945305

Book design by Colin Rolfe

Red Elixir is an imprint of Monkfish Book Publishing Company

Red Elixir
22 East Market Street, Suite 304
Rhinebeck, New York 12572
(845) 876-4861
redelixirbooks.com

PRAISE FOR ON THE VERGE OF THE VERB

"Some books come from a person, and some books come *through* a person. The former are like dried fruit whose wisdom is preserved and always available. They have no expiration date. The latter are like fresh fruit so ripe they must be eaten or lost. Their expiration date is always Now. Gaby Meyer's *On the Verge of the Verb* is the latter. Eat it Now or its Wisdom will be lost." —**Rabbi Rami Shapiro**, author of *Zen Mind, Jewish Mind*

"In this engaging and charming text, Gabriel Meyer uses non-fiction fiction to embark us on a journey, weaving together the real and the utopia on an autobiographical portrait. The book is a play on the mysterious border between the dream as 'illusion' and the dream as 'project,' as a vision for the future. Meyer uses this with politics, spirituality, and love.

"A tour through space, from Argentina to India, Jerusalem, and beyond, and through intergenerational time. From his parents' dream— Gabriel is the son of the visionary rabbi blending human rights with ethics and the spirit—to the son's dream, manifested in song, joy, and sacred activism."—**Rabbi Nilton Bonder**, bestselling author and member of the Brazilian Academy of Literature, founder of Midrash Cultural Center

"*On the Edge of the Verb* is a critical contribution to our collective imaginary. It is one of the most relevant pieces of visionary fiction at a time when our culture is bereft of alternative cosmologies and worldviews that can orient us in times of breakdown and renewal. Meyer's life experience as an activist, musician, organizer, and sacred scribe brings to bear a kaleidoscope of possibility, hope, and presence in the midst of transition." —**Alnoor Ladha**, co-founder of *The Rules, Tierra Valiente,* and *Culture Hack Labs*; co-author of *Post Capitalist Philosophy: Healing wealth in the time of collapse*

"Intriguing, as a journey should be, like a map of the heart, responding to the imagination of reality." —**Tiokasin Ghosthorse**, Mnikhówožu/ Itázipčo Lakȟóta

"This is a brave book about sacred activism, with a stunning vision at its center so persuasive that, after reading, you will say: I want to know this man. I want to meet his friends. *I want to hear his music; I want to have his life.*" —**Roshi Eve Myonen Marko,** founding teacher, Zen Peacemaker Order

"You must read this book. A common songline for peace-activists, connecting with the spring and the river finding their way back home to the ocean, and facing the reality of war but never giving up the love to the tender secret of peace and life." —**Sabine Lichtenfels,** co-founder of Tamera Peace Reesearch EcoVillage

"In his passionate spiritual odyssey, Gaby Meyer dances at the nexus of indigenous, Hebraic, Sufi, and other-worldly mystical wisdom, unfolding stories from a rich lifetime of travel at the edge of the possible. Hilarious, surprising, provocative, and full of longing, the reader cannot resist joining the magic of the adventure." —**Rabbi Tirzah Firestone,** author, Jungian psychotherapist, and Jewish scholar and teacher

"From Buenos Aires to New York, Jerusalem to Portugal, Gabriel takes you on an inner and outer journey in search of the Big Vision. And in the course of his travels, life is always unfolding. Nothing is static—all is in movement, and the destination is collective liberation." —**Stephen Apkon,** Co-Founder/Executive Director of Reconsider, Executive Producer of *Fantastic Fungii* and producer of *Disturbing the Peace*

"You do not want to put this book down. Gabriel takes you on a journey of imagination through multiple dimensions. He invites you to expand your perception of what we think we know by inviting you to enter the realm of lucid dreaming. He reminds you that peace making is about bringing heart, soul and creativity together. This books needs a genre of its own." —**Sami Awad,** Palestinian Peacemaker, founder of The Holy land Trust, spiritual coach, currently Co-Director of Nonviolence International

CONTENTS

Acknowledgments	vii
Prologue	ix
Preface	xvii
Back to My Origins	xix
CHAPTER 1: THE CALL	1
Buenos Aires – 1984	
Sinai – 2018	
CHAPTER 2: POINT ZERO	13
Lisbon	
Marrakesh – 1998	
Buenos Aires – 1987	
Greece – 1988	
CHAPTER 3: DUE SOUTH	23
Brazil – 2003	
Ireland – 1993	
India – 1996	
Cappadocia – 2002	
Eynif Plateau - 2005	
Tantur – 2000	
Dharamsala – 2005	
South Africa – 2014	
1979 and 2017 – Buenos Aires to Tamera	
Gush Etzion/West Bank – 2014	
West Bank – 1998	
Philadelphia – 1995	
CHAPTER 4: DUE NORTH	107
Paris – 1989	

Shaharut – 2006
New York – 1990
Portugal – 2017
Buenos Aires – 1976
CHAPTER 5: DUE WEST   129
CHAPTER 6: DUE EAST   153
Buenos Aires – 1979
Buenos Aires: 1981–1983
CHAPTER 7: SCOUTING   164
Below
New York – 1993
Above
On To Jerusalem
CHAPTER 8: BACK TO SINAI   176
Taos – 1995
CHAPTER 9: NOBEL LAUREATES   196
The Presentation
CHAPTER 10: BACK TO PORTUGAL   205
CHAPTER 11: LAUNCH OF THE CARAVANS   208
CHAPTER 12: BEYOND GRIEF – CAVE OF MACHPELAH   213
CHAPTER 13: AS BELOW, SO ABOVE   218
CHAPTER 14: THE HEART OF THE MATTER   221
EPILOGUE   225
SONGS FROM THE BOOK   227

ACKNOWLEDGMENTS

I'm in deep gratitude to the midwives of this project.

First, to the wise and generous Sufi heart of my dear brother, whom I will not name to honor his desire to annihilate identity.

Thanks to all the early readers and editors of the embryonic stages of this book: Shira Jacobson; Guy Liberman; Rabbi Nilton Bonder; Jane Isay for her expertise and always timely, loving, and generous advice and encouragement; and many others who just heard or read my prologue, preface, and epilogue and cheered me on.

Thanks to Ruth Gordon, the book's first editor in the early stages of my manuscript, for her dealings with an English-as-a-second-language writer and all that entails.

In gratitude to Tiokasin Ghosthorse and Chief Arvol Looking Horse for their Lakota wisdom. You can find more here: www.worldpeaceandprayer.com.

In gratitude to my blood family and all my relations who supported me along the way.

In deep appreciation to the wonderful real-life and fictional characters who fill my book with their wonderful vitality and wisdom. I did my best to be accurate and reflect your ways. If anyone is not happy with the results, I ask for your forgiveness.

I'm in deep gratitude to my editor Kirsten Webb, who showed up at the right time, with the right flow, empathy, grace, and encouragement to wrap this book up for the publisher.

Lastly, thanks to my publisher Paul Cohen and his team at

Monkfish Publishers for believing in my writing and getting it into print, to Colin Rolfe for the fitting and beautiful design, and to Ganesh Dass, Carly, and Jon Bleicher of Prospect PR for helping me get the word out.

Note: This book was finished before the horrific events of October 7th, 2023, and the bloodbath that followed and continues as I write these words. The book's vision for healing the prophetic land remains current and awaits the right timing for radical imagination to lead all living beings into a safer, freer, more just and beautiful reality from the Jordan river to the Mediterranean Sea.

PROLOGUE

Careening through wild geography and time, we had arrived at the heart of Jerusalem, in pilgrimage from the four corners of the Earth. We had witnessed, in awe, the Pope kneeling in front of an Amazonian Indigenous chief and a council of Indigenous elders, weeping, then nullifying, tearing up, and burning the Doctrine of Discovery[1] in front of our very eyes.

Three days later, most everyone was gone. It was just me and my friend Tiokasin, a Lakota elder, musician, and practical mystic. There we were: Tiokasin on a handsome and abandoned rocking chair, and me laying on my favorite hammock under the generous shade of the old olive tree near the spring, "verbing" it away in what felt like an ongoing conversation without beginning or ending.

While immersed in global pandemics, social revolution, and climate catastrophe, you who are reading these words might feel these to be uncertain terrains for a lucid conversation.

Tiokasin had been part of our whole adventure through the fertile crescent. One of the first Indigenous elders we had contacted, he was a Lakota sundancer, a proper elder, a friend, and one of the few hundred last carriers of the old Lakota language. He still remembers the old ways from his grandparents, and in his presence, one can sense this. He exudes a simple and practical mysticism, combining

---

[1] The Doctrine of Discovery was a document written by the Pope in 1453 declaring all savages in the newly "discovered" lands inhumane, thus allowing them to be killed, taken as slaves, baptized, and their lands made available for any Christian to take freely.

humor, lightness, and joy in a generous and abundant life. His resilience derives, in part, by the traumas of oppression he endured on the Cheyenne River Reservation as he tried to make a life in the colony that once, five hundred years ago, was a free land called Turtle Island—a land woven in awe and humility with the Creator's original instructions.

It had been quiet and cool for a while under the olive tree near the spring. The breeze massaged our arteries as we delighted in rest. We shared the silence, our hearts beating in sync.

"Wow," Tiokasin said, smiling widely.

I "wowed" back.

"Man, those camels!" said Tiokasin.

"And those boats!" I replied.

"Oh, man!" Tiokasin's mood was contagious and visible. Though his demeanor is usually calm, his joy spills over like a child's when his heart feels heard and trusted.

"The Doctrine of Discovery—burnt!" he added.

Watching the Indigenous Council of Elders, and Arvol Looking Horse's face when the Pope knelt in front of them and incinerated the original document of the Doctrine of discovery, had given me goosebumps. It felt like we were witnessing the rewilding of Jerusalem. The collective imagination had magically experienced a beautiful leap, both ancient and newly relevant. These were building blocks of peace and trust based not on the principles of *Pax Romana* but created from real, whole, aboriginal Hebrew and Arabic *salaam* and *shalom*.

Although overwhelmed and exhausted by all that had transpired in the last three years, and especially in the last weeks and days, we were still elated and overflowing. The birds, the wind, and the magic of Ein Karem's layers of culture enveloped, nourished and soothed us as we gazed at a minaret still standing above Mary's Spring in the mostly Jewish neighborhood on the outskirts of Jerusalem.

The feminine waters, in their abundant and sacred hospitality, held us beyond our friendship, beyond our encounter as allies. It felt as if Lakota and Hebrew angels were hovering above us and climbing up and down our spines. Tiokasin began to dwell on the mysteries of water, or *Mni* in Old Lakota. As he delved into *Mni's* relational ways, I was reminded of the "wasiswillbe"—the fluidity of the divine Hebrew Tetragrammaton *YHVH* as an ever-changing verb, and the sacred, primordial breath—infusing and creating all that is, was, and will be.

Tiokasin explained, "Water is not a noun. Lakota is a verb-based language. We have no noun logic. The 'm' is the relationship between all creatures. The 'n' is living, like the 'ing' verb, always in motion. The 'i' is voicing—giving voice to the living relationships between you and me and all creatures. *Mni* is part of the Lakota creation story. It offers a shining transparent mirror to the Universe. *Mni* carries the whole of Creation in her womb: oceans, rivers, lakes, ponds, creeks, streams, rains, floods, waves, humidity, wetness, hurricanes, tornadoes, rainbows, and the teardrops of babies."

"So beautiful!" I said, relishing my dear, tall, northern friend's words. "Yes, water is not a noun—no thing, or rather no one, is a noun. Everyone is 'interbeing,' as Thich Nhat Hanh says, constantly in motion. When nouns, concepts, objectification, and ideas rule, verbs die. Nouns are the cemetery of verbs," I declared.

Tiokasin kept going. "*Mni* is in your breath, your tongue, your fingertips. *Mni* is dreaming within you, safeguarding your memories. *Mni* makes us humble when we think we are important. As soon as we respect the Indigenous cultures again, the human species will return to the original instructions given to us. This is the language of Mother Earth, which was ignored for so long in the scientific, political, and religious explanations about life. *Mni* is now considered to be a resource instead of a source of life."

I chimed in, "You know, according to Hebrew legend, water is *mayim*, which was divided at creation into rain, the upper waters, and springs, the lower waters. *Shamayim*, sky, can be read as *sham mayim* meaning 'there is water.' Sun, *shemesh*, can be read as *sham esh*: 'there is fire.' We call water *Mayim Chayim*, living waters, similar to *Mni Wiconi*. And just as water is the source running through our veins and arteries inside our blood, the rivers and seas run through the body of the Earth, infusing it with sacred Life."

Tiokasin continued, "Makes sense to me. Every morning I splash *Mni* on my face and cool the fire in my eyes. I sprinkle drops over my head and body in recognition and gratitude for life. I ask for permission before drinking *Mni*. *Mni* is a loving and cleansing powerful living being, a liquid full of stars."

"You know," I said, "Martin Buber, in his book *I and Thou*, says we constantly have the opportunity to be in real relationship with every single creature, seen and unseen, not as a resource but as a source, like you said—a living being like us. *Same same but different*." I humored myself, using one of my favorite Indian expressions.

"I am because you are" could be Martin Buber's Hasidic version of *Ubuntu*, the Bantu African maxim of interdependence, which echoes the phrase *In Lak'ech Ala K'in* ("I am another yourself") in the Mesoamerican tradition and chooses relationship rather than objectification as the guiding ethical principle.

I continued, "We've been, and are still trying, to live through times and civilizations whose systems exile the heart. The mind has taken over, not as intelligence in service of the heart, but as the boss who severed us from our sacred origins and propelled us towards the brink of annihilation."

"If we really listen with the Earth," Tiokasin said, "we can feel its seeds growing in the dark soil, in the bottoms of the ocean, as coral reefs regenerate. We remember our beauty and role in harmony with all creatures, the original way to be human, made of humus. Faithful to our origins, our 'original instructions,' as *Oyáte*[2] calls it."

"You know," I said, "my dad, Rabbi Marshall T. Meyer z'l—his memory is a blessing—was studying with Buber at the Hebrew University in the '50s, right here in Jerusalem. Buber was one of his two main mentors. In fact, he is the reason why I was born and grew up in Argentina."

"Really?" My elder friend was happily surprised.

"My Dad had just gotten his rabbinic ordination and was about done with his doctorate on the philosophy of religion—he just had to complete his thesis to get his PhD. His parents—my grandparents—had

---

[2] *Oyate*: "Our people" in Lakota.

both died recently. He had been offered a two-year job in Argentina. They needed a rabbi there. He asked Buber if he should finish his thesis or go to Argentina to take his new post. Buber looked at him and said in a heavy German accent:

"'Young man, do you want to write about history, or do you want to make history?'

"My father was twenty-nine years old when he arrived in Argentina. He needed to get as far away from his known life as possible. He was already married to my mom, who was twenty-three years old. They packed up their life and left New York City to go to Buenos Aires, utterly ignorant of where it was and not knowing a word of Spanish. Both my sisters and I ended up being proudly born and raised in Argentina. So, there you have it."

"The South, the land of the Condor. Remember the Mapuche youth's song at the double cave?" Tiokasin asked. I smiled in deep gratitude and then remembered Tiokasin flipping Descartes' famous Enlightenment dichotomy with the words "We thank therefore we are."

"Someday I'll be able to visit again," he said, "and we can sit on the Earth's sand and smoke a pipe. We will ask it to rain, ask it to dance, ask it to shine, to glisten in the dawn, and to restore memories that she never forgets. Peace with Earth, not just peace on Earth. No more and no less anymore."

We stopped speaking and listened to the birds for a while, relishing the silence between us. They charmed us with their songs; there was no competition in their singing, and they fit perfectly together without any one bird trying to outdo the other. Together, they were an amazing, sacred, living soundscape, accompanied masterfully by the melody of the wind, "magic carpeting" us into relationship with all things, rooting us into our voices and emerging from our throats as words.

Tiokasin continued, "You know, in this extractive way of thinking, even in the so-called new age 'spiritual' and 'medicine' circles, people go to 'Nature' to listen to her. We don't have a word for 'nature' in Lakota. It pains me to even say that word as a noun. So they go to

Nature, to get something, tame it, and bring it back as a trophy into their lives. It's all about what can give them more power. In this paradigm of Western civilization, we are always thinking of our growth, our profit, 'what can we get out of it.' It's an intrinsic and essential ingredient of our anthropocentric civilization.

"In our native culture, we humans are just a tiny part of it all. The emphasis is on the harmony between relationships, on each being fulfilling our sacred work to re-member that the food grows us, makes us who we are. We don't grow the food.

"We humans are the youngest creature, the last to arrive at the hoop of life. We should be learning and getting counsel from our elders: the rivers, rocks, trees, animals—beings who are still imbued with the original instructions.

"You know, I grew up on a reservation, and we had the biggest herd of buffalo on Turtle Island. The *rez* was surrounded by white man's cattle and their ranchers.

"One day a buffalo calf lost its way and, without being noticed, strayed into the cow herd.

"The ranchers saw the shift in the cattle herd. The cows were acting different, wild. No one knew why this was happening until the ranchers finally spotted the buffalo calf and got it out of the herd. The cows immediately returned to their domesticated habits, far estranged from the 'original instructions' which the buffalo calf still carried intact."

It felt calm around, inside, and between us. We both usually receive deep nourishment through our time together. Accepted for who we really are, when trust is the trampoline of our encounters, we can shine our beauty and put our inadequacies and insecurities to rest. Words are a "shout out" to the Divine in everyone, everywhere; the Sufis call Moses *Kalim Allah*, or Speaker of Allah[3]. As we are initiated into maturity, as our ancestors springboard us into our elderhood, as we become part of it all, conversation becomes prayer.

Indeed, our conversation felt like an ancient, ongoing, and present field of liminal celebration. Celebration of breath. Celebration of

---

[3] *Allah*: Arabic for the Divine, specific for Islamic culture.

the Great Mysteries. Celebration of Great Spirit. Celebration of life, water, fire, air, animals, plants, rocks, and Mother Earth—and ultimately, the celebration of our vulnerable, humble, and broken selves in right relation with all else.

"I feel we just witnessed a glimpse of whole alignment—races, guilds, and religions reemerged to bring about spirit action in an archetypal stress spot. Acupressure, massaging one knot at a time. The Cave of the Machpelah, the Old City of Jerusalem, and the reversal and healing of thousands of years of 'power over' and domination. Conquest, crusades, inquisition, oppression, repression, and violence since the times of the Sumerians. The theft and hoarding of power through the fetishes of writing, patriarchy, rationalism and hierarchy. Apartheid of the heart and the feminine principles, the government of private property. A 'forgetting' that we are embedded in Mystery and our heartbeat oozes radical amazement at each breath."

PREFACE

PEOPLE OFTEN ask me to describe my gifts and work in the world. This is the latest version I've come up with: "Flexitarian Global Minstrel, Cross-Cultural World-Bridger, Celebrating Spirit, Beyond Enemy Lines."

"Ha!" they respond. "WTF is that? No, seriously."

So, I add into the fold: musician? Peacemaker? Sacred activist? Poet? Keynote speaker? They all sound pretty off, petty and incomplete.

Needless to say, most people see me as someone who is not easy to confine to a label.

"Married or not? Monogamous or polyamorous? You never had any kids?" They ask, often with disappointment and pity. With each of these questions, my soul shrinks, my intrinsic light becomes opaque. The flow of my pulsating life dehydrates.

Binary classification usually takes the wonder away from any breathing being. We become as lifeless and inert as the tone of our "inquisitor." It's uncomfortable for most people to let our identity hang loosely in their perception.

In general, people have a hard time relating to someone they cannot pin down and "de-scribe" or "ex-plain," someone who doesn't fit in one of the well-organized drawers of our brains' filing cabinets. Furthermore, most humans never redesign their brains. They stay with the same interior decoration and look-alike furniture for most of their lives. Their conditioning of learned concepts, ideas, identities, stays as frozen as Walt Disney after death.

To illustrate, here's a story of one of my most important teachers, the late Rabbi Zalman Shachter Shalomi, his memory is a blessing, on his visit to Brazil.

At great peril to his job and at a great financial cost, Rabbi Nilton Bonder had convinced his board of directors to bring his friend and teacher, the iconoclastic Rabbi Zalman, to Rio de Janeiro. He gathered the mainstream Brazilian media for a press conference to get to know the rabbi. At the press conference, whenever a journalist would ask a question, Reb Zalman would play with his white beard for what seemed like minutes but no answer would come out of his mouth. Next journalist, same story: question, white beard, no answer.

As the Q&A continued, Nilton started feeling really frustrated with his rebbe, who had always been critical towards the cultish following of a teacher. When the journalists started leaving, Nilton understood it was all over. He took the microphone and thanked everyone for coming.

He then approached Zalman, visibly disturbed.

"Reb Zalman, you know, I could lose my job for this. I brought together the most important journalists so that people in Brazil could get to know you. I convinced my board and raised the money to bring you all the way to Rio for this? What happened? You were fondling your white beard as any cheap guru would do! You, who have always looked down on the adoration of disciples for their gurus who bypass their own spiritual responsibility."

R. Zalman looked at Nilton with a smile and said, "Do you want to know what happened?"

"Yes!" Nilton answered impatiently.

"Well, whenever a journalist asked me a question, I went through the following process: first, I thought 'have I been asked that question before?' Then, I tried to remember what I had answered previously. Finally, I reflected on how I would answer this question now.

But I guess my process was too slow, because you kept calling on the next journalist to ask another question—so I couldn't respond in time."

Back to My Origins

AS FOR my beginnings, I was born and grew up in Argentina. Because my parents were both from the US, though, I was never Argentinian enough.

When she picked me up from school, my poor mother couldn't talk to me in Spanish because she had a terrible American accent. Little me, trying to fit into the social mold, also instructed her not to talk to me in English either, "cause it's weird." Basically, I told her not to talk to me at all. In school, I was the only son of a rabbi. I was too religious to go to my friends' birthdays on Shabbat, and in high school, too committed to human rights to ignore the military dictatorship. I was always quite different from everyone else. The odd one of the pack. The rebel in my family. I was even kicked out of kindergarten!

When I got to Israel, as I tried to carve out my role, voice, and space in Israeli culture, I felt deeply misunderstood. Are you religious or secular? Ah...then you are "reform[1]"? Are you spiritual or a cynic? After many nomadic adventures, my status was simply "based" in Israel. I never became "Israeli" enough. I had neither the childhood jokes, TV culture, nor the army lingo to share with my Israeli peers. I wasn't enough of a "musician" for my musician friends and not enough of a "theater person" for the theater world. In my Spirit pursuits, I was not "Jewish" enough, or "Sufi" enough, not "Buddhist" enough, not "shamanic" enough, not "secular" enough, not a "gardener" enough, not "activist" enough...the list kept piling up. My art wasn't "Israeli" enough, and it wasn't "international" enough either. I wasn't enough of a leader or a winner as I played soccer as a defensive midfield, made very few goals, and was always afraid to take a penalty kick. I was always more of the "adviser," the closest to the

---

[1] Reform: One of the more open religious movements in Judaism, born in the nineteenth century.

leader. More Robin than Batman, more ping pong than tennis, more poetry than novel.

Playing hopscotch through my spirit's itinerary and random chronology: from my native Argentina to my parents' New York, from Marrakesh to India, from Ireland to Brazil, from Paris to Taos, from South Africa to Turkey. From Sufis to Roshis, from shamans to artists, from rabbis to activists. From city to desert, from jungle to island. Skipping through the map of what became our prophetic adventure: Buenos Aires, Sinai, Portugal, Galilee, Crete, Bethlehem, Rome, Hebron and Jerusalem. In any case, here it is: a faithful and transparent rendering of fact and fiction beyond victim, perpetrator, or hero.

CHAPTER 1

THE CALL

Buenos Aires – 1984

IN MY native Argentina, the dictatorship had crumbled. People were living with tremendous collective trauma and yet nurturing hope for the recently reborn democracy.

Throughout those horrendous years, my father, Rabbi Marshall T. Meyer—his memory is a blessing—had saved many lives and become a beacon for human rights. His main mentor, his *rebbe*[1]—the late Rabbi Abraham Joshua Heschel, a true *hasid*[2], among other things—had been a close ally of Martin Luther King Jr. and Father Berrigan, and had worked for human rights, civil rights, and against the war in Vietnam.

My father was now part of the "Conadep"—*Comisión Nacional Sobre la Desaparición de Personas* (National Commission on the Disappearance of Persons)—a presidential commission of about a dozen illustrious citizens from many walks of life who had raised their voices against tyranny in those sinister years, when the government of

---

[1] *Rebbe*: Yiddish term of endearment for a rabbi who serves as a spiritual and life guide.
[2] *Hasid*: Part of the Jewish devotional movement initiated by the Baal Shem Tov in the eighteenth century, including dancing and singing in the forests of Eastern Europe, as an alternative for illiterate pious Jews. A Hebrew term meaning loving kindness, grace, and unconditional love. As the late Rabbi Zalman Shachter Shalomi put it, explaining one of the ten spheres called Hesed in the Sefirotic Tree of Life, when a mother breastfeeds her baby she doesn't count how much milk she's giving the baby, but feeds it unconditionally.

the *juntas* massacred the best of a generation. The Conadep was now investigating the horrific crimes of the unelected military *juntas*.

I was seventeen years old when the phone rang.

"Hello. Who is this?" I asked.

"Can we speak to Rabbi Meyer, please?"

"He's busy right now."

"Who is this?"

"His son. My father can't talk, but I can pass him the message."

"Okay, but please write it down and make sure he gets it. It's important. We are the Doughnuts."

"Who?"

"The Dough-Nuts—we have a lot of dough, and we are nuts!"

"Okay." This sounds good, I laughed to myself.

The Doughnuts woman continued: "We are organizing a secret multifaith prayer gathering for peace in Mt Sinai, with leaders of different sacred paths and religions, and we want to invite your father to join. Among our guests are Dean Jim Morton from St. John the Divine, Chief Oren Lyons from the Onondaga Tribe, Pir Vilayat Khan from the Sufi Order of the West, Rabbi Zalman Schachter Shalomi, Shinto priests, Buddhists, Palestinians, Syrians, Israelis, and other very special 'sacred activists' who've been invited to pray collectively for peace in the Middle East in the aftermath of the horrible massacres of Sabra and Shatila in Lebanon."

"Wow," I said. "Sounds amazing and very important!"

"You're sure your dad can't get on the phone for five minutes?"

"Don't worry," I said. "I'm very excited about this and will transmit the full message to my father today!"

After a good one-hour talk in the bathtub, I convinced "Ata" (that's how we, all three siblings, addressed our father) to attend. The tub was one of the prime locations of our home, where we had our coziest space for deep, uninterrupted, and intimate conversations. My dad would soak in the bathtub, and I'd sit on the toilet—closed lid of course—as we nurtured our kinship and close friendship. He was a yes! He would be in the Cairo contingent—and unfortunately, it was clear he wasn't taking me with him.

Eleven years later, my beloved father passed away.

I had rebelled and sought distance from him since I was eighteen, including the two years we were both living in New York City, almost until his death.

The year before he passed away was the year I lived in Sinai. I had dreams of bringing my father to the magical desert and re-friending each other by creating a theater piece together: a father and son relationship play. I had it all thought out. Ata would take a sabbatical from his congregation, B'nai Jeshurun in New York, and come live in retreat with me in the Sinai mountains to create our theater piece. We would have a clear, sustained, and inspiring opportunity to keep mending our deep relationship, which had suffered a "me wanting my own identity" hiatus and lots of frustrating confusion on my father's side.

Sinai – 2018

THIRTY-FOUR YEARS after the wondrous and secret "Sinai Gathering" my father took part in, there was going to be a similar encounter. This time, leaders of different sacred traditions had been invited to remember the human family's purpose through a "spirit camp" and a sacred action in Sinai. Many would be arriving through Israel, some through Jordan, and others through Cairo.

The call was out. The scouting had been done. We were supposed to meet in Wadi[3] Meliches, the magical valley where I had lived on and off for almost a year before I moved to Israel. Our Tarabin[4] Bedouin friend Musallem had already started buying mattresses and extra blankets for the guests. But then, the WhatsApp text came in:

"Just to clarify, the donation wasn't 10,000 dollars, but 10,000 shekels!"

Yet another call came from LA: the benefactor who was supposed to give us $5,000 had canceled her donation with no explanation.

---

[3] Wadi: Dry riverbed. "Valley" in Arabic.
[4] Tarabin: One of the eight Bedouin tribes of southern Sinai, supposedly originating from Yemen.

That night, the three main organizers—Mena, Peter, and I—had a conference call. I dug deep for courage, and as the designated curator of the spirit camp, said: "We have to cancel it. We'll have to call everyone involved to tell them it's not happening." It was a sad day.

Mena and I had already been to Sinai twice in the last month to scout and set everything up for the spirit camp and the prayer. We had even held a private event in Dahab to recruit some of the local community there. The project itself was the fruit of Peter's imagination. Peter was an environmental activist and "aerial artist" known for using human bodies arranged in formation to create incredibly vast works of art only viewable from the air. He had been on Mt. Sinai twelve years before and had dreamed that in 2018, for the one-hundred-year anniversary of the Grand Armistice, he would create an aerial art installation for peace on the mountain inspired by the Grand Armistice signed by the rival armies at the end of World War One—"the war to end all wars"—in Paris: "On the 11th month of the 11th day, at the 11th hour, the Great War ends."

Peter kept his vision alive for twelve years. I heard about it from him at one of the most biodiverse oases left in North America, in Baja California, Mexico, two hours south of the Tecate border. The beautiful Canyon de Guadalupe is host to fifty magical hot spring pools, a myriad of different birds, a plentiful array of date trees, and eight waterfalls. I was invited there as a "minstrel" for a gathering in support of saving the oasis from being sold to build a big hotel which would destroy the harmonious life of the place.

As soon as Peter mentioned the word "Sinai," I got a "heart on." I immediately told him that I could support with scouting and most everything else needed for the project. Later that month, I was touring the USA with my music. In LA, I stayed at Peter's home for a couple nights and we worked together on a fleshed-out proposal. That's when I came up with the "spirit camp" for his vision. We only had enough funds to bring two elders instead of ten: a Sufi Mexican Sheika and a Diné[5] Indigenous elder based in New Mexico. We would climb

---

[5] Diné: Indigenous tribe from Turtle Island. Original people from the land which is now called Arizona. Referred to by white people as "Navajo."

the mountain and be together on Mt. Sinai for two nights before the aerial art action, and take part in a ceremony led by Lynn McCallister at sunrise, at the heart of Mt. Sinai, right near Elijah's cave.

For security reasons, the event unfolded on November 9—two days before the official date, to confuse the authorities. Everybody in the region is well aware that the Egyptian authorities' paranoia runs deep towards any kind of religious, spiritual, or political event they don't understand. November 9 also happened to be the day of Kristallnacht: the Night of Broken Glass, when the violence against the Jews in Nazi Germany first erupted.

We arrived in Dahab on November 5. The next evening, we met up with our friends from the film, stills, and music crew at our mountain camp in St. Catherine. There, we were joined by Bedouin musician Milad, and our one and only guide, Musallem.

We climbed the mountain slowly and with gusto, sensing each one of the trees on the way, connecting intimately with the mountain. Everyone led and shone in their own way, and at their own pace, weaving a web of trust between us. A small group climbed from the main camel road, escorting our two elders who were excitedly mounted on camels for the first time. We met near the top of *Jebel Musa*—Mt. Sinai—around sunset, and after a great dinner, a work meeting, and some music, we opted for an early night.

Sunrise on November 8 was the designated time for all those who wanted to climb the last few meters right to the top of Mt. Sinai. Some, like Sheika Amina, walked up in real heartfelt pilgrimage. I stayed. At mid-morning, Peter and Musallem came back with good news. They had found the perfect spot for our human aerial art. The next morning, we moved the camp to a beautiful and spacious canvas to receive our two hundred participants, about a fifteen-minute walk from Farsh Elias (Elijah's Basin). According to legend, in that basin there was a cave where the Prophet Elijah had hidden to escape the wrath of Queen Jezebel, who wanted to kill him. In the mountain cave, Elijah experienced the great wind, the great noise, and the great fire, which according to the story were far from being divine clues despite their grandiose visibility and power. Finally, he sensed the divine within the subtle sound of silence in the "still small voice". Some in the Sufi tradition relate him to *El Khadr*.[6]

It was the perfect place. At sunset, the first group from Dahab arrived—except there was a slight problem. Upon seeing a bunch of young Egyptian hippies with a couple of African drums, three policemen had followed them all the way up the mountain. They thought that we were a satanic cult gathering to hold a ceremony on the mountain, so they trailed our suspicious-looking friends to find out. Contributing to the confusion, our big Israeli contingent coming from Taba arrived almost simultaneously. The policemen at the St. Catherine checkpoint had instructed them to come back down from the mountain before sunset.

As we were preparing for the ceremony and the aerial image, we had to deal with three hungry, cold, lost, and discombobulated Egyptian policemen, in their impossible pursuit to understand what the hell was going on. The sun had already set, it was quite dark, and they couldn't see well. The policemen tried to identify and threaten some of the Dahab "hippies," to no avail. We offered them blankets and a place to sleep, and shared a hot meal with them. They warmed up around the fire, right next to us.

Before sunrise, Peter and the whole team walked to the site. I arrived a bit later to tune my guitar and find a place for the musicians: Tim the spoken word artist, Milad with the oud, and Naomi the singer, along with a couple other vocalists. At sunrise, we ushered the big group up. In the lead were seventy Bedouins in traditional attire who took their place around the canvas, looking ancient and archetypal as they each sat on top of the beautiful granite boulders. Israelis, Egyptians, and internationals followed them. I got the cue from Patrick to start. It was a big group of people, and my task was to set the tone with a heart song:

I hear your call, I see your face
In your embrace wisdom and grace
Now is here, here is now

---

[6] *El Khadr*: The mysterious green prophet in the Sufi tradition.

One being this truth and bliss[7]

My brother Amir's song worked as a charm. It had created a heart field, a fertile ground for Lynn to begin her part of the ceremony. Our Diné elder proceeded to invoke Spirit through sacred song with her drum and smudge the Bedouins. It was a truly radical bond, from Indigenous Turtle Island to Indigenous Sinai. They represented the eight local South Bedouin tribes, one for each tribe: Tarabin, Muzzeina, Jabaliya, Gararsha, Aligat, Sualha, Suarka, and Ualad Ali.

We were aiming to write the word "ME" with our bodies, next to a "pause" button sign, before moving to transform it to "WE" with a "play" button sign: a message to the world to re-align our values as Creation. We started playing music again, as Peter ushered the people into their proper positions for the first image of "ME" and the pause button drawn with our bodies on the mountain canvas. After that, we formed the Arabic word for "life," *haya*. Then Tim got the cue to start the transformation rap, which led us into the image of the "play" button. Finally, our bodies' contours inscribed the "WE" image onto the mountain.

At that point in our ceremony sequence, a trio of whirling dervishes[8] was supposed to start spinning while Milad, Amina, and I played, sang, and led *zikr*[9] in Hebrew and Arabic. This proved impossible, unfortunately, as the trio of whirlers from Dahab had left the mountain in a frenzy, scared by the police who had threatened to arrest them. Consulting quickly with myself, I came to an extreme executive decision. I started whirling with my guitar myself, while playing. Yes, it looked a little silly, but it was playful, and the collective prayer kept us going.

Not long after I started spinning, from the corner of my eye I saw a policeman in full uniform, gun and all, entering the canvas of our ceremony! While I kept turning in 360-degree circles playing my guitar and singing, I saw on the other side, above the musicians' area,

---

[7] To listen to "One Being This," go to page 251.
[8] Dervish: Sufi devotee generally not interested in material affairs, whose primary relationship is with the Divine.
[9] *Zikr*: Sufi heart-cleansing ceremony to remember the Divine through breath, movement, and repetition of the names of the One God.

two more policemen surrounded by about thirty Bedouins, arguing in high-pitched voices. It was getting worse by the minute. I felt an urge to do something. As I looked up and saw the "Hummingbird" (the codename for our illegal drone). I stopped whirling and approached the policeman head-on, without stopping my singing or playing. I just hooked my pupils into his and got really close to him.

"*La Ilaha Ila lah*,"[10] I kept singing at the top of my lungs, right in his face, just a couple of breaths away from him. As two hundred people sang together, I made him focus on me, so he wouldn't look up at the Hummingbird. I blocked his way, swaying first to the right, and then to the left. It was as if I was waltzing him. Finally, I literally started trotting after him with my guitar, still in intense *Zikr* prayer. He wanted to smile, but instead, his face was twisting and contorting. He was supposed to be angry but wasn't, not really. He was unable to stop us. After all, we were declaring the oneness of *Allah*, the *tawhid*,[11] the highest tenet of Islam—and he was a believing Muslim.

A few moments later, I felt our dancer the policeman was getting close to his patience limit, and I returned to my place with the musicians. Peter signaled that we had to end soon, and the utterly flabbergasted officer didn't know who to follow or how to stop any of this "madness." Sure he had seen the Hummingbird up above, he tried to detain Peter. For the remaining ten minutes of the ceremony, Peter just kept dismissing him politely. When it was over, Peter said "thank you" to all who had made the tremendous effort to show up for this love letter from Sinai to the world.

Musallem whispered in Peter's ear that we had to start climbing down immediately in twos and threes from the backside of the mountain. As Hari, an Israeli German and experienced peace activist, tried to walk our confused policeman the other way, our team started leaping down the mountain from the opposite side. I recognized the silhouettes of Mousa and Said, our sweet guides, far away down the mountain. Raaba, a Palestinian Christian sister from our team, was

---

[10] *La Ilaha Ila lah*: There is no God but the One God.
[11] *Tawhid*: The intrinsic oneness of Allah, the Divine.

right behind me. I put my guitar on my shoulders, about to start my own frantic descent.

"You think I have time to go down from the main camel road with Lynn?" Raaba asked me.

"No!" I said in desperation. "Don't you realize the police are after us? We need to go down now! From here. Let's go." We quickly started making our way down.

I saw Peter coming behind me as Hari distracted the policeman and took him by the shoulder. He promised the officer that the whole group would return to gather at Farsh Elias, our basecamp, where we had slept the night before.

In a matter of five minutes, the whole team was on our way down the back way of the mountain. We stopped at our beloved almond garden Farsh el Looza, named after a four-hundred-year-old almond tree. There was a little monk's refuge there. In that haven, I had had one of the best siestas of my life, on our scouting journey two weeks before.

We regrouped and noticed we were missing Teena, our cinematographer and drone operator. We had figured she had enough time to relay the Hummingbird to our Bedouin friend, who would then deliver it to the alpinist in our team. Teena had the camera, and most importantly, the aerial footage on her—and we were worried she hadn't made it down the back way with us. Amidst our worry for Teena, Musallem's commanding presence and charisma remained intact. He was still leading with trust. With his million-dollar smile, he sounded his favorite mantra: "Life is gooooood!" It was as if he said that phrase with more conviction and ease every time, and after a while of hanging out with him, it seemed there was no choice but to start believing him. Maybe it was true after all. "Life is gooooood!"

As our descent continued with trepidation, the bliss of skipping down the mountain grew on me, and I started hopping down ecstatically. It wasn't long before I fell flat on my face. Boom! My head and body crashed into the stone. I had my heavy hard guitar case strapped on like a knapsack over my arms and shoulders, so when I fell, the case landed right on top of me. I heard a choir of voices swirling around me:

"Hey...hey...what happened? Are you okay? Can you move?"

"Let's at least untangle your guitar from your back."

I realized that I couldn't answer them, and I couldn't move either. I was in full shock. The good news was, I was calm inside and had decided not to try to talk, move, freak out, or fight it. It must have been a full minute or so until I managed to say, "Please give me a minute. Let me be still." After that, someone untangled my guitar case for me, and Musallem helped me to sit down. There was a little blood on my knee and on my hand, which he cleaned and bandaged. I finally stood up, and Said, our young and sweet Jabaliya apprentice guide, volunteered to carry my guitar. I was a bit clumsy for the first ten steps, but without the guitar, I felt extremely light. Soon enough, I came back to myself.

At our next stop on the way down, we met some Jabaliya Bedouins who had been with us on top of the mountain as part of the ceremony. After a quick tea and a joint, I was feeling even better. We reached the camp, took a shower, and the James Bond movie continued. We heard the news from the checkpoint at the camel tourist road: they were stopping everyone and looking for our Hummingbird. The policeman had told his superiors at the checkpoint that he had seen a drone. About seventy Bedouins and another eighty Israeli and other international tourists, though, had utterly denied seeing anything. "Just some tourists singing and taking photos and videos," they'd said. Fortunately, Teena had put all our footage in her bra before she went inside the questioning room. The policemen also searched our Israeli friends, asking politely for forgiveness in an uneventful routine security check.

Everyone—including Teena, thank goodness—had arrived back to base camp. In a hurry to catch their planes, the film crew was frantically trying to transfer all of the footage onto Teena's computer so she could edit the video. One by one, everyone departed. The people from Dahab had already left. Most Israelis made their way back to the Taba border. Finally, it was time for us. I oversaw the transfer of the Hummingbird from our climber ally to the Bedouin Sheik. Atua literally grabbed it from the climber's hands and shut the door, disappearing into his house. Mena and I were the last to leave. Tim, Naomi, and Maggy from our film crew joined us. All in all, it was a great adventure. Our Dahab friends were okay, all two hundred participants had arrived at their home countries, no one got arrested, and the footage was safe with Teena. Or was it?

As we waited anxiously on 11/11 and the famous day ended without the video's release, we realized something was wrong. Days passed. Then, we finally heard from Peter, who told us that with the rush the sound was never transferred to Teena. It was still on Tim's computer, who was now volunteering in a little Palestinian village near Tulkarem with very little Wi-Fi reception. Though it was eventually completed and released, out of paranoia about possible backlash we decided to take it down from social media.

And as I write these words, this book has caught up with my present. It has ended its life as an artistic project. The book has fully synced with my life and is becoming an integral part of it. And for you, too! Yes, you, reading these words. You have become part of the "Big Vision." But I'll tell you more about that later. For now, let me say that although there was beauty and value in our "sacred activism," our Sinai adventure was far from impeccable. Emotionally, it had been very messy. There had been some very uncomfortable moments with some of my old friends and with myself, including lashes of anger which I thought I was done with. At times, we forgot that if we want to call our activism "sacred," it needs to be sacred each step of the way.

And as I write this, it hits me: our sacred action at Mt. Sinai was just a rehearsal for learning to be a "we" in preparation for the "Big Vision." We were still learning to work with ease, even and especially when the conditions are extremely stressful. Like my Sufi waltz with the policeman at the mountain, embodying the message at every step is the work, and the play.

So, acknowledging the messiness, and my own obsessive tendencies, here goes some *Ho'oponopono*[12] for my old friends who I still love dearly. Some *metta*[13] meditation in compassion for their journeys, and for yours and ours too! We are in this puzzle together. To be healthy and balanced as a whole, we need all of our "sacred agents" along the way embodying and shining their authenticity. As R. Zalman—his memory is a blessing—used to say: "The only way to get it together is together."

---

[12] *Ho'oponopono*: Hawaiian healing modality focusing on love, forgiveness, and gratitude.
[13] *Metta*: Buddhist form of meditation based on loving kindness and benevolence. Active wishing well to other beings.

CHAPTER 2

POINT ZERO

Lisbon

BY THE end of summer, a peace research community in southern Portugal had become a hub for activists involved in systemic change focused on celebrating and protecting the sacred. Spiritual activists of all races and cultures and Indigenous elders converged for the encounter, and were landing in Lisbon almost every day. One of them was Ibrahim, a famous retired Moroccan soccer star who had played quite a few seasons at Paris St. Germain. This was the first time that a sports-celebrity-turned-activist had joined the global alliance.

I was sipping my *vinho verde* with my friend Bruno on his cozy porch when we saw the famous soccer player get out of a taxi and ring the doorbell. Bruno went down to help with the luggage, greeting Ibrahim before disappearing into the kitchen to cook dinner. Ibrahim put his big bag down, hung his jacket up, and sat next to me on the sofa. I broke the ice:

"You're a soccer star, right?"

"Yup. In Paris, but originally from Morocco," Ibrahim answered.

"I'm from Argentina," I told him.

"So, you know about soccer?"

"*Iiiiwa*! Got my first big ball when I was four! And played in a team until age fifteen. I saw you play. You're really talented."

"*Shukran Habibi*,[1]" said Ibrahim.

---

[1] *Shukran Habibi*: Thank you, my dear.

"I heard you've retired?"

"Yes," he said. "I got tired of training so much, not eating well, and living only for soccer. I'm hungry to expand my views and experiences of the world."

"Hmm, that rings a bell," I said. That's what happened to me when I was a teenager. Although I have to admit, I learned tons about leadership, communicating, and planning while playing midfield—not to mention singing to the rhythm of the drums and the ecstatic chants of thousands of fans at La Bombonera[2] stadium. But you said 'expanding experiences?' Tell me more."

Ibrahim continued. "I'm interested in new perspectives. I want to be politically and socially responsible. My father was of Jewish origin and died when I was very young. I was raised Muslim by my mom. My big dream is to contribute to peace in the Middle East. With my name, I might be able to serve as an amplifier for tolerance and pluralism. This is why I was invited to Portugal, and why I'm here to talk to you about the "Big Dream." I heard you presenting the vision the other day." I thought back to when I'd shared what I thought was my raw, and unarticulated talk on creativity, spirit, and peacebuilding for the Holy Land in front of the alliance a couple days before—but I had no idea the famous soccer legend was among those listening.

"Wonderful!" I said.

"You might think I'm a bit indiscreet," began Ibrahim shyly, "but although I didn't join you guys, I saw you laughing with the 'pirate crew' at the gathering. So I have a hunch, and I am ready to take a risk. I also just saw you smoking a *'petard'*[3] out on the porch when I was unloading my bags and thought I could open up to you. So here it goes, straight up. Ready?"

Ibrahim was warm and present, exuding a natural joy embodying the beauty and depth of what I remembered experiencing while visiting Morocco. The color of his voice was crisp and kind. Seeing my anticipation, he continued. "A dear friend gave me magic mushrooms

---

[2] La Bombonera: Boca Juniors soccer stadium in the neighborhood of La Boca in Buenos Aires.
[3] *Petard*: French slang for cannabis joint.

last month, which we ate near my native Marrakesh. In short, from this new vantage viewpoint of my life, I can't really see myself going back to playing soccer games, training, or even coaching." I was happily surprised to hear this. A professional soccer player impacted in such a way by the holy mycelium was a first for me.

"I've been in Marrakesh," I told him, delighted. "I absolutely loved it!" Going deep into my memories of my time in Morocco, I began daydreaming.

Marrakesh – 1998

WE WERE a small team of musicians, film crew, and producers, with two movie projects on our hands and a month and a half of funding in magical Morocco. Arriving in Marrakesh still giddy from our stay at the Atlas Mountains, we took a few rooms at the Afrikia Guest House just a two-minute walk from Jemaa el Fna.[4] We spent every single day of the two weeks in the square, which led to the most amazing market I have seen in my lifetime: each door leads to a corridor, which in turn opens to the stairs of a hidden basement, where there is a coffer, which becomes a staircase through a small door into another magical space.

At our abode, even the ceilings were vibrant with art and sculpted patterns. There was an exquisite patio in the middle of the *riad*[5] with beautiful plants, colorful mosaics, and exquisite proportions. Remarkable characters rented the rooms. One of them was an eccentric genius professor who would draw and lecture on his mystical theories and far-out sacred geometry with chalk on the floor of the square. He was often surrounded by fans, enthralled with his designs and inspiring talk. When we discovered he was our neighbor at the guest house, he became our friend. We filmed him praying next to us with *tefillin*[6] on, for one of our movies (which ultimately was

---

[4] Jemaa el Fna: The main square and entrance to the immense market of Marrakesh in Morocco.
[5] *Riad*: Traditional Moroccan villa serving as a guest house with many rooms.
[6] *Tefillin*: Phylacteries, or traditional Jewish hide ritual straps. Tied to the left arm next to the heart as remembrance and on the third eye for balancing thought with Divine principles. Originating from the biblical "Totafot."

"never-to-be"). He complied willingly, as any ordinary mystic Sufi wizard professor would do.

A few days later, we hung out with the *Isawis*, a brand of ecstatic "fakir" Sufis who we met at the Jemaa el Fna doing their thing for the tourists. They would bring themselves into a trance through drumming, singing, and dancing, then work their prowess with knives, swords, and snakes. We took them to the waterfalls of Sti Fadma[7] and filmed a trance snake ritual, except this time, the three actors—me included—were the ones who had the snakes on their bodies. Every day at that legendary square, we continued to meet wild, delightful characters: from mountain-dwelling toothless violinists to Sahara lizards, plant-peddling witch doctors, and spontaneous street "dentists" sitting on a rug and offering to pull out your aching molars.

My heart fully opened, though, with the *Gnawa*. According to oral stories, the *Gnawa* are Sufis who came as slaves from Sudan a few centuries ago. Their healing ceremonies include drums, sung incantations, and dancing with the *caracab*: big castanets made of steel which they hold in both hands and play while they dance. The *caracab* serve as the memory and sound of the chains they wore as slaves, and induce trance. They wear a hat covered in seashells with a cloth-threaded pom-pom spinning from it, twirling like a fan every time they do a full turn or a high jump and a whirl. At the square, they make their living by playing and dancing for tourists with their *gimbri*, *sintir* bass, *caracab*, and drums. I made a point of hanging out with the *Gnawa* every day, and became friends with their elder and leader, Hassan. After he saw me dancing to their music, he invited me to join them when they performed for the tourists. Later, we danced and filmed with them for a full day at a fire ceremony in the beautiful Palmariva, near Marrakesh.

One morning, I wandered into the market with my musician friend Mosh. We bought a *gimbri* for him and a little Moroccan ceramic drum for me, and as we tried the instruments in the little shop of the *suk*, dozens of people gathered around us. The next day on the

---

[7] Sti Fadma: Breathtaking waterfalls in Morocco's Atlas Mountains, next to the shrine of Ibn Lachnes and the Ourika valley.

square, Mosh sang and played his new instrument, and I danced like there was no tomorrow. Not long into our show, tourists and even some locals began handing us money. We had been accepted at the ancient and mythical Jemaa el Fna.

As my memories continued to wander, Ibrahim sneezed and brought me abruptly back to Bruno's porch in Lisbon. "So why did you leave soccer?" Ibrahim asked.

"Back to my native Argentina," I continued. "When I was sixteen, I started studying theater seriously. I also began going to human rights demonstrations with my theater teacher and my friends from the theater classes. Argentina was opening up to me, especially the non-Jewish aspects, the political situation, the weed, my creative side, the erotic...all of it took precedence over the soccer world."

"I see," said Ibrahim. "For me, after my mushroom experience, I started reading about other medicinal plants for expanding consciousness, from the Amazonas, from the Mexican desert...do you know anything about them?" Ibrahim asked.

"Well," I said, "I did have an adventure with LSD...and soccer." I grinned.

"Tell me, please!" Ibrahim exclaimed with glee.

Buenos Aires – 1987

IN 1987, I worked as an actor in a terrible telenovela on Argentinian TV. I was getting paid well because it was filmed outside, and exteriors always paid better. It was my day job, and we filmed once or twice a week. To satiate my soul, I was also writing for an underground magazine called *Cerdos y Peces*. My life then was a mix of counterculture, grass, cocaine, poetry, crazy friends, and acid.

One time, a special convoy of lysergic "oms"[8] had arrived from Amsterdam to Buenos Aires. They had the reputation of being very pure and strong, and somehow, through my roommate, they landed in our fridge. We started dosing quarter acid portions—and then one

---
[8] Lysergic "oms": a very pure strain of LSD.

more quarter, and one more, and yet one more—for two weeks. On one of those "after acid" mornings, I had to film for the telenovela *Tiempo Cumplido* at River Plate, on the training field, right next to the "Monumental": the biggest soccer stadium in Argentina and the second largest in South America.

I was playing the part of a soccer player on a youth team, and most of our filming involved playing soccer, which I loved. In general, I tried to be in the scenes as much as possible so that I would be paid, but avoided speaking parts when I could as the content was terrible and the dialogue utterly stupid. That morning they wanted to film a real game, and had our team of actors play a ninety-minute game against the technicians, who were well-known for being the best team in union soccer. When we started the game, I was still under the influence of LSD—specifically the "morning after" effects of the journey, when insights and "aha moments" abound.

I played the most amazing soccer game of my life. My perception could intuit what would happen with the ball before it happened and exactly where the players would run, as if I was seeing and knowing what nobody else could. I simply arrived before everyone else to the ball and knew exactly where to pass it. Usually, I was a defensive midfielder—*número 5*—so my job was to steal balls in midfield and make long passes to the wings. That morning, though, the most unusual thing happened: I scored three goals! Nobody could stop me, and nobody knew what the hell happened to me!

"Wow...*Mezuian*!" said Ibrahim as I wrapped up my story.

Our other guest at Bruno's was a video artist, Vasilis. Like Ibrahim, he had been at my presentation in South Portugal. He was part of the media team and interested in the "Big Vision" I had shared. Vasilis was from Greece, and was well-built, well-read, and well-traveled. He was a very solar being, radiating like the sun, and the few times we'd interacted at the gathering I'd had a warm and positive feeling about him. He also came well recommended by dear friends. When he arrived, this time I was the one to run down and open the door. Bruno was in the kitchen when I came back up with a cheery Vasilis.

"Hi! My name is Vasilis," he said with a heavy Greek accent. "We met briefly at your presentation."

"*Yasu file*,[9] I remember you," I answered. "Our host is making dinner and will be right out."

Bruno came out of the kitchen and said his daughter was arriving on a surprise visit from Berlin, and he had to go meet her. The three of us said in unison: "No problem." Ibrahim announced, "I'll take care of dinner. Do you like Moroccan food?"

"Yes!" Vasilis and I answered together.

Bruno waved at us and was out the door. Vasilis and I went back to our conversation. He told me about his first job in a movie with Costa Gavras, as an assistant to famous actress and activist Melina Mercury. The last project he co-created was a docu-fantasy movie about the magical and nonlinear origins and nature of Parmenides and Empedocles, the well-known Pre-Socratics. Vasilis also shared his love for rembetiko music and the late-90s Night Arc ensemble. I had recently set lyrics for a song called "Liminal Grace" to a beautiful melody by Ara Dinkjian, the great Armenian oud master from Night Arc.[10] There was clearly a deep resonance between Vasilis and me.

"I lived in Ios, in the Cyclades for four months." I told him, inspired by our deepening bond.

"Really?" Vasilis asked.

"Ready for a story?" I asked.

"Shoot," he said.

Greece – 1988

WHEN I left Argentina for good, I was twenty-two years old. Bombs, a lost lover, and police were all to blame. I had also spent a couple of days in prison in solitary confinement, and a bomb had exploded at the underground magazine I wrote for. I was utterly depressed, and I was suffering from photophobia; my eyes were constantly burning and wouldn't open completely. I felt like Harry Dean Stanton in the

---

[9] *Yasu file*: Greek greeting meaning "Hello friend."
[10] To listen to "Liminal Grace," go to page 251.

movie "Paris Texas" walking aimlessly through Buenos Aires with the only certainty I had, which was to leave Argentina as soon as possible.

After promising my father to stay until my sister's wedding, I was trying to decide on my destination. It needed to be a place where I could be naked in the sun. This was my clearest and only discernible wish. I thought of my nudist travel biography. The Virgin Islands? No. Sinai…maybe? And finally, my favorite: the Cyclades Island of Ios in Greece. My sister hooked me up with a travel agent friend and I went to meet him. He offered me free deals for Moscow, Amsterdam, and even northern Greece, but I would have none of it. I just knew I wanted to get to the island and get naked in the sun as fast as possible. The travel agent made the arrangements, and I was on my way. On my layover in Barcelona, I bought a tape recorder, and with my fifteen cassettes, fifteen books, and very few clothes, I landed in Athens. From there I took a taxi to Piraeus Port, and after getting very drunk in a lowly bar full of smoke and sex workers, I slept for the night and took the ferry at eight in the morning to the island.

It was April—so early in the season that not even the Greeks from Athens had arrived yet. It was just me and the locals. I rented a room in the empty guest house. Over the next two weeks, I witnessed the island village come back to life as the hotels, restaurants, bars, and discotheques began to re-open. I couldn't really tolerate any human interaction at the time, though. I could still barely open my eyes without excruciating pain. My eyelids were burning; reality was too much to behold. My only conversations since leaving Argentina had been with the airport authorities, when paying for my room at Piraeus, and with my landlord in the village. By now I was sure I had to move out of the village. The next morning, I went for a walk to the other side of the island. Sitting on the beach, I focused my aching eyes on a few tiny homes in the valley. I approached a man at the beach bar and asked him about rentals, and he told me the owner's name was Panaiotis: the same owner of the guest house where I was staying in the village.

I returned to talk to Panaiotis and told him I wanted to rent his little home in the Mylopotas valley. He gave me a strange look and said, "There's no one in the valley. Besides, all the girls are already arriving in the village and the party is about to begin. So where are you going?" I responded with certainty that I wanted to move out from the village; I needed silence. I asked for the price of his house in *drachmas*[11]. After a long pause, he finally said, "Okay, if you pay in advance. Pack your stuff and I will take you there."

I settled in and was content in my little white refuge with bright blue windows. There was even electricity for my cassette player. Still, my heart was extremely heavy, and I couldn't open my eyes fully without feeling an overwhelming aversion. Any type of light still made my eyelids very uncomfortable, and anything I saw related to humans gave me the creeps. My daily routine became pretty much the same every single day: I read at home, went to the beach, and lay in the sun for days on end without talking to anyone. Any interactions lasting longer than ten seconds felt dreadful. At night I tried different bars in the village, got drunk, danced anonymously, and then rolled back down the mountain to sleep reality away in my little white and blue cubicle. About two weeks in, I was laying in the Greek sun with my eyes closed when I heard a man speaking over me. I glimpsed his shadow above my body as he gently said in a soothing bass voice:

"Sorry to bother you, brother. What's your name?"

As I responded, I realized that he was the first person who had asked my name in over a month. For some mysterious electromagnetic reason, some voices resonate better than others. This one found a calm resonance within me that I could receive without resistance.

"My name is Reiner," he told me. "I'm your neighbor. I saw you walking by a few times. If you need anything...I'm here."

"Thanks," I answered shyly.

As he talked for a while, gentle ease overtook me. He was older than me, in his forties, which gave me a sense of trust. He told me he painted. Among other things, I told him I was studying deep tissue massage in Argentina before I left the country. Apparently, that stuck with him.

The next morning, as I was lying lifeless on the sand with my eyes closed as usual, I heard a feminine voice:

---

[11] *Drachmas*: Greek currency.

"Can I have a massage?"

"Hmm...sorry...what?" I mumbled, emerging out of my limbo state.

"Yes," she said, "your sign." She pointed as she read it out loud: "One-hour massage."

I looked at the sign. It was a drawing of a naked woman in the sun getting a massage. At the top, it read "Massage" in big letters, and at the bottom, "60 Drachmas – 1 hour." I suddenly got my senses back and said, "Yes...sure!" I saw there was even an oil bottle next to the sign. Wow! I thought to myself. This was surely the work of Angel Reiner. That's how I literally opened my eyes for good and began working and earning money on Ios. I became quite a popular massage therapist on the island, and known as the young esoteric Argentinian with great sophisticated music, wild guided meditations, and good deep massage.

"End of story," I concluded.

"*Hela re, poli orea!*"[12] Vasilis exclaimed as he gave me a warm and friendly clap on the upper back.

After more good conversation and dinner, Ibrahim and Vasilis left for the airport to catch their flights home. After Bruno returned, we stayed up late sipping some more *vinho verde* on his porch, sharing insights and stories as usual. The next morning, I flew back to Israel—back to my Galilean home. A few months later, I was starting to feel overwhelmed with daily life. After repeated failed attempts to ignite the "big vision" in my head and think of the relevant "sacred agents" to invite, too much online life, and too little paid work, I decided it was the right time for a well-needed vacation at my usual beach in Sinai.

---

[12] *Hela re, poli ore*a: "Hey there, very beautiful!"

CHAPTER 3

DUE SOUTH

I DROVE all the way from the Galilee, stopped at a friend's home in Pardes Hanna, had a last stop in Eilat, and finally crossed the border to Sinai. As always, the Bedouin crew seemed to be waiting for me at the Ras.

"*Salaam Aleikum, Djibril!*"[1] they called, using the name by which the Bedouin in Sinai know me.

"*Aleikum a salaam, Kif halkum?*"[2] I answered. I was excited to be back in Sinai.

"We'll get some tea. Leave your bags and your *guitarra* here meanwhile."

"I prefer to put my bags in the *husha*,"[3] I said. "Which one is it?"

"*Husha* 16—the one you like, overlooking the sea."

"I'll be right back," I said, and left my guitar with them. I unpacked quickly and came back—to a different scene altogether. Now there were even more Bedouin friends gathered, along with tea, and most importantly, a beautiful woman playing the viola. I sat down silently and listened to the haunting music, a kind of gypsy oriental sound with a lot of soul. (Later, the violist told me that she had a Senegalese father and a Czech Roma mother.) She finished her tune, put down the viola, and turned to me.

"You just arrived, right?" she asked. "You play guitar?"

---
[1] *Salaam Aleikum*: Arabic traditional greeting meaning "Peace be upon you." Djibril: Name of angel who brought the Koran to Mohammad—"Gabriel," in Arabic.
[2] *Kif halkum*: Arabic plural for "How are you?"
[3] *Husha*: Hut made of reeds and straw, typical of Sinai beaches.

"Yeah...well, I'm not a guitarist. I just accompany my singing with it."

"I'm Mona," she said with a warm smile, in graceful command. "I'm a nomadic artist."

"Nice to meet you. Is this your first time here?"

"Yup," she said. "I'm taking a break from my touring and came to Sinai to replenish."

"You chose well. You're a nomadic artist, and...I'm a Global Flexitarian Minstrel," I told her."

"What do you mean you're not a guitarist? That's all you do here!" one of my young Bedouin friends, Sayed, complained.

"Actually, I learned how to play guitar at age thirty-seven!"

"Really?" The violist said. "Amazing!"

"You wanna hear how it happened?" I asked.

"Sure," the violist answered. Sayed and Ahmed gazed at each other and, in tacit agreement, suddenly left the scene. Bedouins have an uncanny sense of timing: a way of disappearing like the wind, with no goodbyes. They are there, and then they are gone. It was pretty clear that I was upstaging them with my story, and so they left me to Mona.

Brazil – 2003

A BIG trauma had been festering in me longer than my sanity could hold, and I was trying to get back to my true self. Five years earlier, my beloved girlfriend had been in a tragic accident. She had been in a coma for over two months, then underwent an intricate and never-ending rehabilitation process in a hospital, only to finally lose part of her memory through a brain injury. She remembered nothing of us living together for a year, and her parents had taken her back home and had locked me out of any contact with her. In the years since, I had been a mess; I was hospitalized for a liver abscess twice and was traveling the world to find solace.

My journey to Brazil was one of my attempts at re-claiming myself. I had signed up for a two-week ayahuasca experience near

Rio de Janeiro, an "intravaganza" that included Carnival in Rio and samba classes. After three intense sessions of "the tea" and ten days of Brazilian samba and carnival, I went to the musician serving the tea, Carioca, and asked him if he could teach me guitar. He lived in Saquarema, an hour from Rio de Janeiro, right next to the *pousada*[4] where we were staying, and was a second-generation professional guitarist. He told me to come the next morning at 9 AM with my guitar. I was early, as usual. Carioca got there at nine and said, "Okay, show me what you know."

"But I don't know how to play!" I protested.

"Anything," he insisted. "Come on."

"I can't even hold the guitar," I complained, "Everything hurts. My hair, my hands, my toes, everything."

"Okay, relax," he said with a smile. "Did you like any of the songs we sang during the sessions? Can you sing one song you liked from the session for me?"

"I can happily do that," I said, and started singing a melody.

"Now play it," he instructed.

"I can't!" I said, beginning to get frustrated. "I don't know how."

Carioca got behind me and my guitar. He placed my left-hand fingers on the A minor chord and pressed forcefully. "Don't let go," he said as he showed me a right-hand fingering movement. He signaled for me to keep repeating the movement. Trying to keep my left hand in position while fingering with my right hand felt excruciating. My fingers weren't responding to my brain, and I was suffering. "Keep going!" Carioca urged me. With his full strength, he started massaging my shoulders while telling me to keep picking the A minor chord.

I thought I wouldn't survive my growing exasperation, but his fierce rubbing and kneading kept opening neural pathways from my brain to my fingers until I was playing the fucking A minor! Yup, it took about fifteen minutes, but I was now playing a guitar chord! After that, we did the same sequence with the E minor chord. He placed my left-hand fingers in position, showed me the right-hand sequence of plucking the strings, and didn't stop massaging me until

---

[4] *Pousada*: Brazilian or Portuguese guesthouse.

I got E minor fifteen minutes later. We then went to D minor. By the time I had that one down, it was the end of the class. My hands, arms, shoulders, and back were full of cramps; it felt like my whole body was a cluster of knots. Carioca gave me a couple of exercises, which I did over and over all day until I fell asleep that evening, guitar on top of me, fingers bleeding.

The next morning, I was back again for my second class. Carioca asked me to play the song I had learned the day before, then inquired what song I wanted to learn next. I decided on a new song, and we began the same process as the day before. This time, with the help of Carioca's relentless shamanic massages, I managed to learn two more songs and four new chords. The third class was more of the same. I learned to play three more songs—and was also singing them. To my surprise, my voice had totally changed. It was coming from somewhere else, a totally different place within me. Its source had moved from my throat to my heart. Carioca finally said, "Okay, we're done, but let me tell you something: you are crazy, and you will do a lot of harm to the world if you don't sing and play as much as possible. Now bye-bye!"

I paid him for the class and left, exhilarated. Back on the patio near the pool of the pousada, I took out my guitar and started showing off what I knew. My heart was open to the songs I was singing. There was no effort in my voice, though I was still in tremendous stress while playing guitar.

"I survived, though, and eventually got to a place where I can play guitar, both picking and strumming...while I sing...onstage!"

"What a story!" Mona said "Unbelievable!"

Things felt a bit unbelievable to me too: I was at my favorite beach camp in Sinai which had been my second home for more than twenty-five years, sharing my stories with a very beautiful and present woman who was now soloing to my chords with her viola. She played extremely well. I felt good and ready for life.

"I'm going to get some goodies," Mona said. She came back with hibiscus tea and some potent *charas*[5] which she had brought from India. She also materialized a bag full of delicious dried apricots, brazil nuts, pumpkin seeds, seaweed crisps in olive oil and wasabi, and other succulent, organic munchies. Mona mentioned she had missed the Rainbow Gathering in India. She hadn't arrived in time to attend because she'd been at a climate justice and regenerative agriculture educational program in Costa Rica. She was curious, but like most people (including me), wasn't sure what to make of Rainbow Gatherings.

"Have you ever been to one?" she asked.

"Yup," I answered.

"Where?"

"Well, the biggest and the first one outside of Israel I've been to was in Ireland."

At the mention of Ireland, Mona's face lit up. "Tell me about it," she asked. I sensed that she was flirting with me. It wasn't crass or obvious, but was simply her shine: a wonderful blend of presence, confidence, and grace mixed with an elegant naughtiness. We had high-quality smoke, healthy munchies, and no expectations. The situation kept getting better, and the excitement of telling my story to a new, special, and sassy lady was growing.

Ireland – 1993

"SEE YOU in Ireland!" I heard Molly say as I was leaving the Tel Aviv party. Molly was the first woman I had met when I arrived at the Rainbow Gathering in the forest near Jerusalem. According to my inner logic, she was my benefactor. She got rid of my headache at 3 AM and welcomed me to my first gathering with a glass of water, and because of her, I decided to stay. I admired her clarity and compassion, and I was impressed by her eloquence. None of that was of any help, though, as I arrived in Dublin from the airport and grumpily rented one of the ugly, cheap bunk beds in the dorm room of a tourist hostel downtown.

[5] *Charas*: Potent cannabis paste made in India.

I went out into the streets of Dublin and started walking. The first thing that caught my attention made me happy: a young guy busking with a *didgeridoo*. I recognized the instrument from the Rainbow Gathering I had been to near Jerusalem. It seemed natural to stop and ask him a question, which I had selected carefully. In those days there were no cell phones and no internet, and even though I'd been to one already, my understanding of the Rainbow Gathering was at best very loose. I figured it was a secret gathering and I could only come by myself. I had ascribed mystical stature to my journey to Ireland and was excited by my first question:

"Hi...do you know where the enchanted forest is?"

"You're in Ireland, brother, all forests are enchanted! But you definitely won't find anything in Dublin. Go south, to Cork," he said with confidence.

"Thanks!" I said.

That same morning, I got on a bus to Cork. It was smaller than Dublin, but still a city. Reluctantly, I got a bed in another hostel dorm, praying it would be my last one of this trip. It was getting dark, and I went out to the nearest pub. I sat in the bar next to an English bloke with big dreadlocks. Like the didgeridoo, dreadlocks were another sign I was on the right track. I ordered a Guinness, beginning to get the hang of Irish pubs. This one was a bit empty. At the bar, it was only the blond guy with dreadlocks, me, and a drunk woman in the corner.

"Sláinte!"[6] toasted the dreadlocks guy, and raised his beer towards mine. I was proud to be getting my first dose of Celtic culture.

"What's your name?" I asked him.

"Sean."

"Where are you from?"

"England...and you?"

"I was born in Argentina, and I've been living in the Sinai desert."

He asked me if I was coming to the Rainbow Gathering, and immediately answered himself: "It's not happening this year." He told me that he'd met the scouts, who'd separated when tensions between

---

[6] *Sláinte*: Celtic way of toasting.

them became too much. The Swiss, the German, and the French were gone; the Norwegian was sick, and the last two scouts remaining, an English couple, were stuck somewhere in the middle of Ireland and had stopped looking for the site. The people, two thousand of them, were supposed to be arriving soon, and there was still no site for the gathering. He was sure that the gathering would be called off.

By the third beer, I decided I didn't like Sean. His vibe was murky, and it didn't rub me the right way. I said thanks for the info, paid, and left the bar uneasily, thinking to myself, "WTF?" As experience teaches us, though, better not to reach conclusions or make big decisions after three large pints of Guinness. A much wiser idea was to collapse in bed and figure it all out in the light of day.

The next morning I got up, had some bad coffee, and went for a walk. In those days, I used to trust books much more than people. So when I saw an artsy little cozy bookstore, I immediately went in. There was nobody there but me and the owner, busy at the cash register. Browsing around, I saw a book that caught my full attention: *Rainbow Nation without Borders* by Alberto Ruz Buenfil. I had heard of him; he was a Mexican alternative pioneer who had led an artistic caravan of performers called "The Illuminated Elephants" from a *ting*[7] meeting in Scandinavia overland to India. They eventually founded the Huehuecoyotl community in Tepoztlan, Mexico. (I would meet his son Odin at India's first Rainbow Gathering a few years later.) I started flipping through the book. This caught the attention of the bookshop owner and for the first time since I came into the store, he seemed to be checking me out. Excited, I brought the book to him and asked, "How much for this one?"

"That one is for you," he said.

"What do you mean?"

"Yeah, for you. It's free. I have only one copy," he said intriguingly.

"Really?"

"Yes."

"Can I ask you a question? Do you know where the enchanted forest is?"

---

[7] *Ting*: Revived Scandinavian traditional gatherings.

"If you are looking for the Rainbow family"—he had pronounced the magical words—"you have to go west to a town called Bantry, to the 5A Cafe. They'll tell you how to get there." I left with a smile, packed my stuff at the guest house, and started hitchhiking west. The first car held a cheery old Irish woman and her dog. They were both kind, but my question seemed irrelevant. They dropped me forty kilometers later at a junction. I thanked them and continued raising my thumb. This time, an older man picked me up, and I asked him straight: "Do you know where the enchanted forest is?" He called Ireland "the land of rainbows" and told interesting stories about leprechauns spiced with mystical humor, but it wasn't what I was looking for. He dropped me half an hour later, next to the road.

My third ride was epic. A van picked me up, and the man driving it was extremely positive and upbeat. "Hop right in!" he said. His rearview mirror had a peacock feather on it, and his van felt at least as alive as he did. We started driving, and he matter-of-factly asked me if I was coming to help with the Gathering.

"What do you mean 'help'?"

"Well," he said, "you know the gathering starts in August, which is now one month away."

"What?" I said, completely confused. "I got here a month early?!"

"You're just in time," said the man driving the van. "There's no site yet for the gathering. The scouts fought with each other and abandoned their tasks. Two thousand people are coming from all over the world and there's still no place to gather. You've got to help us find a location."

"No! you don't understand," I explained, "I've only been to one gathering, for five days in Jerusalem. I know hardly anything about the Rainbow. I got to Ireland one month early by mistake."

"Listen," he continued, "there are only three scouts left...but here, we've arrived in Bantry already." The ride had gone by too quickly. "Across the street is the 5A cafe—they surely can help you there."

"Thanks so much!" I said. As I got out of his van, I realized I didn't even know his name—and I never would, because I never saw him again.

Bantry was no Cork, but rather a picturesque little town in the west of Ireland. I walked into the 5A Cafe, a typical new-age village chai[8] shop, with yoga and massage ads everywhere. I ordered a chai and sipped it slowly. Although the cafe was pleasant, my mind was racing. What was this place? Not the enchanted forest for sure! Suddenly, out of the kitchen thundered a powerful voice. "They say you come from the land of our fathers…from Sinai! Come with me."

Through the doorway emerged an impressive middle-aged man. His hair was badly combed, but he had a demeanor about him—a certainty I couldn't place. I felt compelled to follow him outside to his little Volkswagen Beetle. In the back were his two kids and sweet wife. He got into the driver's seat and invited me to sit in the front, next to him. Then he turned on the car, lit up a Marley-sized spliff, and announced dramatically, "Now I will tell you the story of Ireland. By the way, my name is Mike, and I was born in England." Mike was an ex-English professor at Oxford, who got kicked out for smoking ganja[9] with his students. With his hair blowing in all directions, he began telling me with much passion about how the English had destroyed the forests of Ireland. They cut all the trees down for wood to build the mighty British fleet that would conquer, pillage, and enslave much of the known world. Mike had created a company called "Future Forests" to plant new forests all over Ireland. His land was in the Kelkille hills. The people who lived in the forests were called "the little people," he said. The women were the carriers of plant wisdom, medicine, old folktales, and songs. They had also been systematically massacred and burnt at the stake.

We drove for about an hour, until it was getting dark. Mike dropped his wife and kids at his neighbors' and me at his place, telling me that one of the three remaining Rainbow scouts, Austa, would explain everything. He rushed out the door and left me in his dark living room with a lit candle. Here I was, alone in Ireland. Not in the city, not in a dormitory, not even in a village, but in the hills. I had no idea what would come next.

---

[8] Chai: Tea in Arabic, Hindi, and quite a few other languages as well.
[9] Ganja: Cannabis, in Jamaican Rastafari slang.

Austa was Norwegian, and seventeen years old going on seventeen thousand. She was very blonde and pale, maybe more so now because she was recovering from amoebas after a recent trip to India. Mike had told me she couldn't continue scouting because she was sick. As soon as she eased into the room and said hello, Austa started asking me about different people she knew. When I told her I was from Israel and didn't know any of the people she mentioned, she seemed disappointed.

"I don't know much about the Rainbow or its people at all, actually," I confessed.

"Hmmm," she frowned.

I felt like my remark had discouraged her even more. Trying to explain myself but only making it even worse and more awkward, I added, "I've only been at one gathering, for five days near Jerusalem, and arrived here in Ireland a month early by mistake."

After a few more failed attempts at name-dropping, she said, "You know that guy with a big purple hat like Merlin, and a *djembe*? His name is Gil."

"Yeah! I do remember him from the forests of Jerusalem." Now, at least, I felt we had someone in common.

"You need to go to the center of the country. Yes, it's true," she continued, "all the scouts left except for Michael, who's staying near Ushnagh. I can't go with you. But Andi, my neighbor, and Sally, who's from Wales, will take you there. I know he'll be able to find a place for the gathering…two thousand people are coming from all over the world for it, so you must succeed."

We talked a bit more about my Argentinian origins and her Norwegian culture, and how the north and the south meet naturally at the poles. Then she sang me a beautiful old Norse song. I felt elated to be in the presence of something ancient, deep, mysterious, and beautiful. I was already charmed by her when she broke open my heart and sang to me the Chilean hit, Violeta Parra's "Gracias a la Vida," in my native Spanish. We were now more than comfortable, moved, and intrigued by each other. But Austa was very weak, she was not feeling well and had exhausted her last reserves before bedtime. She excused herself for the night and told me to get ready for tomorrow. We would meet Andi and Sally and begin our long drive to the center of Ireland, to Ushnagh.

Andi was a good guitar player, and really nice to be around. Sally was trying too hard to be cool. It's not that she wasn't, but her extra efforts made her clumsy socially. We were a nice team, though, as Cromwell, Wales, and Argentina coalesced on our way to the center of Ireland; the meeting place of the five kings, in Ushnagh, where Ireland was unified. We finally arrived at a farm, not far from there.

In the house's big kitchen, Michael was making toast and spreading his marmite and butter. He was obviously English.

He greeted us with a radiant smile on his face. "Your timing is perfect!" he told us. "I found the location this morning! It's beautiful. You wanna come see it?" After a short drive, we arrived at a stunning farm next to a little town called Rosenallis. It belonged to the sweetest old Irish couple. They were both short, with white hair, and beaming with shining smiles. "Welcome, Rainbow Family, to Ireland!" they greeted us. Apparently, Mike had closed the deal already and had rented their farm for a couple of months for a really good price.

We moved there the next day. Slowly but surely, the seed camp gathered enough people to set up the kitchen and the main structures. My role, self-designated like everything else in the gatherings, was to launch a listening circle almost everywhere I went. In one of those circles, we decided to pitch Mike's tipi on the northern part of the main fire. Three more tipis arrived soon after with powerful and responsible crews. They pitched them around the main circle at the four corners of the main fire. It created the sense of a village. The clearest and most grounded people stayed around the main fire with encampments of concentric circles outward.

The gathering was beautiful by all accounts: abundant and luscious art, music, and an amazing sprout kitchen from the English family. A caravan of Roma people, who had arrived by horse and wagon. The introduction of the Mayan calendar "dream spell" game which had just arrived from Jose Arguelles in Mexico. And my first *temazcal*[10], led by a Peruvian, who had lived in Sinai and the Galilee, and who sang *Pachamama*[11] and *Elohim*[12] in the same breath. We were thirteen people sitting and sweating according to the thirteen moons of the Mayan Calendar. It was a life-changing and very healing experience. We came out of the *temazcal* and right into the gentle waters of the crystal-clear creek. My liver pains from my stagnant hepatitis were totally gone!

Mona proceeded to roll an aesthetic joint. "Amazing," she said. I sipped on my tea and ate some chocolate. "One more story?" she teased.
"Well, I was at this amazing healing retreat in India," I said.
"I want to hear about it," Mona encouraged me.
Now I could see her complexion. We were sitting quite close to each other, and her face was blooming at a perfect angle with the sun.

India – 1996

INDIA WAS becoming inevitable. All roads, signs, omens, and friends were leading to *Mata Bharat*.[13] My dear brother Amir had summoned me to an "invite only" retreat in Satapada, Orissa. Amir had taken part in Chamba, the first Rainbow Gathering in India, the year before. They were so inspired by it that, together with Odin from the Huehuecoyotl community in Tepoztlan who was now living and studying Indian music in Orissa, they had decided to organize and host this first-of-its-kind healing retreat.

It was my first time in India, and I had arrived two months before the retreat (this time on purpose). I landed in Bombay and went straight to Karnataka. I didn't get off the bus in Goa, and instead

---

[10] *Temazcal*: Indigenous mesoamerican purification and healing sweat lodge ceremony.
[11] *Pachamama*: Earth Goddess in Indigenous Andean Culture, related to the feminine fertility of Mother Earth, Creation, and sustenance of all life.
[12] *Elohim*: One of the Hebrew names for the Divine. In Kabbalistic numerology, "Elohim," or "gematria," has the same value as "Nature." In the sefirotic tree of life, Elohim corresponds to "Binah," the left brain, understanding, and discernment.
[13] *Mata Bharat*: Mother India.

continued straight to the beautiful village of Gokarna, eventually arriving at "Om Beach." Sacred open fires, or *dunis,* glowed at each encampment. Live music and interesting people abounded: the kind of travelers I love meeting, each one on their own wild journey.

After a month at the beach, I amassed some courage to venture into hardcore and holy Varanasi. My dear friends Avishai and Anita received me and eased my landing. We were all staying in Nagwa, near Assi Ghat on the Ganga River. Our daily routine was yoga, music, music, and more music! I started studying Indian classical music with the late *shenai*[14] master and performer extraordinaire Ali Abbas Khan. Every day I had a one-hour singing class with him, accompanied by his percussionist, the almost one-eyed Mr. Khadim. In each class, Ali Abbas would choose a specific raga. Then we would sing in call and response. At the end of the class, he taught me songs fitting the raga. He especially preferred old tunes from Indian movies, which got everyone in the 'hood excited. I practiced on my way to the chai shop, showing off and creating relationships on my daily excursions in Nagwa.

Although Ali Abbas's instrument was the shehnai, he gave me seminal singing lessons. He had been second *shehnai* player to the great Bismillah Khan and had married and then divorced Khan's daughter. In our daily classes, beyond singing, we would laugh a lot, eat *samosas,* smoke *bidis,* and drink chai. "Too much laughing!" Ali Abass would say in our short breaks, then "*Tora* (little) rest and then continue," in his flamboyant, endearing, magnetic Indian accent. Mr. Khadim and *Guruji* loved to chew *pan,*[15] so every time they laughed, they would spit a mysterious red goo, coloring their teeth and gums red. In the evenings, I joined the Indian music programs and jam sessions at the Antonelos guest house where I was staying.

I had spent a full month in Benares: a city where everyone (including me) gets intensely sick at least twice. The malaise encompasses vomiting, a horrible sore throat, and spitting green mucus. Varanasi is also the holy city of Shiva, where they burn dead bodies on the sacred

---

[14] *Shenai*: Indian reed instrument with a piercing sound.
[15] *Pan*: Indian chewing tobacco.

Ganges River. By the end of my stay, I was really ready for a cleansing retreat in nature, surrounded by like-minded friends. Govinda (as Mexican Odin was called now) and my brother Amir had invited about thirty people from sixteen different countries to the retreat. Each one of us was a teacher, a natural leader, or had the potential to be one in our own field and community. We began arriving at the quiet and clean (anywhere is cleaner than Varanasi) city of Puri, where we hung out for a couple of days in a cool guest house near the sea until all the invitees arrived, and I reconnected with a few Israeli musician friends. Finally, we departed by bus, followed by a little boat to Satapada: an island with very few locals. We reached our secluded location on foot.

For the next two weeks, we were in a retreat setting. We cleansed—meaning no sugar, coffee, smoking, bread, black tea, or fried food—and basically had two meals a day of rice, dahl and vegetables, some fruit, and herbal tea for the whole stay. This felt really good in my body. Each participant was encouraged to sign up to teach or offer something to the group. Through these workshops we were initiated into Reiki, Indian music, overtone[16] singing, African percussion and dancing, meditation, yoga, massage, shiatsu, and lucid dreaming. In daily listening circles after breakfast, we became aligned with one another and as a group.

By day seven, the musicians from Israel had left the retreat for Kasol in the Himalayas, to create what would become the groundbreaking *Sheva* world music band. I had my own challenges with music: I didn't play an instrument (having not yet learned guitar), and my singing was still quite unstable and insecure. I was also dealing with the unhealthy aftermath from my last co-creation of ritual theater with a couple of the Israeli musicians. It somehow made painful sense that I wasn't invited to Kasol to be part of the band. I reached out to Amir, who had invited me to the retreat, and made him promise to stay until the end of the two weeks. He said he had no intention of leaving.

---

[16] Overtone: Sound harmonics above the normal tone, present in every sound. Can be used for healing and centering. Traditionally from Mongolia, Siberia and Tibet, it was also used in those places to communicate with horses.

The last night of the retreat, Govinda announced that we would be doing a *temazcal* ceremony. The day after, as a celebration, we would all ingest magic mushrooms together. After the very intense and transformative *temazcal*, we all slept like babies. Rested, we got ready for the full moon mushroom celebration. Anita had decided not to take the *niños*[17] and offered to take care of us. Jai Dass was the firekeeper and had built an enormous bonfire which could be seen from almost anywhere on our little island.

When the mushrooms kicked in, I found myself with a small group on the beach: Marisse, Revital, Pascale, and Amir. It was a full moon, and it was raining; we had dropped our clothes and gone into the ocean. When we left the water, our clothes were nowhere to be found. Laughing, we started running back as fast as we could. Catching my breath in the rain under the full moon, I tried to figure out where we had left our clothes. They were really far away! Thanks to Jai Dass's impressive fire, we finally found our way to our clothes and eventually to the camp. It was late in the night. Jai Dass and Anita dried us off, covered us with blankets, and after we all woke up, served us some delicious hot chai.

After that, I decided to sign up for *Vipassana* insight meditation, Goenka style, in Dharamsala. I left again for Varanasi to continue my music studies until the Vipassana retreat began. I still had about ten days until the retreat. A concerned friend had told me, "You in Vipassana...silent for ten days? You'd better start sitting and meditating at least ten minutes a day and increase your time every day, or it will be a very big shock for your system in Dharamsala." I was already practicing a little yoga routine of about 45 minutes, to which I added sitting for ten minutes in silence.

When I got to the Vipassana retreat, they immediately took away our passports. That's it! I said to myself. No way of leaving here for the next ten days. The first few days were intense. We slept very little and got up in the dark to sit in meditation for hours on end. The silence, though, was surprisingly soothing. After the first few days,

---

[17] *Niños*: magic mushrooms, the "playful" members of the psychedelic family. Niños also means "children" in Spanish.

though, they instructed us to sit in stillness without moving our body position. This was agonizing for me. My body was in horrible pain—even parts I wasn't aware of. Sitting up straight was a killer. At some point, perhaps by day seven, I stopped paying attention to my body. The pain had faded from my consciousness.

On day nine, we were allowed to start talking. I met with an old friend who was also there and ranted at him for about two hours. Poor Inbal was Israeli, played sitar and lived in Nagwa. He had worked with us as a chef in our ritual theater company, Metatron;[18] the company had been my main reason for staying in Israel, but was over for now. "So," I told Inbal, "Either I leave Israel, or I create a nurturing container which will hold me in a space of creativity and spirit, where I'm seen, and where I can contribute to the new Israeli alternative culture." Inbal just listened and nodded. Within the hour, I had decided to stay in Israel. In the following hour, I told Inbal everything I would do over the next five years.

One of the main things I felt was missing for me in Israel was my relationship to its essential Spirit. At the time, my way of celebrating Hebrew wisdom, and the theology I grew up with, were unheard of in Israeli alternative circles. My peers were flourishing in India, Africa, Sufism, and shamanism, but didn't have any positive experience of including Judaism in their spiritual holistic mix. By now, Judaism was becoming—even for me, the son of a Rabbi—an obsolete expression. However, I was determined to change that. These were the days when rock and roll had shifted to world music, my meat-eating habits had turned vegetarian, God gave way to Great Spirit, and Judaism surrendered to Hebrew wisdom. I was on a roll and wasn't about to stop.

"So," I told Inbal, who only managed to interject the word "yes" and nod. "The vision is to create a vehicle to celebrate the Hebrew calendar in a relevant, creative fashion. A way which is comfortable and coherent with my values, my theology, my ecology, my activism, my emotions, and my spirit."

Inbal added "hmm" to his lexicon. Before he could say a word

---

[18] Metatron: The angel who, ancient Hebrew legend says, used to be Enoch, the Prince of Presence, father of Methuselah.

more, I continued, "The soup to be cooked will include the depth of reflection of American Jewish renewal, the few Israeli professors initiated in Spirit, my musician friends of Sheva, the core of the newly born Israeli Rainbow family as staff, selected new age incoming Israeli teachers, and our mainstream fans and participants." These were the radical and roaring '90s. Together, we would become one community celebrating a few selected Hebrew holidays, holistically, in nature, in color, reliving and recreating Hebrew living legends, myths, and ceremonies. As Rabbi Kook had envisioned, "The ancient shall be renewed and the new shall become sacred." I even went as far as deciding that the first Hebrew holiday that we would tackle would be *"Tu Bishvat,"* the new year for the trees. I hugged and thanked Inbal, who just looked at me and smiled.

On day ten, we all parted ways. Pascale, who I had met at the retreat, surprised me by waiting for me right outside the gates of the Tushita Center. She was a brilliant Belgian choreographer, and one of the original legendary Zap Mamas.[19] "I couldn't miss you!" Pascale said. "Coming out of Vipassana, I have a few days free here in Dharamsala." As I came back down to daily life from the heights of Vipassana, Pascale and I spent the next couple of days singing and hiking together.

I also passed through Delhi, briefly. I was excited to get back to Israel, to co-create an ecological village with a retreat center at its core together with the tribe that was becoming a brilliant, powerful community—or so we thought. We met, blended with one another, and eventually created a bank account to purchase land in the Galilee at Har Hazon—Vision Mountain—after scouting possibilities in the alternative villages of Kadita, Clil, and Har Shokef. We never got the permits to build there, though, and our adventure ended by returning everyone's money to them.

The Hebrew holiday gatherings happened in full force, beginning with *Tu Bishvat* in Kibbutz Beit Oren in 1997. Our same group then organized and hosted eight gatherings for the renewal, rehydration,

---

[19] Zap Mama: African women-led percussive and experimental voice-oriented band based in Belgium, prominent in the '90s and early 2000s.

and re-sacralization of Hebrew wisdom, creating ceremonies for certain Jewish holidays that rehydrated ancient wisdom with contemporary creative language. Around two thousand people took part in these beautiful holistic gatherings out in nature, which kept me based in Israel for a while.

At every turn of my stories, it felt like soul-stripping, and I could sense my life force getting juicier and brighter. Of course, Mona's presence helped; her deep listening and beauty inspired me. She told me about a new regenerative community in Costa Rica she was involved with, which sounded grounded and exciting.

Temperature shifts are sudden in Sinai, and it gets cold quickly after sunset. We had to get dressed accordingly. I got to my *husha* and my joy was alive! I felt my heart pumping. By then I had already seen that Mona would be a really good addition to our "Big Vision." In those days, I was only talking about it with the special few who would be directly involved. Until now those few were Ibrahim, Vasilis, me, and a couple of others including Lakota elder Tiokasin who had shown up to hear my informal presentation in Portugal. My vision was to get the core team together and have a vision retreat, with no more than 20 people. We would ignite our spirits and souls for the Big Vision. We would listen to Grandma Sinai, and build trust and cohesion amongst our team.

The location of our "Spirit Camp" was still a conundrum. Should we hold it in the Sinai desert, the perfect secluded and inspiring place? But then it would be almost impossible for Palestinians without a foreign passport to attend. Crete was the other possibility. I had a friend with a big piece of land there. It even had its own river. It would involve some flying, or boat travel, but it looked like that could be the right location! A boat from Haifa? A plane from Amman? I had some research to do.

All this was going through my head as I began putting on my heavy socks and a couple of layers. I packed my songbooks too—by now four, filled with songs from around the world I'd learned by direct transmission for thirty years. I made sure my guitar tuner, capo, and flashlight were all in the case, ready to go to the fire to sing and play with my newfound friend the alluring violist.

I ordered a big *barrad*[20] of ginger and lemon tea and sat down near the orange and blue flames. They seemed to be in sync with the colors of the majestic crack between worlds, also known as sunset, happening in front of me. The sun had already gone down but the afterglow remained. And Mona? *Patience*, I told myself. The sky shone and I began playing. And there she was, walking by the sea, hand in hand with a tall, blond, handsome man. My heart cringed. *Shit, not again*, I said to myself. They went to sit by the sea in a *zula*[21] quite far from the fire. I could still see her radiant glow, smiling and happy as a clam with her new gorgeous guy. *Let it go*, I said to myself. *She's not for you now*. I went back to playing a new song I was working on. Closing my eyes, I started improvising with the plethora of emotions I had in me. Passion, anger, frustration, yearning, sadness—it was all in my voice.

You might be thinking, "You just met her! How can you get so emotional about someone you hardly know?" But the heart is irrational, and all the traumas of rejection from women in my past had risen with full force to my solar plexus. Even deeper knots popped up in my abdomen and neck as I recalled the countless times that women I was attracted to and became close to had voiced their appreciation for my "amazingness," my heart, and my friendship. And no, they didn't want anything intimate, erotic, physical, or romantic with me. The old wound of rejection was now reaching my throat. I closed my eyes even tighter and forced myself to keep singing.

A couple of tears ran down my cheeks. After about fifteen minutes, which seemed longer than the world's history since the big bang, I stopped singing, put the guitar down, and finally opened my bleary eyes. It was already pitch black except for the fire and some candles glowing in the dark. The moon wasn't up yet. A luminous couple of white-haired elders were smiling at me—Murat and Kurdi. They

---

[20] *Barrad*: Arabic for "teapot."
[21] *Zula*: Cozy space, Arabic for "hangout." Same meaning in Israeli slang.

didn't blink or stop smiling until they stood up and approached my side of the fire.

"Can we sit next to you?" Murat asked.

"Sure," I answered. The captivating witch and magnetic wizard sat next to me. They were beaming, and I felt their goodness and warmth. It was traveling up my body and landed right at my gut.

"Your soul perforated us through your song, and we had to come closer and let you know," Kurdi said with a contagious giggle.

"Where are you from?" I asked.

"From Turkey on the border with Syria," Murat said. "We're Kurds."

"Are you hungry?" Kurdi inquired. "I want to order some fish for us. You want to join us?"

"I would love to," I said, happy to let go of my drama.

I put the guitar back in the case and followed Murat to a quiet cozy corner with a candle and more than enough pillows. There are moments when you know you are in the right company—and this was one of them. Kurdi joined us and they asked me whether I minded if a couple of new friends joined us for dinner. They had just met them a few days before, they said.

"If you like them, then me too!" I replied without thinking.

"Great," Kurdi said with her sweet laugh, and went to look for the surprise guests. Murat had gone to the seashore to pee. I followed Kurdi's trajectory with my eyes. She was walking in the direction of Mona and her handsome, athletic, tanned new man. I prayed out loud, "Please, not them! I'm not ready yet!"

Sure enough, they were precisely the ones she invited to join us. I tried breathing out strongly through my nose, releasing any negativity, and breathing in a smile. It wasn't happening. The three of them arrived at once and sat down. I was very uncomfortable and trying to hide it, which made it even worse, and it probably showed. Kurdi broke the silence.

"Mona is an amazing musician, and this is our new friend, also a sacred musician. We just met around the fire."

"We also met today," I said, glancing slightly at Mona, trying to seem nonchalant.

"This shiny powerful being is Rowan," Murat added. "He's a man of the sea."

"Nice to meet you," I said.

Mona kept looking at me and smiling, which made me feel uncomfortable and magnetized at the same time. I was still under her spell.

"Rowan," said Mona, "is my half-brother."

Wow! Was I relieved. The ball of tension in my gut abruptly melted. I was breathing again—and I think everyone in our magical intimate circle felt my release. I realized my crush was strong, and I couldn't hide it.

"Ahhh, so good to meet kindred souls!" Murat said, helping me out in brotherly solidarity by dissolving the awkwardness. He took out a bottle of Raki and five little shot glasses. Filling them up, he passed them around, and suggested, "Let's toast to new friendships!" We all drank to that. Murat started telling us about a project they were leading together with the youth of Kurdish Rojava. "Amazing," Rowan said. He had also worked with youth. In his case, it was with refugees and boats, in Greece and Turkey. I was thrilled. I felt a rush of freedom above my belly button, which propelled me to tell them about my adventure in Cappadocia. Mona encouraged me with another of her all-conquering smiles.

Cappadocia – 2002

It was a first for me: I was part of a proper tour group. We went to encounter the *Bektashi*[22] Sufi order during their annual festival in breathtaking Cappadocia. The group consisted of about thirty people, led by a guide who had met the Bektashis a year before. I had joined the group with three old friends: Gil and Udi from the band Sheva, and Boaz, who had entered village life in *Amirim*[23] a few years

---

[22] *Bektashi*: Nontraditional Sufi lineage rooted in the Sufi saint Haji Bektashi from Cappadocia, Turkey, whose first disciple was a woman.

[23] *Amirim*: Vegetarian village (moshav) in the northern mountains of Galilee.

before. We were "behaving," and had been part of most of the official daytrips with the group—including to the mesmerizing caves of Cappadocia. Haji Bektashi, we learned, was a thirteenth-century Sufi who had lived for some time in isolation in a cave. When he stepped out of his time in retreat, the first person he met was a woman. She became his first student, and because of this, women in the Bektashi order had the same opportunities as men. They were allowed to sing, play, and dance in their *Semaa*[24] ceremonies. Bektashis are even prone to drink wine on occasion.

On our first evening, our gentle and informed guide told us we were going to visit the *Dargah*[25] and that Dede Munir Baba himself, in direct lineage from Haji Bektashi, had invited us to join them in their *Semaa*. It was love at first sight. The *dervishes* danced in the midst of the circle in mixed-gender couples, to stunning music played on the *saz*[26] and sung live by women and men alike. They were some of the same famous Turkish musicians who played on the main stage of the festival. After we had been there a while, one of the local pilgrims asked Dede Baba what Israeli Jews were doing present at their sacred ceremony. Firmly, he responded that we were their special guests and part of the family from beloved *Nabi Musa's*[27] side.

The ecstatic night was pulsing through our hearts, woven through with hypnotic songs and ceremonial couples dancing, Sufi tales, teachings, and prayers intertwined with blessings. As the spirit wave increased in intensity, I was suddenly shaken in awe from within as I stood next to the circle, ready to explode. Dede Baba sensed my trembling presence and signaled with his staff, daring me to dance alone. I disassembled my body into a trance in the middle of the circle. It was my sweating prayer.

When Dede Baba saw that some of us had brought our musical instruments, he generously invited us to sing a prayer from our own tradition as part of the ceremony. This felt completely unexpected

---

[24] *Semaa*: Turkish Sufi ceremony whose name means "a deep listening," and includes music, dance and breathwork. A kind of Zikr, a heart cleansing.
[25] *Dargah*: Sufi abode where initiates eat, pray, learn, engage in ceremony, and gather.
[26] *Saz*: Turkish traditional string instrument.
[27] *Nabi Musa*: Arabic for the prophet Moses.

and surprised everyone in the room. Udi took the guitar, and we sang the priestly blessing from Solomon's temple times—one of the oldest prayers we have in the Hebrew tradition. The music was written by Jai Uttal while visiting us in Israel, the first song he ever wrote in Hebrew (but that is another story).

Our Bektashi brothers, sisters, and musicians were deeply moved—and so were we, by the elegance of their spirit. Tears were flowing all around as the dervishes reached out one by one to hug and bless us. Abraham's Family[28] was shining. The aura of re-encounter was filling the *dargah*, our bodies, and our spirits. In liminal space, I glimpsed broken images of Ishmael meeting his brother Isaac and burying their father in the *Cave of the Machpelah*. A gentle old dervish who, like most of them, only spoke Turkish, gave me his prayer beads with the ninety-nine names of Allah, which I have to this day. A brilliant female vocalist and true sister reached out and hugged me with the warmth and nourishment of deep spiritual family. It was collective bliss in the form of prayer, kindness, and community.

As we were about to break bread together, Dede Baba instructed the director of the Halevi[29] annual national festival, who had come to pay his respects, to give us fifteen minutes to sing on the main stage of the festival. Excited, we discussed amongst ourselves what to play. The consensus was the song "Love Your Neighbor as Yourself." Udi said he wouldn't dare to play *baglama*[30] in front of the best players in Turkey. So guitar it was. Boaz, neither a musician nor a percussionist, played a couple of wooden spoons—his worldwide debut, and also his farewell performance, in front of a massive audience of fifteen thousand people.

Five minutes before we were supposed to go onstage, magic happened. We met Eyal, the percussionist who had recorded that same song in 2001 for my first album, *Merkavah*. He was traveling with his girlfriend through Turkey and had come as a spectator to see the festival. I

---

[28] Abraham's Family: Isaac and Ishmael were the sons of Abraham from two different mothers, Sarah and Hagar. They were the forefathers of the Hebrews and the Arabs, who are all descendants of one of the sons of Noah, named Shem (the Semites).
[29] Halevi: The Halevi belong to a lower class and ethnic group with most of their constituency living in Cappadocia, and are quite active socio-politically.
[30] *Baglama*: Turkish string instrument. Also called Saz.

spotted him in the first row and ran quickly to say hello. I told him we were going onstage very soon and asked him if he would play with us; he said he would love to but didn't have a drum. "We have one!" I said, as I had brought mine. Gil introduced us onstage, and our translator announced us with a Turkish accent—"Israil"—then mentioned each of our names. We played and sang for about fifteen minutes, including my solo African dancing and Boaz's debut on spoons. Fifteen thousand people, mostly Kurds and Halevis, went berserk.

The next morning, we went with Gil to the *dargah*. An ancient attraction of pure love was pulling us there. We relished the next few days, in the presence of whoever was taking care of the *dargah*, of our hearts, and of each other. The Bektashi were very poor materially, but they shared everything with us, even what little food they had. Our *dost*[31] also spoke the language of hospitality, simplicity, and spirit. It was our heart family. We were home.

The nights were a whole other matter. We were staying at a shady establishment on the outskirts of town. The cheap hotel had an oriental cabaret and bar with very sensuous belly dancers, and we indulged the habit of shifting to our *Zorba* personas by going to drink at the hotel bar. We felt like some kind of celestial hooligans. Sufis by day, enamored with simple spirit and heart, and drunk with worldly pleasures by night.

In a tragic turn of events, though, the last night of the festival was canceled after thirty-two of the people who participated in the *Semaa* with us that sacred night had died in a bus accident. The mystery of tragedy devoured the story and our experience. The rest of our Israeli tourist group left for Istanbul, and the four of us stayed in Cappadocia. We continued to meet dervishes from Syria and all the way to Albania until our departure.

The fish arrived as I was finishing the story. We ate lavishly and drank some more of the Raki that Murat had opened earlier. For dessert, Mona had brought some sumptuous white chocolate with passion fruit inside. (She had kept it safe and chilled in the kitchen fridge,

---

[31] *Dost*: A Turkish Sufi term referring to deep friendship, and spiritual family.

which, for Sinai, was a miracle in itself.) As a digestif, she rolled yet another immaculate joint. Her spliffs lasted for hours, even though we were a group of five. That was an even greater miracle at this Sinai camp.

Then Mona said, "Can I borrow your guitar? I want to sing you all a song."

"Of course!" I said.

As she leaned over to get the guitar, she lightly brushed her hair over me. I felt my blood moving. She played and sang so enchantingly that Kurdi was crying as we all grinned in delight. Rowan encouraged her to sing another song from their childhood. Her voice was deep and clear with a unique translucent color. After her song, she gave me back the guitar. "Lead the way," she said. I played some chords, and as Mona joined in and deepened the music, Murat took out his *dumbek*. Although he wasn't a virtuoso, he kept perfect time and held his own as a pertinent launchpad for Mona to fly far into fantastic worlds of melody. Rowan and Kurdi joined us in some choruses and giggles—but mostly, as the warmest, loudest, and most present listening ears I have ever felt. Music, I recognized in that moment, is influenced and sculpted by those who actively listen and receive it.

Enter laughter. Kurdi and Rowan were penetrating the skies with high pitched chortles, we were all quite high, and even the million stars seemed to be enjoying the evening as they shone brightly and proudly above us. It was bedtime. We hugged warmly and truthfully.

"I feel so nurtured," I said.

Mona came straight to me and gave me the warmest and most present hug I had experienced in a long time. It felt sufficient, and so I just said a funny goodbye and prepared to leave for my *husha*. As I strapped my guitar case on my back, Murat said, "It would be nice to go to the desert together, no?"

It was unanimous. It was the end of fall, and the beach was almost empty: just a few volunteers, the locals, and a couple of visitors. The next morning, as I went to get my coffee, I glanced at the two last tourists leaving in a taxi. Wow! It really seemed like it was just us there now. I took my coffee close to the water, staring into the horizon over the Red Sea. My back was to the camp when I heard a very familiar voice.

"*Salamtak habibi!*"[32]

It was our dear brother Musallem. Those last ten years, he had mostly been staying and working in the mountains and was very rarely seen at the beach. He was wearing his million-dollar smile as he delivered his classic "Life is gooooood!" Truly happy to see him, I laughed and got up to hug him. For some good reason, his timing was usually impeccable. It felt as if he'd heard our call for the mountains and was coming to get us. So I went right ahead!

"Hey *achui*,[33] are you free to go to the mountains?"

"*Aiwa!*[34] Why not? Always happy to go to the desert with you."

"There are some other friends," I added. "Fantastic people I just met yesterday who want to come too."

"Sure, of course, why not?" He smiled again. "*Yahara beitak*,[35] I missed you, man. *Wenak?*"[36] said Musallem with joy and his big smile. "Peace be with you, your house is shit!"

"I'm here, bro!" I said as we hugged and laughed again.

"We can leave tomorrow! What do you think? You can bring your friends and meet me at sheik Suleiman's *maagad*,[37] my brother's in Tarabin, you remember the place…at 9 AM?"

Kurdi and Murat approached us. "*Salaam Aleikum!*" they both said. I could see Musallem was puzzled by their accent.

"*Alaikum Assalam*," he replied, intrigued. "I hear a nice Arabic… with a twist…where are you from? *Shami*? *Suria*?"

"We are Kurdish, and yes, very close to the border with Syria in Turkey," Murat answered.

"Wow, *Alhamdulillah!*"[38] Musallem said. Then Rowan and Mona appeared, and both introduced themselves to Musallem. Each of them

---

[32] *Salamtak habibi*: "Peace be with you, beloved" in colloquial Bedouin Arabic.
[33] *Achui*: "My brother" in Arabic.
[34] *Aiwa*: "Yes" in Arabic.
[35] *Yahara beitak*: Literally, "Your house is shit." Used in Bedouin slang as a term for affection.
[36] *Wenak*: "Where have you been?" in Arabic.
[37] *Maagad*: A dwelling and sitting place where Bedouins and guests gather.
[38] *Alhamdulillah*: "Divine sweet grace" in Arabic.

hugged me with a warm good morning. This was a great team, and we could all feel it.

"Check this out, Murat," I said. "You thought it would be nice to go to the desert. And Musallem showed up this morning just in time. What about leaving tomorrow morning for four days and three nights? We're in the best of hands."

"I've known this man for twenty-five years and we are good friends," Musallem told everyone. "I felt I had to come to the beach today. And now, I know why."

"Musallem is the best Bedouin guide I know! He truly loves Sinai," I said, proud of my dear friend.

"Thank you *habibi*," said Musallem. "And you know who is getting married tomorrow? Remember Said our young guide from the *Jabaliya?*[39] I just got him a fancy *Jelabia*[40] from Dahab!"

"*Enjad?!*"[41] I said, excited.

"We can go to his wedding!" He continued. "We are all invited to *Wadi El Arbain* for his *Farha*[42] tomorrow evening! Then we can go to Hodra, Meliches, wherever you want. We'll be back here at the sea in four days."

"*Mumtaz*! Perfect," Kurdi said, and we all laughed, infected by her contagious giggles.

Musallem left as suddenly as he had arrived. Bedouins are Indigenous desert people. They sit still like mountains and move like the wind.

I went to the kitchen to order orange juices for us all. It was getting sunny, and we were starting to shed layers of clothes. When I came back with the drinks, the others had arranged mattresses to create a comfortable, cozy space. They had paired up and were giving massages to one another, a bottle of arnica oil between them. The scene looked auspicious. Kurdi was working on Mona, and Rowan was working on Murat. It really felt like a spa. I pulled out the guitar, sat on a cushion,

---

[39] *Jabaliya*: Bedouin tribe from the St. Catherine mountain range in the high mountains of Sinai. Probably got to Sinai from Europe to build and protect the monastery.
[40] *Jelabia*: Bedouin traditional tunic.
[41] *Enjad*: "Really?" in Arabic.
[42] *Farha*: Arabic for wedding celebration.

and played some healing chords which matured into a deep quiet song. After they were done, we remained in silence for a while. All of a sudden, the four of them got up and surrounded me with the best group hug I had ever had. We sat in silence for a bit longer.

"Time for drinks!" I said and passed the juices around. "I'm really feeling you guys. I have the strong impulse to tell you about a big dream which I'm getting ready to manifest. I have a sense that you will be a part of it. I will tell you more when we get to the sandstone desert. But for now, can I share with you the story of The Iranian-Israeli Love Conspiracy?"

"Love your stories," Mona said with her usual grace. Her encouragement and attention made me feel strong, and was beginning to have a serious effect on my shine and courage.

Eynif Plateau – 2005

THIS WAS the first time that a World Rainbow Gathering had taken place in a Muslim country. We had arrived to gather in Turkey, and it finally felt more real: we were not just privileged Judeo-Christian white counterculture hippies from the West who had an inspiring go with psychedelia, Native American spirituality, or mystical India. This time around, it was different—especially once the Iranians arrived.

One morning about a week into the gathering, I woke up feeling totally out of place. This usually happens to me at a gathering, a spiritual workshop, and often in ordinary life as well. I didn't fit, and wanted to leave. What was I doing there, anyway? In a tent with a bunch of privileged new agers trying to play "harmony in nature," I felt hypocritical and awful.

That's precisely when I decided it was time to lead a workshop. I got to the breakfast's main circle early and announced that we would meet after breakfast for a *Sulha*[43] workshop rooted in my peace work. The location I chose was out of the way, a bit far from the main fire,

---

[43] Sulha: Indigenous Middle Eastern ritual form of mediation used to resolve conflict involving a shared meal, three cups of coffee, forgiveness, and a council of elders or "j'aha" recognized and accepted by the two feuding parties.

where there was enough shade and the ground was flat and suitable for movement. I began by singing a song to create an attention field and ground our journey in Spirit. Following a little icebreaker game, I proceeded to tell the story of the *Sulha*. After some time for questions, we were all ready for some hands-on work.

I guided everyone to form a circle and told them about *Zikr*, calling it simply a "heart cleansing remembrance ceremony." We were already holding hands in a circle, and I was about to start the movements. The participants were getting restless, as anarchists usually do when they have to follow anything or anyone. Suddenly, I heard loud voices getting closer. Everyone in the circle began staring towards the direction of the main fire. "What's going on?" I asked. As I turned around, I saw a truck at the main fire! This was unheard of, as the gathering is supposed to be car-free, and the main fire is meant to be sacred. Though I was upset, my intention was firm, and I told the participants to focus and bring back their attention to our circle.

The noise grew louder. As I glanced again, I saw people coming out of the truck and walking toward us, carrying heavy luggage. Then they sat right outside our circle. What's going on here? I thought to myself. A truck at the main fire? Why are they coming here, straight to my workshop space, of all places in this enormous mountain range?

At that point, it was hard to continue talking. More than twenty people had sat down around us with their knapsacks. Dolphie, who had gotten up to try and tell the newcomers to be quiet, whispered at me from across the circle, trying to alert me without them noticing. He rolled his "r's" with a heavy French accent: "Gabriel…Iran, Iran." It was hard to understand him, and I was starting to find the whole situation ridiculous. Dolphie insisted, though, and whispered more loudly. "Ask them where they are from!"

To give some context, these were times of imminent war when, encouraged by the media and the governments' narratives, Iranians and Israelis had become sworn enemies. Other than a few meetings in India or the West, Israelis and Iranians weren't meeting face to face at all.

I finally gave in and asked them, "Where are you from?"

"Iran," several voices answered from outside our circle.

Our group transitioned suddenly into a loud silence and then a bewildered collective sigh of radical surprise.

One of the recent arrivals reciprocated. "Where are *you* from?" he asked us.

"Israel," several of the people inside the circle answered. Now it was the Iranians' turn for surprise. Just as the Israelis had done a moment ago, they gasped.

I invited everyone to get up, and asked the Iranians to leave their bags where they were and come join the circle. "Make room for them and open the circle," I said to the mostly Israeli participants. As we re-ignited our *Zikr* again, I started turning my head to each side, calling in the Divine Oneness in Hebrew and Arabic: *Alla Hu, Ya Elohim*. Then I began another simple movement, bowing up and down with *La ilaha ila lah*. We chanted different divine names in Arabic and Hebrew along with simple movements which everyone could follow. After almost half an hour of praying, singing, moving, and breathing with increasing intensity, we reached a trance-like state, eventually landing on the ground in deep surrender.

I asked everyone to slowly get up in silence and saw the faces of the people across our circle. A few were crying—one here, one there, and then another and another joined the weeping. As the tight group surrounded me, we concluded by singing the *Priestly Blessing*[44], ending with *Shalom*[45] for blessing and protection.[46] By this point, I was crying too. Priya, the one responsible for bringing these twenty-three Iranians straight from Tehran to Turkey in a truck, was hugging me, tears flowing in a cascade. We sat down side by side, crying and smiling, then laughing. We all hugged again, and decided to camp next to each other. We showed the Iranians where our tents were, and helped them with their bags. And so it was: the Iranian-Israeli Love Conspiracy was born. Our camp offered the best meals and parties,

---

[44] Priestly Blessing: One of the most ancient Hebrew prayers in temple times. Known as "Birkat Hakoanim," it was performed by the priests at the temple. A blessing for protection and wholeness.
[45] *Shalom*: Hebrew for "wholeness." Peace in its most profound sense. Rooted in the Hebrew "Shalem," or whole.
[46] To listen to "Shalom," go to page 251.

the most amazing music and goodies. It was truly a love affair, and no one else in the gathering could believe it.

Five days later, Priya and I decided that Israelis and Iranians should meet once a year. I suggested to her that we go to Cappadocia to visit Dede Baba at Haji Bektashi. We would ask his spiritual permission to start a peace gathering for Middle Eastern people in Turkey, the only place Iranians and Israelis could meet without visa issues. It would be cheap to arrive overland for Iranians, and would also be affordable for Israelis. The rest would follow.

When we finally arrived at Haji Bektashi after many relentless hours of driving, Sadegh, Priya, and I asked for Dede Baba, who wasn't hard to find. He remembered me and asked about the other Jewish friends that had come from Israel to the festival a few years before. We asked him if he approved of peace gatherings between Iranians and Israelis in Turkey. In broken Turkish, Sadegh translated to Dede Baba. "Yes," replied Dede Baba. "No problem." After another tea, we asked Bubu if he was ready to drive us back. As usual, our big-hearted friend was up for it. We traveled the whole way back to Manavgat and the Rainbow Gathering.

Priya and I remained steadfast in our intention to create a Peace in the Middle East Gathering in Turkey the following year. We even had a date, and already our Turkish brother Aykut had a strong hint for the location. A veteran traveler, German Baba Hans, supported our vision and sat with us in the vision council, where consensus to gather in Turkey happened in less than twenty minutes! It was probably the fastest decision-making process in the history of the Rainbow. We had a location, the date, and the local scout inviting us in the name of the Turkish family. We were ready to go.

"And did you guys end up meeting in Turkey?" Murat asked.

"Yup! We gathered there for four years in a row," I answered.

There was a moment of silence, we all looked at each other and smiled, inspired in our friendship.

"Okay," Rowan said. "I'm ready to go to the water. Who's coming?"

We all went to the lagoon at the beach next door. After some swimming, Mona offered to give me some *watsu*.[47] I was in heaven. Rowan went for a snorkeling journey through the coral reef with Murat and Kurdi, then we all met again for sunset and had dinner together. It seemed like we couldn't separate. I imagine you know the feeling, when you bond with someone, feel increasingly more comfortable in your own skin, and joy takes over. Every time we met, I felt less tired. We waited for our food—and in Sinai, where the rhythm is slow, you can wait for quite a while. While we waited, I told them another story—this time, one that happened in Jerusalem. The Big Vision was getting closer.

Tantur – 2000

THE '90S were over and so was the peace hype and the new wave of Israeli cultural flourishing. Hope was in freefall since the assassination of Prime Minister Yitzhak Rabin. It was the beginning of the Second Intifada.[48] As violence took over the country, relationships were crumbling in the peace camp.

I was living in the Galilean vegetarian village of Amirim, recovering from terrible heartbreak after the tragic story with my beloved girlfriend. With two liver abscesses and an ocean of inconsolable tears and frustration, I had traveled the world looking for medicine to ease my pain. Her tragic accident had happened only a couple of years before, but I was getting stronger—and this conference was about to shift the direction of my life.

One afternoon, I got a call from Eliyahu MacLean, an old friend and interfaith activist I had met in Berkeley. Eliyahu was a Hawaiian neo-Hasidic *Jufi*[49], and had been commissioned to convene and organize the first interfaith global peacemaker conference in Jerusalem. When I asked who was behind it, he said, "Roshi Bernie Glassman." I

---

[47] *Watsu*: An aquatic modality of healing that blends acupressure and water. Watsu was born in the alternative community based at Harbin Hot Springs in California.
[48] Intifada: "Uprising" in Arabic. Used by the Palestinian people as a means for fighting the Israeli occupation.
[49] *Jufi*: Jewish Sufi.

had heard my dear dad mention this name; they had worked together with the Coalition for the Homeless in New York City, and had great respect for each other. When I asked Eliyahu if I could come to the conference, he said it was by invitation only. I told him to tell Bernie who I was and mention my father. Eliyahu called the next day and told me that Bernie said I could come as a guest observer.

I arrived on a Friday at Tantur Monastery, whose walls still had fresh holes from gunfire. Tantur was situated between Gilo and Beit Jala, and was important strategically as one of the only safe routes for Palestinians to cross from East to West Jerusalem without having to pass a checkpoint. Soon, other participants started arriving: rabbis, sheiks, nuns, Buddhist monks, Europeans, Middle Easterners, and North Americans. The organization had spent fifteen thousand dollars to bring everyone together. And Roshi Bernie Glassman was not your typical Zen Roshi;[50] he had a Brooklyn accent, smoked cigars, and joked often. As soon as I saw Bernie was available, I went to say hello. Bernie told me that he loved my father and was delighted to meet Marshall's son, then gave me a warm hug. Everyone was fully present and looking forward to Bernie's words at the opening session.

"Welcome!" Bernie said. "We have come together here to launch a global interfaith, international order of peacemakers. This is the last time I will be talking in this gathering, as I won't be leading this initiative. It is all up to you."

Everyone was in shock.

"This is Purna," Roshi went on, gesturing to an American in jeans and sandals who had just stood up. "He is going to facilitate this conference and help us get to know each other and our synergies. Thank you."

Purna was apparently an American expert in teamwork for major high-tech firms, and his name and sandals made up for the spiritual persona. It certainly wasn't enough. By the second afternoon, we had met in several sessions under the leadership of our dear Purna. We had played confidence games, indulged in trust exercises, and practiced body warm-ups. The Europeans and the Arab clergy were getting

---

[50] Zen Roshi: A teacher of an order of Buddhists from the Japanese spiritual lineage.

impatient. I overheard a radical Franciscan French priest talking to a Buddhist activist from Switzerland in the monastery's hallways during the break. "What are we doing here?" asked the priest. "There's a war going on and we're here playing new-age games?"

"I don't know," the activist answered. "Not knowing is one of our tenets. We need to trust the mystery."

Other Palestinian and Jordanian faith leaders were done with politeness, though. We went in for the next session. As usual, Purna was leading, and I could see everyone getting restless as he explained the next exercise with seriousness.

And now, dear reader: will you grant the sacred fool coming from the heart a place of honor? Might you give the medicine of humor a chance to play its earth magic? So...enters the heyoka,[51] the classic *bouffon*,[52] the *badchana demalka*,[53] the only one who can say whatever he wishes to the king without being beheaded—even if it's "politically incorrect," even if it breaks all the rules of ideology, or the rightful protocols of privilege and race, or worse, just to crack reality up and reshuffle perception for the higher cause of balance, for a more nuanced, multidimensional, and polychromatic experience with earth. Ready or not...here we go.

My inner "prophetic rabbit", the jester, burst out in wild surprise—and as the sacred fool's spirit took me over, I got up and said in a loud voice with my funniest Indian accent, "If we don't start smiling here, there will never be peace, there will never be a global order of peacemakers. "The extremely tense room collapsed in laughter. First the Italian nun, then the Palestinian sheik and the American rabbis, until finally even Purna had to stop his explanation and laugh. At that moment, Bernie—who hadn't said a word since the opening

---

[51] Heyoka: The contrarian. An "anti-natural" trained by the Earth. In Lakota tradition the "heyoka" may subvert even the most sacred ritual for the sake of Earth's balance. He's a necessary and respected part of ceremony.
[52] *Bouffon*: In Middle French it was *bouffon*, which came from the Italian *buffone*, meaning "jester." The original root is the Latin *buffare*. Think of the stereotypical court jester, the person who makes jokes and acts the fool to make the king laugh.
[53] *Badchana demalka*: Its source is in the Kabbalistic masterpiece, the Zohar. Aramaic for "jester" of the king. In the Zohar, there is also a love for celestial hooligans and holy rascals who go against everything seemingly appropriate and sacred for the sake of truth, and ultimately, love.

session—jumped up from his chair, took a red clown nose from his pocket, and put it on. Three others who were sitting in the circle did the same. They started dancing and laughing around me as Bernie put a red nose on my nose and finally said, "You are now initiated into the *Order of Disorder*."

Bernie declared a break, and then we divided into focus groups. I joined the vision group and came up with what would become the *Sulha Peace Project* one year later, then presented its full-fledged vision about a gathering of Israelis, international participants and Palestinians, including many from the West Bank and Gaza. By 2008, the annual five-day gathering would embrace over six thousand Palestinians and Israelis in a holistic micro-world of peace. From 2001 to 2009, when I left the organization, more than fifteen thousand people had participated in the adult and the youth *Sulhita* programs. The gatherings were multidimensional with facilitated listening circles to address the emotional world. We met on the mind level through workshops that dissolved our ignorance about each other. We addressed the physical dimension through body practices in the early mornings, and a shared kitchen. Finally, we focused on Spirit through a multifaith prayer tent in the daytime, cross-cultural and interfaith ceremonies at sunset, and celebration through live music, poetry and dance on the main stage in the evenings.

My thoughts and body meandered back to the Sinai beach. That night, we had a simple dinner together: just *tabag bedoui*,[54] one of the camp kitchen's standard dishes, and some sauteed vegetables with tahini. We had to be in Nuweiba by 9 AM to meet our dear guide Musallem, and were expected at Said's wedding in the evening, in the high mountains of Sinai. It would be quite the journey, and we were all extremely excited.

Our taxi driver arrived at 8:30 AM. We had our coffee and then started packing the taxi with our desert luggage. It was winter in the mountains, and we were planning on trekking for four days, so we

---

[54] *Tabag bedoui*: Bedouin dish made out of an assortment of tiny portions from all that is in the kitchen that day.

had quite a bit of gear. The sky was deep blue, and the sacred sun was warming up our bones. We got to Sheik Suleiman's *maagad* and met our superstar host Musallem. He received us with his winning smile and served us some Bedouin tea. Before we left, it was time for another story. Rowan had told us about his Buddhist meditation practice. He had lived in Ladakh for a few months, supporting a local Tibetan school. In turn, I decided to tell them about my five-day trip to Dharamsala, my second time in India.

Dharamsala – 2005

AS WE were waiting to board the plane in Amman, my South African *jubu*[55] friend Guy who had custom-tailored our private audience with the Dalai Lama, was "preparing" me for the great meeting. Guy Lieberman had a years-long relationship with the office of the Dalai Lama and with His Holiness himself, and had been instrumental in bringing the Dalai Lama to South Africa for his meeting with Nelson Mandela.

The journey was long, and we had just boarded our plane to Delhi. Next to us, Ihab was already sleeping and Senegalese sheik Fara Gaye was mumbling deep prayers. I had met Fara Gaye at the Waldorf Astoria, in New York City. He was a Sufi from Senegal and had been in the city participating at the Millennium Peace Summit of Religious and Spiritual Leaders, the first time the UN had ever held a spiritual conference in their building. This was an unusual team on a very special mission.

Guy concluded, "So when His Holiness says 'photo,' you all stand next to him for a picture, and it is over. The meeting will last between ten and fifteen minutes."

"What?" I said. "All the way to India for fifteen minutes?"

"Yup," he answered. "It's the Dalai Lama. His days are full of these meetings. You're not the only ones." I was upset, but didn't respond. Later, I mentioned my frustration to Ihab, who nonchalantly advised with a smile to just count our blessings. I was having none of

---

[55] *Jubu*: A blend of Jewish and Buddhist.

this, and the thought of those mere ten to fifteen minutes bothered me until we landed in India.

Ihab Balha, co-director of the *Sulha* Peace Project for four years, was a Muslim from Jaffa. His parents' family had lost much of their land in Jaffa in 1948, with the creation of the state of Israel and the *Nakba*.[56] His father was still bitter about their situation, to say the least. Like most other Palestinians, they had gone through exile, forced migration, and loss of land. The declaration of the state of Israel was, for most Jews around the world, an epic source of celebration after two thousand years of exile and particularly after the horrors of the holocaust. For Palestinians, it was a catastrophe.

For most of his childhood and adolescence, Ihab had hated Israeli Jews. After a couple instrumental Israeli Jews confronted Ihab in his twenties and challenged his views, though, he focused on learning how to embrace the paradox of two peoples in love with the same land. I met Ihab when he owned a restaurant in Tel Aviv. The restaurant had since been burnt in an accident, and now Ihab was finally actively engaging in peace work. After a deeply atheistic and communist youth, he became more interested in Islam. I got to know Ihab at a time when he was in deep debt and working at his uncle's grocery store in Jaffa. He came to the second *Sulha* gathering as a participant; by the third, he'd volunteered to translate and MC on stage. He began leading the annual *Sulhas'* gathering workshop content in 2004. By 2005, I had offered him to co-direct the entire *Sulha* Peace Project with me. Ihab is now known as Sufi Sheik Ihab Balha and is married to an Israeli Jew, Ora Balha, with three beautiful boys. He runs four mixed kindergartens for Arabs and Jews together with his wife, and teaches Sufism at his cultural center in Jaffa.

Arriving in New Delhi, our group felt mixed responses. I had been in India for five months a few years before, but for Fara and Ihab, it was their first time. After all the airport bureaucracy and a taxi, we finally got to Delhi's humongous main train station, where

---

[56] *Nakba*: "Catastrophe" in Arabic. This is how the Palestinians refer to the state of Israel gaining independence, which marked the beginning of their exile and the occupation.

they experienced their first real India shock. Hundreds of vendors, thousands of people, beautiful ones, crippled ones, begging ones, and a myriad of smells, animals and colors bombarded our senses all at once. We boarded the train to Pathankot, and Ihab was amazed by the sheer numbers of people and vastness of the land as we journeyed out of Delhi.

From Pathankot, we transferred to a minivan heading for McCleod Ganj. Then, we finally stopped for our first chai—and our first taste of the majestic Himalaya Mountains. On the last segment of our journey, we boarded our final minivan to our guesthouse in Dharamkot, where we met the rest of our crew: Ian, Guy's South African partner in charge of video documentation; and Guy's mom, who would hold the boom for the sound and who came along as an excuse to get into the private audience with HH.

Just before sunset, Ihab and I went for a walk around Dharamkot. I showed him Rishivabhan, where I had stayed for a month a few years before. It was right next to where I had done Vipassana on my first visit to India. Ihab was in awe. "Look at this! Man, it's incredible!!" He couldn't get over the size of the mountains, the valleys, the views, the massive Himalayas. We were both in bliss!

We had dinner with the whole crew and then turned in, as we had to wake up for an extremely early breakfast before our private audience. After breakfast, we took our passports and went through security at the Dalai Lama's official government office (back then, the Dalai Lama was still the political head of the Tibetan government). As soon as we got into the Dalai Lama's office, Ian, Guy, and Guy's mom set up for the video shoot. Present in the room besides the video crew was the *geshe*[57] who had been at the *Sulha*. (We had always invited "spirit holders" to our *Sulha* gatherings who were not involved directly in our regional conflict. We had Irish, Zulu/South African, Native American, and Tibetan "spirit holders" who had experienced racial, ethnic, or religious conflict in their land.) The Dalai Lama's personal translator

---

[57] *Geshe* (Tibetan *dge bshes*, short for *dge-ba'i bshes-gnyen*, "virtuous friend"; translation of Skt. *kalyāṇamitra*) or *geshema*: a Tibetan Buddhist academic degree for monks and nuns.

and Tenzin Takla, who eventually became the head of the Tibetan government, were also there. On my right, an arm's length away from our sofa, was HH himself in his own armchair.

As protocol had it, and Guy was our "protocol", I began by giving HH some gifts: first, olive oil harvested from the land at our third annual two-day *Sulha* at Mghrar; then an Abraham, Sarah, and Hagar "mandala" made specially by Muslim, Christian, and Jewish women. All to which HH answered, "Thank you, beautiful, thank you very much."

Finally, I delivered my one-minute prepared speech, integrating my greatest hits of all time in one paragraph. As I spoke, I got excited and stood up. "Interesting," said the Dalai Lama. "Please sit down." I did. After me, it was Ihab's turn. He spoke from his carefully crafted Palestinian perspective. "Thank you," HH said. "Very interesting." Finally, Sheik Fara Gaye stood up and put a pair of little shoes on the table. "This..." said the Dalai Lama. "Fantasy? Reality?"

"This child couldn't come, so here are his shoes," Fara said. He proceeded to tell the story of his Sheik who went through exile like HH, and gifted him with a book by Senegalese Sheik Abdoulai Jai on Sufism in Africa.

HH yet again: "Very interesting, thank you!"

Right smack in front of our sofa was a big clock. It was hard for me not to notice it, and to look at it every few seconds. It was now twelve minutes since the meeting had begun. We were all done saying our piece, and the Dalai Lama's only words had been "Thank you, very interesting, sit down please." We couldn't go back to Israel this way. I had to do something. I closed my eyes and started singing at full volume:

"*Achilayo, amdo macha*!" It was a well-known Tibetan folk song I had learned from a Tibetan flutist in Dharamkot, during my first stay there a few years back. As I later found out, The Dalai Lama had grown up in the Amdo region of Tibet. One minute into the song, I stopped and heard the Dalai Lama ask something in Tibetan and the Geshe answer. I asked the translator, "Sorry, but I don't understand Tibetan—can you translate please?" "His Holiness asked who you are," the translator answered. Ha-ha...he had no idea! The Geshe proceeded to tell the Dalai Lama how he was invited to *Sulha* gatherings through Mark from Earthville at a chai shop in Mcleodganj, and so forth.

"I see," said HH. "Very interesting." Immediately, he burst into a story of his spiritual experience with the Virgin of Fátima at a church in Portugal. He told us about the importance of sharing the spiritual experiences of other traditions. Becoming fully present, I shared with him our youth project proposal. It entailed working with youth of cultures in conflict—such as white and black South Africans, Native and white Americans, Protestant and Catholic Irish, Palestinians and Israelis, and Pakistanis and Hindustanis from Kashmir—and hosted in Dharamsala.

HH approved immediately, and offered the orphanage his sister ran to host the week-long retreat and festival the kids would produce. He then told his personal secretary Tenzin Takla to write it all down for official approval. Our spirits were boosted. Ihab, Fara Gaye, and I started proclaiming our visions for the family of Abraham, and the support it could share with the Tibetan people and their essence of compassion and insight. We invited HH to come to Jerusalem. He said he'd been, and would come again with his friends, the Nobel laureates, when the right time came. The meeting went on for one full hour, and we left the Dalai Lama's office in bliss.

"Wow, *Chok Gozal!*[58] Kurdi exclaimed. "Did the project ever happen?"

"So...on our return to Israel, the board members of the *Sulha* Peace Project didn't approve the program, which needed $100,000 to become feasible. They told us we were dealing with the cherry on top of the cream on the cake. Furthermore, they insisted there were much more pressing issues to deal with in our volatile region. Ihab and I experienced their response with deep frustration, and the collaboration was buried," I concluded.

"Are we ready to go to the mountains?" asked Musallem, who

---

[58] *Chok Gozal*: "Very good" in Turkish.

had been busy packing for us. Elated to be going to the desert together, we all jumped into his run-down but beloved jeep, which had no front windows.

Musallem began telling us about Bedouin weddings. He said Said was very happy we were coming. I'd had a really good connection with Said during my last time in the high mountains. A few months before, on one of our scouting trips at *Wadi Looza* (where I had the best siesta ever), he told me that he would love for me to be at his wedding. So here we were—a dream team.

Mona took out the viola. Rowan joined with Murat's frame drum, and they played a Czech Roma tune from their mom's repertoire, who was a musician too! It was a very joyous one. Musallem looked at me and said, "*Salamtak, Eize anashim ebeita,*" in a mix of Arabic and Hebrew. "Peace be with you, amazing people you brought!" Of course, Kurdi led the infectious laughter, and we all caught the virus.

We made our first stop at a stunning valley, not far from the road to St. Catherine. There, we found a bunch of Bedouins sitting around a fire drinking tea. "This is one of my favorite restaurants," Musallem told us.

We went through all the hellos, standing up, shaking hands, some double cheek-kissing. The Bedouins have so many ways of greeting, and a very rich and intricate way of bestowing blessings upon arrival. Their departure is usually without ceremony. They are not very big on farewells: life goes on, with no goodbye dramas. Some of the old ones remembered me from a couple of decades ago, some of the young ones from a few months ago. It was so good to be seen and recognized in the middle of the desert by these warm and cheerful Indigenous people. I felt at home.

The food arrived, and it was delicious. We all ate from one big plate, using the *libbe*—traditional bread made under the coals—as spoons. Some of the amazing salad greens, like the *gargir*[59], were grown right next to the Bedouin tent where we were sitting. There was also rice with onions and baba ganoush made of eggplants from

---

[59] *Gargir*: Arabic for the bitter herb family. Potent cleanser and vitality provider.

the neighboring Ein Khudra oasis and good tahini. It was all fresh, simple, and scrumptious.

As usual, we had some tea after the meal. Then the Bedouin women came to show and sell their crafts: hand-sewn rugs, bags, keychains, dresses, scarfs, beads, and more, in a wild palate of colors. The five of us decided to pitch in and buy their biggest rug for our camp.

Rowan, Murat, and I went back to sit around the fire with Musallem and the men. Mona and Kurdi stayed with the women. After buying some things, they disappeared with the women into their tent. This didn't seem like just the normal tourist-Bedouin rapport; they had bonded. Between Kurdi's contagious laughter and Mona's radiance, the women had created a spontaneous and real connection. It probably helped that Kurdi's Arabic was fluent. She had a Syrian twist, and of course a Kurdish accent. They seemed to really like her; she made them laugh. And Mona, she was…well, I can't be objective. By then I had a real attraction to her.

The Bedouin men started telling stories. One of them, Abu Hamdan, said, "You say you lived in *Wadi Meliches* twenty-five years ago? And you knew Saleh Abu Awad, right?"

"He was my friend," I replied, "and his camel, Hemran, too." They all laughed, and Abu Hamdan continued. "Let me tell you a story about Saleh." Wanting to get all the little details of the story, I asked Musallem to translate.

"Saleh, as you know, was a very good guide from the old-school. One day a young man came to Tarabin asking around for a guide. Someone recommended Saleh to him. When they met at the beach, the young man said, 'I would love to go on a five-day camel trip into the desert.'

"And Saleh, in his usual cheery and open friendliness, said, '*Ala Kefak!*'[60]

"'Can we leave tomorrow?' the young man asked.

"'Sure,' Saleh answered.

"The young man asked for the price and Saleh told him it was £30

---

[60] *Ala Kefak*: "Great" in Arabic slang. Used also in Israeli slang.

per day. The young man thought a bit and then said, 'That's £150. Hmmm, I only have £50. So, sorry.'

"'It's okay,' said Saleh. 'I'll take you.'

"So generous. Thanks!"

"The young man was excited. He went back to his camp. They met the next morning and had a great journey together.

"When he was saying goodbye and thanking Saleh, he handed Saleh the £50. Saleh looked at him, and said, 'But this is all you have. Take your £50, it's okay,' and gave it back to the young man.

"A few years later, the young man came back to Sinai and asked around Nuweiba for Saleh's home. It was a very shabby and poor tin house, where he lived with his family. While Saleh was away in the mountains, the young man re-built Saleh an entirely new home. He paid for all the building and material costs and hired the workers too."

Abu Hamdan looked at me across the fire. All the old men nodded in agreement as to the prowess of Saleh's heart. Hearing the story, I remembered my friend's kindness and a couple of tears flowed down my cheek. Murat came close and gave me a warm, present brotherly Kurdish hug.

The women came back glowing and giggling with all sorts of gifts in their hands. We said goodbye to our hosts, left the desert restaurant, and climbed happily into our jeep.

"Next destination: Fox Camp. We'll be there in forty-five minutes," Musallem said.

The others looked out the window in awe of the mountains, the way only someone who is in Sinai for the first time can. I was dreamy and dozed off as Mona started singing a Senegalese lullaby she had learned from her dad. Rowan joined her.

When we arrived at Fox, the whole camp was gushing with joy and preparations. After all, Said was one of their own: the camps' star guide and beloved young host. Saadala, the sweet and attentive manager, received us. The rest of the staff helped bring our luggage to the beautiful new rooms they had built. Even Suleiman the owner came to greet us, proud of his new rooms. The internationals working for Sinai Trail had made flower arrangements, and the place looked beautiful.

The Jabaliya tribe is not well-known for investing in aesthetics and facilities, so this was an auspicious shift for them. It was probably because of Musallem, who had developed a great business partnership through their company Sinai Trail: an international prize-winning tourist trekking co-op involving the eight main local tribes of South Sinai. Musallem, a Tarabani, was very used to aesthetics, as well as making Europeans and Western tourists feel comfortable. He had run a couple of beach camps in his youth, and at the sea, everything is a bit more upscale, up-to-date, and artsy.

We all settled in our rooms and napped during the hot hours of the day. After our well-deserved siesta, one by one we indulged in the new showers and began preparing for the wedding. Kurdi said, "I think we should all dress local style, as Bedouins." We all agreed. We still had a couple of hours before the wedding, so we took a taxi into town, five minutes away. We found a typical Bedouin store and bought *djelabias, keffiyehs*,[61] and *kuchul*.[62] Kurdi and Mona bought *farwas*.[63]

We came back to the camp all dressed up. Surprised, Saadala and the crew at Fox laughed when they saw us pass on our way back to our rooms. We had put some black *kuchul* on our eyelids and felt beautiful and ready. We went to the cafe, had some tea, and were about to leave when Murat stopped us. "One minute!" he said. "Not that quickly!" He pulled out a new bottle of his special Kurdish liqueur and we all toasted and drank to Said's new life. Musallem shouted, "*Yalla*, guys, time to go!" We finally climbed on the back of a little pick-up truck and followed a caravan of Toyotas into Wadi al Arbaeen.

Many Bedouin tents were set up, surrounding a flat desert canvas. Their tents are made of camel wool and are very warm; Musallem signaled us to go in and settle in one. He said we could also leave our

---

[61] *Keffiyeh*: Traditional Arabic cloth headdress.
[62] *Kuchul*: Traditional Bedouin black eyeliner.
[63] *Farwa*: Traditional Bedouin winter overcoat.

things there for the night. Inside, there were mattresses set up and it felt really cozy. Then Musallem disappeared.

It was already dark, and we decided to venture as a group into the middle of the action. There were many pick-up trucks coming and going, and a few camels as well. Bedouins were walking around, intermingling. Music was coming out of different tents. It was all working seamlessly, an organic chaos. No wedding planner or linear program. Musallem returned. "Come with me," he said. He took us to Said, the groom. Said was radiant, dressed in pristine white. The hosts were serving goat for everyone, from their own herds. The goats were slaughtered in a *halal*[64] manner on the spot, then cleaned and cooked for the wedding. There was also a big tray with delicious rice. We all ate from the same pot with our right hand, then were served the customary Bedouin tea.

I managed to give Said a big hug before he was taken to his special tent by the men. We saw rows of women all dressed in black, facing the rows of men and dancing frantically. The women contorted in front of the men and they both went back and forth towards each other. The men had a particular step and a clap. Murat, Rowan, and I joined the row of men, while Mona and Kurdi went off dancing freely.

The excitement was palpable. There were many dancing rows going on simultaneously. Everyone sang ancient wedding songs and drummed on old metal water containers. As we fell into a collective trance, we transitioned from group to group, from row to row. Eventually, our group of friends sat in a circle on the dirt, with our *farwas* as mats. Murat took out his Kurdish drink and shared, while Mona rolled one of her impressive joints. Musallem managed to bring Said, the groom, into our little circle, where we had a powerful blessing for him. After that, we kept dancing for hours in the wild desert.

When we went back to our tent, it might have been 4 or 5 AM—and it was freezing. We all cozied up in the tent, close to each other and right next to the fire that Musallem had lit. To my delight, Mona was beside me this time, and we fell asleep next to each other. We

---

[64] *Halal*: Dietary laws according to Islam. Mostly parallels the concept of Kosher food in Judaism.

woke up a couple of hours later with the dawn and had some tea around the fire. We were incredibly happy, but exhausted and hung over. We agreed we would go back to the camp and rest properly for a few more hours until lunch, but ended up sleeping the whole day and waking up for dinner. Musallem announced that we would leave for the sandstone desert early the next morning. I was thrilled. We had an early night, and the next morning, we felt like ourselves again. While we waited for breakfast, we saw three camels being saddled for us. Inspired by the beautiful camels, I began telling my new friends about my incursions into interspecies dialogue.

South Africa – 2014

WE HAD just finished an intensive and beautiful week with the *Lemba*[65] youth for Passover.[66] I had helped design the week, and co-led workshops and music at the beautiful Thlolego Educational Center twenty kilometers west of Rustenburg. A very friendly white Jewish couple, Paul and Steph, founded the center in 1989 and had turned it into a regenerative educational community. The mostly black live-in staff were also community members. Over the years, Paul and Steph had built the residences of their staff first and had left their own home for last, which was still under construction.

The day after the *Lemba* youth had left, Paul, Steph, and I sat at breakfast, harvesting and celebrating the week's success.

"Today we go visit the wild animals!" Paul said. "We are in Africa, after all. There's a great wildlife reserve about fifty minutes away. Would you like to go?"

"Sure!" I said, thrilled.

"Okay then, let's make a move! The park closes at 5 PM," Steph told us. "Get your stuff ready. We'll meet next to the *bakkie*[67] in ten minutes."

---

[65] *Lemba*: African tribe ascribing their origins to the ten lost tribes of Israel.
[66] Passover: Jewish celebration commemorating the passage from slavery to freedom of the Hebrews out of Egypt. The beginning of the spiritual year. One of the three main pilgrimage festivals to Jerusalem in Temple times.
[67] *Bakkie*: Jeep.

When I arrived at the jeep with my guitar case, they both seemed puzzled.

"Hey, why did you bring that today? Today we are resting!" Paul said with a big smile. "We're going to be driving in nature on a very bumpy road. It might get damaged."

"Just in case," I said. "Don't worry about it. I'll hold it on my lap in the back and keep it safe."

They both smiled, and then Paul said, "Okay then, hop in the back."

We were all quite exhausted from the intense and fruitful week and the bustling energy of the *Lemba* teens. We drove through beautiful and ancient lands, just taking in the magnificence of Africa in silence. After a while, Paul said, "Okay, we're almost there. We'll drive into the park. It usually takes a few days of roaming this park till you encounter the big wild animals, so we may not see much. Since we got a late start, we're only going to be around for a few hours. No expectations, okay?"

As they paid the car fee, the ranger told us, "You have to be out of the park by 5 PM *shap*." (South Africans have a habit of dropping the "r," as you might know.)

We drove in deep silence. The park was utterly breathtaking. After about forty-five minutes, Paul said, "Wow! You are really lucky—see? A young elephant!"

"Where?" I said.

"There...on the other side of the river," Paul answered, pointing.

"Yeah!" Steph had just spotted the elephant too.

Exhilarated, I instinctively opened the window and started toning. The others looked at me in awe. "What's that?" Steph asked. "Sounds crazy...Om?"

"It's *overtones*," Paul answered. As I kept breathing for air and starting another round, the overtones got louder. Then, the young elephant's ears started to flap back and forth! "Wow," Steph said, "look at his ears!" I kept going with the harmonics. The young elephant was pacing back and forth near the river. Suddenly, Paul said, "Look over there! There's another elephant coming over the hill!"

"Oh yes!" Steph said. As she spoke, several more elephants were approaching—a whole herd! Big mamas, enormous papas, young ones, even baby elephants were making their way toward the river. I could only say *"Elefantes!"* as I caught my breath after ten minutes of overtones. They kept laughing with joy and imitating my Spanish: *"Elefantes!* Haha, *elefantes!"* I asked them to turn off the motor. Paul agreed reluctantly, as the elephants seemed to be crossing the river and coming our way. Meanwhile, I took the guitar out of the case and started singing my song "Skin of God"[68] for the elephants. *"Llegan manadas de elefantes,"*[69] I sang. It was a concert just for them. It seemed that I had written the song for this very moment.

The elephants kept coming closer. Paul was concerned. "You know, elephants can be really dangerous and can attack a jeep too," he said, uneasy.

"We need to move on," Steph insisted.

I finished the song as the elephants were just about to reach us. I put the guitar back in the case, and as they came within literally 150 meters of our vehicle, we moved slowly away. Throughout the afternoon, we had similar overtoning experiences with zebras, giraffes, and antelopes. My hosts couldn't believe what was happening. We had seen and sung with so many animals within just four hours! Now it was time to go back home to Thlolego and tell our fantastic tale to the other members of the community. We were awestruck by what had just transpired.

"This is a gift from Africa to you," Paul told me.

I held that experience of interspecies overtoning, music, and cultural connection in my heart for many years.

"I love elephants," Kurdi said.

"And I love Africa," Rowan said. He told us of his adventures sailing around Africa with a small crew, training orphan refugees from the Red Sea. They had started at Port Said, Egypt, and sailed all the way to the Seychelles on the Indian ocean. On another trip, he had

---

[68] To listen to "Skin of God," go to page 227.
[69] *Llegan manadas de elefantes*: "Herds of elephants are arriving," from my song "Skin of God" from Amen's album *Hatevah – Skin of God*.

gone north from Cape Town all the way to Sagres in Portugal by way of the Atlantic Ocean. He described how the refugee kids had found their self-worth in learning how to sail, falling in love with the ocean, and working on their intense relationships at sea.

The kids had created a storytelling, music, clowning, and acrobatics talent show and performed in all the ports of Africa they anchored in. They also handled all aspects of production, including going to the nearest towns and attracting local youth to come to their show. It usually took ten days to prepare the show, identify a local school or community center, and persuade some of the local youth to participate. They also spent part of the trip on the boat prior to the landing in research about the Indigenous and local cultures at the next port of entry.

"I'm really impressed," Murat said.

"That's my dear brother!" Mona added.

"Yes, Captain Rowan!" Kurdi said, and started giggling so loud that we felt compelled to join her. She had just baptized him. From then on, Rowan became our "Captain."

We had enjoyed our breakfast, getting to know each other in the desert way by weaving in marvelous stories and breaking authentic Bedouin bread together. By the time we'd finished our tale-telling, all the bags, our big carpet, and the blankets were perfectly tied to our camels' saddles. "Ready?" Musallem asked as he started walking out into the desert. Feeling the excitement of our brilliant caravan of camels and humans, we walked for what seemed like two hours. During the first hour, silence enveloped us.

On the second hour of our journey, it was time for the flora. Musallem pointed to some beautiful purple wildflowers that we passed, and introduced us to other medicinal plants and their uses: the well-known *batharan*, a medicinal plant indigenous to Sinai often used as a remedy for the stomach; the amazing *habag*, a mountain mint great for the throat; and the *chandal* fruit, which looked like little desert watermelons and are useful as a compress for rheumatism and joint problems but poisonous when eaten raw.

We finally arrived at a beautiful little canyon and stopped. Musallem said this was the tribal land border between the *Jabaliya* and the *Muzeina*. (In Sinai, all Bedouin tribal borders are specified in maps that are kept at St. Catherine's monastery.) We had some tea in the canyon and rested a bit. "Come on, guys," Musallem encouraged us. We wanted to make it to the oasis of Ein Hodra before dark. This time, Captain Rowan and Murat helped prepare our sweet camels for the road. The camels were fed at every stop; we had packed some special food for them, and they went especially wild over orange peels. I fed one of them the peel from the four oranges we'd just had for breakfast. Using his big tongue as a gigantic spoon, he scooped the peels from my hand, taking great care not to hurt me. Camels can be very gentle. Kurdi and Mona also took their turn in feeding the camels straight from their hands.

After they were done, we took Musallem's lead and started walking. On the way, we met a group of *nagot*.[70] Our dear guide explained how the Bedouins left the female camels free to roam, using only the male camels for riding and carrying luggage. We spotted an adorable baby camel next to his mama. He was tiny, compared to the other camels, and Musallem told us he was only a couple of months old.

After a few hours, we reached what Musallem called the "closed canyon." It was on the outskirts of Ein Hodra, a big and beautiful oasis. Some thought it had been one of the stops of the Israelites, or *hatzerot*, as they wandered on their biblical forty-year journey. The closed canyon's floor was clean white powder sand. We set up camp there, and after unsaddling and unloading the camels, we went to fetch *chatab*[71] for our fire.

Musallem was a good cook and started preparing dinner. Kurdi helped to cut the veggies, and Rowan went for a walk. Mona and I took out our instruments and Murat joined in with his frame drum. The fire kept us warm, and we had another great dinner. Then it was story time. Murat and Kurdi told us of their work with refugees at the Turkish Syrian border. This was right next to Rojava, the free Kurdish territory. The people there, led mostly by women, had fought in the frontline against *Daesh*, or Isis, and defeated them. They were also

---

[70] *Nagot*: Plural for "female camels" in Arabic.
[71] *Chatab*: "Firewood" in Arabic.

involved in Rojava's radical direct democracy experiment, based on the philosophy of Ocalan, a Kurdish political leader and philosopher who had been jailed by the Turks. Kurdi and Murat had created a camp for refugees fleeing Syrian territory, using a regenerative design which included a water retention space, a vegetable garden, and fruit trees. They grew their own food, and Murat—also a great chef—taught cooking at the camp. They had created a garden and soil-to-table restaurant which they managed to run sustainably, serving the communities surrounding the camp. Kurdi was an amazing clown and stand-up comedian and would keep the restaurant patrons, cooks, and staff laughing till the wee hours of the night.

We all lay close to each other watching the stars. There was no moon that night, and the lights in the sky were breathtaking and kept us entertained for a while. Mona had put her sleeping gear next to me again. We were literally getting closer, and the pace of our encounter felt healthy. The field created by our amazing friends was so supportive that organic time was governing the beat of our meeting. We were not rushing anything, and it felt good to go slow. That night, we simply slept next to each other.

Ein Hodra is divided into different orchards, each one owned by a different family. In the morning, we went to one of the orchards where a young man received us with tea. As I was greeting him, I glimpsed an older man next to him—and couldn't believe my eyes.

"Farraj!?!" I exclaimed.

"Djibril!" he answered.

Though we hadn't seen each other in twenty-five years, we both recognized each other, hugged, and sat down as old partners of an untold history. We recalled old Atua singing with his *rababa*.[72] Atua used to be Farraj's neighbor, and one of the well-known Muzeina elders at Ein Hodra. When our posse saw me with Farraj, even Musallem and Farraj's son were surprised to see us joking in such a familiar way.

"How do you know my father?" Farraj's son asked.

"I met Djibril many years ago," Farraj said, "before you were born!"

---

[72] *Rababa*: Traditional Bedouin violin.

We had a succulent, celebratory breakfast of an amazing salad with plenty of local *gargir*[73] and *bagdunes*[74] grown in the oasis. We added the olive oil I had been carrying from the Galilee and plenty of lemon. It was delicious, and so healthy! Eating in the barren desert is always an empowering experience. No matter what you eat there, it feels like a big miracle and tastes completely clean, immediately nourishing you and giving you lots of power.

After that, we rested for a bit. It was hot; our hosts had just cleaned the pool coming from the spring, and it really looked enticing. We put on our bathing suits, went in, played, splashed, dunked each other under the water, and laughed. Farraj, seemingly without reason, told me to go for a walk and check out the landscape around us. Desert Bedouins have a very strong intuitive side, and usually know what you need, so I followed his advice. On the walk, I deeply took in the beloved oasis of Ein Hodra where I had had so many peak experiences in the early '90s. When I came back, Murat, Mona, Kurdi, and the Captain had already packed and loaded the camels, and Musallem was saying goodbye to his Muzeina friends at the oasis. I joined the farewells, and we were off. We passed by the gorgeous white canyon, shared a moment of tranquil joy full of vitality in the pristine white sand, and continued.

We were finally off to Wadi Meliches, where we would spend the night. Meliches had a beautiful mountain, Jebel Meliches, next to it. I had once called this place home for almost a year. First, though, we stopped at Wadi Ruahbeia,[75] where some Bedouins were living. More than twenty-five years before, my closest neighbors in the valley, Salem Abu Atwa and his beautiful shepherd daughters, had their tent pitched there. Since then, though, the Bedouin encampment had grown considerably and there were at least four new families living there. They had a guest tent set up to serve tea for tourists and for the women to sell their crafts. After a short stop, Musallem signaled to me.

"You can lead the way down to Wadi Meliches from here," he said. Addressing me directly so no one would hear, Musallem then

---

[73] *Gargir*: arugula.
[74] *Bagdunes*: parsley.
[75] Wadi Ruahbiya: Next to Wadi Meliches in the sandstone area of southern Sinai. About a two-hour walk from the road to St. Catherine.

spoke softly. "You remember the way, right? I'll come later with the camels from the other side."

We went down surrounded by the colorful sandstone: pink, white, yellow, brown. The colors changed as the sun moved. The sandstone desert is a natural palace—Allah's museum—with shifting shapes that change each time you look at them. You can see the whole universe in those stones. Elephants, eyes, a man sitting in a chair, ears, wings, lions with spears—whatever your imagination is open to. A walk that usually takes thirty minutes took us an hour and a half, as we kept stopping and marveling at the colorful stones and many shady nooks and crannies, big enough to lay down in.

When we got to Wadi Meliches, Musallem, who had already arrived with the camels through the camel path, was making a fire and some tea. It was sunset, and we all went on a wood mission, preparing for a long intimate night around the fire. A good friend of Musallem from the coast had arrived on a jeep with a few tourists and stopped for a short visit. Apparently, Musallem had asked him to bring fresh fish from the sea. After they left, he said, "Tonight: grilled fish!" Rowan said that he would grill the fish. Murat created the most colorful and tasty salad and Kurdi made delicious fried potatoes, while Musallem hung out. Mona and I went for a walk in my old 'hood. Of our desert journey so far, this was really our first time alone. We started walking up the Wadi. I told her how I used to go there by myself and make *libbe*[76] and how I had once seen a family of gazelles.

There are spots in the desert where no one, not even an animal, has set foot for weeks. The silence was loud. We lay down, looking at the majestic *Jebel Meliches*, hearing the wings of a bird flapping over us. It was both exhilarating and calm. We turned on our sides towards each other. I put my elbow on the soft sweet sand, lying down in a favorite Bedouin position known as *enkawe*.[77] Mona broke the silence: "What about your love life?" she asked me. "Can you share some of your intimate history?"

---

[76] *Libbe*: Bedouin bread. The most ancient way of making bread under firewood coals on the earth without an oven.
[77] Enkawe: Slang for common Bedouin reclining position with elbow on the ground.

I thought for a moment. Then I decided: I would be 100 percent honest with her. If she really liked me, she would have to hear about the real me, including my deep shadows. It was extreme, but I went for it. All of it.

1979 and 2017 – Buenos Aires to Tamera

THERE WAS a time when I romanticized sex workers. I even fought for their rights in Argentina when I was twenty-one years old. As a young adolescent, I ejaculated for the first time on a vacation with my family, with a porn magazine. I was thirteen. I had sex for the first time at age fourteen in a vacation adventure in Key West, Florida, with a woman who was completely drunk. When I got back to macho-entrenched ways in upper-middle-class Argentina, the thing to do was to masturbate with porn magazines as much as possible and, if you wanted to belong to the "men's" club, there was the vulgar act of paying a sex worker. As part of the systemically sick patriarchal and misogynistic societal patterns prevalent then, almost everybody in my class did, everyone in the soccer team as well. There was a famous legal brothel in Uruguay, next to Punta del Este. Most of my school peers went there for summer vacation and for a taste of the forbidden.

I peeked at Mona—she wasn't even flinching. This wasn't easy, to say the least, nor at all attractive, but I took a deep breath and continued.

At age sixteen, I made love for the first time with a woman I really liked from my theater class. Estela was also the first woman to share a joint and cook together with me. It felt as if, for the first time, the kitchen at my parents' home had opened up to me. I wasn't afraid of it anymore. I could cook. I could enjoy smoking marijuana and also making love with a woman I really liked…and it was reciprocal! But these experiences were sparse, and I was already hooked on anonymous easy sex in the dark.

"Should I go on?" I asked Mona.

"Please go on," she gently placed her hand on my heart for a moment. "I'm all ears," she said.

I had my first real long-term lover when I was twenty-one. We were together for a year, sleeping together almost every night. We lived in separate rented apartments, and would take turns to visit each other. When she left me, and Argentina, I was heartbroken. Occasionally I would return to my addictive dark erotic experiences, first in Buenos Aires, and then while living in Paris. Then I had my second long-term relationship: one year of "good lovemaking and fighting" in New York, hitchhiking through East Africa, and traveling through Egypt. Highlights of our journey included reading Lewis Carroll's *Sylvie and Bruno* together and discovering the Sinai mountains, before eventually separating in Tel Aviv.

My next long-term girlfriend was in Israel. It was 1997, as my addiction gave way to true love and a real relationship. We lived together in the Galilee for a year. The physical attraction was very strong. She was a herbalist; young, voluptuous, and ravishing. Eros came naturally to her. She was free, wild, and a good belly dancer, half Indigenous and half Jewish. I was in love. We lived together for a year until her tragic accident, ten minutes away from our rented home in Amirim.

Later, I had another long-term relationship in Israel. We lived together in 2012, separated, then came back together three years later, for four months. Although we had our good moments living together in stability and companionship, fighting and sadness were also an integral part of the relationship. My frustration mounted, wanting to connect with her intimately and emotionally much more than she did. The pain in me was almost always present, and we eventually ended it.

I announced to Mona, "Now comes the healing part."
She smiled and continued to listen deeply. I breathed in some courage and continued.

For the past four years, I have been healing from these sexual and relational wounds and traumas through participating in the Global

Love School at the Tamera Peace Research Village in Portugal, and through the International School of Temple Arts, or ISTA. Before that, this area of my being had been neglected and underdeveloped. I had immersed myself deeply at different times and with many different teachers: shamans, sheiks, activists, rabbis, in the spiritual, shamanic, political, social, physical, emotional, and artistic realms. Yet I had never deeply faced the erotic aspects of my development. Instead, I had suffered in these dimensions in an endless loop. These last few years, I was finally learning firsthand about rejection and jealousy.

My first year at Love School, I was focused on how I looked from the outside and trying to fit in with the multiple partner model, but I couldn't really include my emotional self. I had a crush on a woman there, but ended up playing out the same emotional dramas I had been stuck with throughout my life. The second year, I felt more chill and had less fear to engage with the woman I liked. We became friends, and eventually made love. She had other lovers, but jealousy wasn't an issue for me anymore. By the third year, I experienced no drama at Love School—but something felt sad, dry, and missing.

After Love School, I was invited to another encounter at Tamera focused on sacred activism, called "Defend the Sacred." People in the community who knew me told me, "Yup...this is much more your thing than Love School." After the official Defend the Sacred program was over and all my close male buddies— the Lakota elder, the Palestinian wild Christian, the Sufi mystical anarchist, the Peruvian *paco*[78]—had left, I had an embodied sexual and love epiphany. It lasted a full eight uninterrupted and magical hours.

"Yes!" Mona said. "Finally! Please tell me more," she encouraged me, with a tender smile.

I had seen Maria during the Defend the Sacred gathering from afar; she was very attractive, though not a part of my sub-group for the program. After a couple days, I found the courage to talk to her, and invited her to the lake. We talked a bit, then swam naked. I

---

[78] *Paco*: Holder of coca leaf ceremonies and offerings in Andean culture.

noticed her voice was louder than her energy, so with a smile, I dared to mention it. Apparently, she was very impressed that I managed to be sincere with her. She said that usually men and sometimes even women were overwhelmed by her strength—and were often afraid of her. The next time I saw Maria, I was having a jam in the community's cultural center with my dear Brazilian musician friend Claudinho. It became a high-energy celebration night, and when the live music evolved into DJ music, I danced with Maria. It was extremely sensual, though I felt like I was too forward. She told me she wasn't Brazilian, but Portuguese, so she was slow—and I guess I was too pushy and fast for her to handle me. She disappeared, leaving me hanging there.

The day after the official program of the gathering had ended, we all enjoyed a concluding social dance party. Again, I saw Maria showing her moves in a miniskirt, and was deeply attracted to her. I danced with her, but this time I didn't pursue her. As soon as I felt a sign of her drifting away from me, I noticed an older, very sultry woman named Roxane dancing and joined her in motion. "I'm not going to fall into my own trap of going after someone who doesn't want me again," I told myself. So, after a very intimate, creative, and erotic dance with Roxane, I asked nonchalantly, "Do you want to continue somewhere else?" She immediately answered, "Yes." Fortunately, I had my own space, which at Tamera is a big deal. As we got to my space, Roxane said, "Oh no! That orange tent over there is mine and my husband's. It's so close." It was true, their tent was literally right next to my small mobile home.

"Does your husband agree with this?"

"Yes, he really likes you and even encouraged me to be with you."

So we went into my caravan and started kissing. She was very sensual, experienced, and had a quiet joy about her. We started getting hotter, touching and undressing each other. As she held my *lingam*[79] we heard the zipper of the orange tent next door.

"I can't do this anymore," she said.

"Okay, no problem," I said, astonished by how comfortable and understanding I felt. It was clear that this had nothing to do with me.

---

[79] *Lingam*: The divine Hindu word for the male sex organ.

We hugged, I assured her that everything was okay, and she went back to her husband. I went to sleep early, surprisingly happy.

I got up for breakfast at 8 am. It was departure day for most people, and somehow, I ended up sitting alone at the same table with Portuguese Maria. It was just her and me for breakfast. I had learned to be very specific and clear with my invitations. "Can I offer you an invitation?" I asked her. She just looked at me, so I went on. "Would you come to hang out with me and just hug, caress, and talk in my caravan before you go?" Maria started tearing up. Then she said in a vulnerable and soft voice, "Yes." I was extremely pleased. My RV was quite a small space, so we sat down on my bed, as it was the only place we could both fit. Maria spoke first.

"Listen, you were one of the people I was most impressed by in the gathering. I had an amazing time at the jam where you played, and when we danced, but you were going too fast for me." She said she got a bit overwhelmed and eventually turned off by my intensity. She went on, "I've witnessed you going after women who don't see you at all. I want to tell you that I do see you, and you don't have to prove or do anything to impress me." As she caressed my hand and arm, she finally said, "I like you the way you are."

This totally opened me up. I felt malleable and light, my heart pumping at high speed. In an instant, she felt it and started kissing me. And I responded naturally. My jaws were relaxed. My body felt tender and alive, and so did hers. We accomplished so much that day, and it all progressed organically, in a way that was both comfortable and epic. We spent the next eight hours in presence and awe of each other. After we made love, we went for a walk and a swim in the lake, then had cake in the cafe and another walk holding hands. We had a shit each, laughed from the belly, and cried in each other's arms. We even met, on one of our walks, a recent lover of hers whom I knew and really liked. We winked at each other when the three of us understood our roles as mutual lovers. Maria smiled and then we two men hugged in a brotherly embrace. Life was shining.

Maria and I went back to my borrowed caravan and made delicious love again and again. My lion roared from the base of the tongue to my open sphincter, from the heart of my hands and soles of my feet to my eyes. The world was glowing, and I was an integral part of it. Afterwards, we eased into the sweetest siesta I can remember. Maria had to drive back home later that afternoon, so we said goodbye. The most remarkable part of this passionate and authentic love encounter was that we didn't even once mention the future. We had no expectations at all. It was all happening for us right there in full presence of each other. That was the last time I saw Maria. I tried to visit her a year later, but she wasn't into it. I took it well. "I will always be in gratitude for such heartfulness and deep sexual healing," I told her.

I took a deep breath and smiled. Mona looked at me deeply and kissed me with her full lips, then held me in a warm and nourishing embrace. She pinched my nose lightly with a witch's touch and said, "Magical You! It's getting cold and dark, and the fish is probably ready!"

"I'm really hungry," I said.

Mona took me by the hand, and we went back to the camp. It was so good to come back to such a friendly scene; the smell was amazing, and everyone seemed very happy and hungry.

Mona said she had a surprise for after dinner. We ate the delicious meal, rested, joked a bit, and digested.

"So, what is it?" Murat asked Mona. "What's the surprise?"

"I have San Pedro for all of us," she said.

"What's San Pedro?" Musallem inquired.

I grabbed him gently by the shoulder and told him, "Don't worry *habibi*, I think you'll like it."

Musallem, already with a twinkle in his eye, didn't need to ask any more questions. We all recognized our excitement. As Mona gave us each a distinct portion, her approach was unique for each one of us. Like a good medicine woman, she communicated with no need for words. We cleaned the fireplace of dishes and pots, leaving just the teapot on the fire and some water with drinking glasses. The setting was inviting.

It was a long and beautiful night. Musallem began with an old

Bedouin *howg'en*.[80] I played a couple of medicine songs. And Mona, in turn, sang some haunting Roma melodies. Kurdi and Murat danced and giggled like little children, and we joined them. Rowan, the Captain, took care of the fire for the whole night. Some of us disappeared now and then for walking adventures, who knows where. Mona kept distributing extra and blessed portions to whoever asked for more. After a long night of communal ecstasy and bliss, truth came in for a deep visit. It was as if everyone in our constellation took turns playing different roles through the night: we had all been mother, father, grandfather, grandmother, child, brother, and sister, and had embodied Divinity playfully together.

As the sun was coming up, we took turns blessing each other, then cried softly with joy as the mountains around us changed colors and the ball of fire in the sky began warming us up. We fell asleep tucked into each other. When I woke up, I saw Kurdi and Musallem preparing us breakfast. They looked filled with wonder.

After tea, I made sure with Musallem that we had some time before our departure. The moment finally felt ripe to tell them about the Big Vision. I felt that this crew was truly a part of it, and their roles in the Big Story were getting clearer in my head.

We could still leave in two hours and get to the coast in time for sunset. So I decided to tell them the plans for our historic event, which would progress through Hebron at the double Cave of the Machpelah and end in the square kilometer within the Old City of Jerusalem.

As a springboard, I told them a short story from my time in Jaffa.

It was the early years of the second Intifada. Roshi Bernie Glassman, and the incipient order of global interfaith peacemakers, had brought famous Buddhist actor-activist Richard Gere to Israel-Palestine. I was invited to attend the event with him in Jaffa. After it ended, Bernie called me over and introduced me to Gere. "G. has big visions," he said, looking at me encouragingly. "Come on, tell him."

"I'd love to hear," said the actor.

I told him about our multidimensional gatherings, and the surprise leap into a new paradigm for healing: our attempt at a medicinal

---

[80] Howg'en: Traditional Bedouin chant for Spirit invocation and sung poetry.

ceremony for collective trauma, at the grave of our ancestors at Hebron, concluding in the old city of Jerusalem. It was designed to be enormous enough to shift reality for the hundreds of thousands of people who would come from the North and the East in pilgrimage.

Without blinking, Gere looked at me and said, "Sounds good." He continued, as if he was in a meeting with producers and investors on a pitch for a Hollywood movie. "But why not think bigger? Maybe pilgrimages from the four directions?"

Bernie had to go. The three-minute meeting with Gere was over.

"But since then, more than twenty years ago," I told my friends, "I've kept this conversation in a safe corner of my heart. Now is the time to release it. You are the right container for my moral imagination, the pertinent spirit holders, heartfelt witnesses, and 'sacred agents' for this Big Vision. The ground feels safe and fertile enough to share it with you," I said triumphantly.

Mona kissed my heart from the back.

Murat said, "Go on, brother."

The Captain, looking around for Musallem and Kurdi's nods of approval, said, "We're with you!"

So I went on.

"We are now on the south side of the big event.

"The pilgrimage to the Cave ending in Jerusalem coming from the south will be on camels.

"The southern camel caravan people will meet at Jabel Moussa, guided by Bedouins." I looked at Musallem, who was shining with excitement, and clapped him energetically on his shoulder. "The southern contingent will pass through Ein Hodra, arrive somehow at the border, and cross into Israel. One thousand camels, Egyptians, representatives of the African nations, and of course southern Israelis and Bedouins who are active in systemic change.

"The western contingent will come from the sea on boats," I said, looking straight at Rowan. "Our Captain will create a fleet of one thousand boats coming from Crete all the way to Haifa and some smaller ports of entry into Israel. They will carry representatives of

European, American continent, and Pacific peoples on them. The western boat fleet will bicycle from the ports, all the way to the double cave in Hebron."

I was in a trance, and could feel the whole desert listening, the valley palpitating, and my friends protecting my clarity. I kept going. "The third contingent will come from the north by horse. One thousand horses from Rojava, Syria, and Turkey," I said, looking at Kurdi and Murat. Now they were glowing too! "It will include representatives of Iran and Asia, joined by horsemen and horsewomen from the north of Israel. The northern horse caravan will also reach the graves of Abraham, Sarah, and our ancestors at the double cave in Hebron.

"The eastern contingent will start from Bethlehem with representatives of Iraq, Jordan, and ten thousand Palestinians on foot. This walking caravan will join all the other contingents at Abraham's grave.

"From the double cave at Hebron, after the healing vigil for collective trauma, the four caravans will blend into one walking healing caravan and continue the pilgrimage to the Old City of Jerusalem. In concentric circles, they will surround the square kilometer which comprises the Dome of the Rock, the Western Wall, and the Holy Sepulchre Church."

I looked at Musallem and said, "I think we've got to go soon. I'll tell you more tonight of what I know regarding the content of the healing vigil at the double cave and the healing ceremony in Jerusalem."

"Wow!" said Mona. "But before that, just tell us—why do you keep referring to it as a double cave?"

"Well, in short," I said, "there's a Hebrew Kabbalistic legend that tells the story. Ever heard of the three Kings announcing Jesus's birth? They are probably the same ones who came to Abraham and Sarah when they were very old to announce the birth of their son Isaac.

"When they arrived at Abraham's tent, he greeted them, and like a good Bedouin, didn't ask any questions. His tent was open to the four directions. He washed their feet and then went to get some game for them to eat. He asked his wife Sarah to make some *libbe*, most probably, and went into the desert.

"While looking for the *bakar* (game meat) which spells the letters of *keber*[81], he got lost inside a cave. He followed the sweet scent and realized this cave had another entrance inside. A double cave.

"The sweet fragrance led him further in. He followed the delicious aroma and saw two big, flaming torches at the feet of two humans lying down at the entrance of the second cave. They were Adam and Eve, waiting at the entrance to the Garden of Eden.

"Abraham looked beyond them. He saw two cherubs with spinning swords of fire guarding the entrance. He came out of the cave overwhelmed, with a powerful insight. He realized he and his family had to be buried in that cave, at the entrance of the Garden of Eden.

"He came out of the Cave of the *Machpelah*.[82] He finally found the game on the way back and slaughtered it, and Sarah fed the three strangers.

"Abraham, ancestor of the Hebrew and Arab peoples, was buried there—and so were his wife Sarah and their son, Isaac and his wife Rivka, and their grandchildren, Jacob and Leah.

"When Abraham died, it is written in the Torah[83] that Ishmael, who had been banished with his mother Hagar to the desert and then reached the *Kaaba*[84] (as the Muslims tell), came back to this same cave in Hebron to encounter his long-lost brother Isaac and bury their father Abraham together.

"This is the source for the collective trauma-healing vigil in Hebron at the cave of the Machpelah. That is where the principle of peace between Arabs and Jews and their common father Abraham is buried. This would be a wake, a *hilula* for that Spirit—the re-encounter of Isaac and Ishmael and Sarah and Hagar, the mothers of Arabs and Hebrews."

"Wow! *Shukran*," Kurdi said.

Musallem called us and told us to start loading our new friends,

---

[81] *Keber*: grave.
[82] Cave of the *Machpelah*: Ritual grave of Abraham, the rest of the Israelite and Arab patriarchs and most of the matriarchs. *Machpelah* comes from the root of the word "double," or "kaful." The double cave.
[83] Torah: The Five Books of Moses. The Old Testament.
[84] *Kaaba*: Holy black rock in Mecca. First house of worship built by Abraham and Ishmael according to Islam. It is said to have been a local pagan sacred ritual space before Islam.

the camels: Abu Nab, Hemran, and Alashan. We walked in silence, perceiving the sound of each of our steps on the sand, while the desert breeze caressed our faces. We only stopped at Ras Ghazalah after walking for an hour and half. There was so much to digest and process.

Musallem cooked. After lunch, I decided to tell them about the last war in Gaza. I wanted them to have as much context as possible. I told them that during the war I had one of my most powerful sacred activism experiences, which had gifted me new brothers, sisters, and allies in Europe, Palestine, Israel, and beyond. Moreover, it had reignited in me a deep-rooted faith in a holistic way of direct spirit action and courage, fostered in fraternity with our "beloved enemies".

Gush Etzion/West Bank – 2014

It was the horrible summer of 2014. Hate was rampant throughout the Holy Land, and it spilled over onto the internet. We were immersed in it, and trying to swim through the most disgusting wave of animosity you can imagine. My soul felt claustrophobic. Even within the peace-festival-conscious-India-medicine tribe, it hurt to go to my neighbors and see them glued to the news, rooting for Israeli warplanes as if it were a soccer game.

On one of those terrible mornings, as the violence was intensifying, I got a phone call. It was an Israeli percussionist I knew, inviting me to a special peace camp.

"We refuse to be enemies," she said. "Do you want to be part of the music team of the camp?"

"Where's it going to be?" I asked.

"At Ali Abu Awad's in Gush Etzion," she answered.

"If it's at Ali's, I'm coming for sure!" I confirmed.

I had met Ali at our *Sulha* gathering ten years before. He was part of the brave Palestinian/Israeli Bereaved Families Forum. Afterward, he became their spokesperson around the world. In 2008, he was our keynote Palestinian speaker at Latrun Monastery's annual three-day *Sulha* gathering of more than five thousand people. Ali's mother had been an important leader of *Fatah*[85] in the times of the first Intifada, and his brother had been killed at point-blank range by an Israeli soldier. Ali had thrown stones and been quite active in the first Intifada too. He had been in an Israeli prison for some time and had been shot and wounded in his leg. His transformation to non-violent action for Palestinian liberation, which came about in an Israeli jail through the writings of Mandela, Gandhi, and Martin Luther King Jr., was astonishing and inspiring.

On the phone, the percussionist continued. "Well, it's organized by key leaders of Tamera…even Sabine Lichtenfels is coming."

"Interesting," I said. I had met three leaders of the Tamera community at my home in Galilee ten years before. They had heard of the *Sulha* Peace Project, which I had co-founded and co-directed from 2001–2009, and had reached out to get to know me. In the following years they had brought me to their Israel/Palestine peace pilgrimages twice, as a guest speaker and musician.

When the percussionist called me for a second time to confirm my presence, I finally said, "So am I fully invited or not?"

"Hmm…yes!" she said.

As usual, I was the first one to arrive at Ali's land. Born at only seven months, to this day, I have the unfortunate and innate habit of arriving early everywhere. That night, alone with dear Ali, it was all about nostalgia, friendship, and catching up on old and new stories. The next day, most people arrived and pitched their tents. There were about fifty of us all together. As the Tamerians arrived—Sabine; her lovely daughter Vera who I had met at my home ten years earlier; Elke, Tamera's neighbor activist; and Bernd, water lover and expert—the organizing team announced we would meet for our opening circle with Babette (Sabine's nickname) before dinner. It was getting chilly when I joined the rest of the circle. When I looked up, I saw the other musicians, dressed in white, singing "angelic songs" on guitar. As Babette joined the group, the angelic singers welcomed her in song, and people all around me started whispering "Sabine is here…

---

[85] *Fatah*: The Palestinian political party ruling in the West Bank occupied territories; began as a Palestinian revolutionary liberation movement.

she's here." I was feeling very uneasy, though, and finally couldn't contain myself anymore. After all, we were in the midst of a war! Unabashedly, I said, "Excuse me for interrupting the beautiful song, but what are we doing here? Can anyone explain? Is this a workshop? We are in the middle of a war!"

The ones who had invited me and the others who knew Sabine and Tamera stared at me, frozen in terror. Babette then said, "Hmm... we'll begin after dinner. Please enjoy your meal, and we'll meet back here again in two hours."

I was upset and didn't feel like standing in line in the kitchen for food, so I took my guitar and started singing an upbeat traditional Arabic song. Some of the local Palestinians smiled and clapped around me. As I finished the song, Sami Awad, founding director of the Holy Land Trust and a close ally of Tamera, approached me and told me sternly that this wasn't a *hafla*.[86] I had met him briefly at the Dead Sea stop of Tamera's last pilgrimage.

"Please be sensitive," he said. "It's not a festival here."

"Hmmm, okay," I answered.

I'm starting to think these are an imbalanced amount of "hmmms" for one story. But moving right along. The kitchen line was free now. I got my plate and sat down alone in a corner to eat quietly, though inside, I was boiling. As I finished my food, Sabine came from behind, gave me a calm hug, and said, "Thank you for that. I love you!" I smiled, and for the first time, I felt her beautiful and clear spirit. The next day, Sabine and Vera asked me to join the steering team of the camp. We became close, and I learned to appreciate their true activism and the openness of their hearts. Vera became the *Global Kapara*[87] to me, and Babette, a courageous wise older sister.

The next day, Bernd Müller was introduced. He taught us the art and love of living water, planting trees, and the miracles of nature at the height of the Gazan armed conflict. His workshop lasted two days, and Ali's family's land felt happy and nurtured. We planted

---

[86] *Hafla*: Middle Eastern party.
[87] *Kapara*: Used in Hebrew slang as a term of endearment. It actually originates in the concept of atonement. In this case, the nickname I coined denotes a universal loyalty to authentic goodness.

thirty trees and went through a very deep spiritual process amid an increasing level of violence in the region.

Another integral part of the camp was something we called "news meditation." Lee, who lived just half-hour away in Ein Karem on the outskirts of Jerusalem, would go back home each night and collect the news: CNN, Al Jazeera, Russian news, Palestinian news, Israeli news, you name it. Each morning, she would bring the highlights to our circle—a daily news briefing which included deaths, bombs, and the most awful news from both sides. The meditation consisted in remaining in silence for fifteen minutes after the news briefing. We could move, cry, and scream, but no words were allowed. It was as if by harnessing our immediate reactions, we could prevent the violence from spreading. By recognizing our fight/flight/freeze mechanism, we could stop it from leading our communication, our perceptions, and our consciousness.

By then, I was already sensing that the "We Refuse to Be Enemies" camp was a sacred action. I had become part of the press and program steering leadership team with Babette, Vera, Ali, Lee, and Sami. One night at 3 AM, enveloped by the roars of sirens and warplanes and choked by tragic news, he and I met in the middle of the camp. "I can't imagine being with anyone else in a war but you, my beloved enemy," I told him. We hugged truthfully. Sami became my new and dearest brother until this day.

Rowan and Mona were smiling proudly. Kurdi and Murat reached out and joined the others in giving me an eight-hand shoulder rub. The story had landed.

The minivan was waiting for us, and we drove silently all the way to the coast. The silence was only interrupted by the policeman asking us for our passports. Luckily, this interaction was short and uneventful. We got to Nuweiba and Musallem's brother's place, our point of departure for the desert. Over tea, we told Musallem we would be in touch soon after we'd put together the northern and western teams. Meanwhile, he could start arranging as many camels as possible, and find Bedouins to join from the southern tribes of Sinai.

We said our goodbyes to Musallem, who was happy to get back to his family before his next trekking trip. After a restaurant meal, sitting in chairs for the first time in four days, we were ready to go back to the beach. It was already dark when we arrived. Fortunately, we had kept our huts and most of our stuff inside them. We took replenishing showers and had an early night.

The next morning, our muscles felt sore and happy from the journey. I joined the crew after my little morning swim, and we had breakfast together. Rowan was leaving the next day for Cairo, catching a flight to West Africa where he had to finish his refugee project. After that, he would travel to Crete and begin boat scouting, amassing the western sea fleet from Greece. He mentioned some of his skipper and sailor friends he would recruit in Africa. We would meet again, probably in Crete, in a month.

Our remaining group decided to have a replenishing spa day at the beach, and Kurdi and Mona told us to leave it all up to them. They prepared the space at Mona's *husha*, setting up all their oils, *saris*, towels, extra mattresses, and pillows to create a sumptuous and cozy healing sanctuary. To begin, they announced that this time, they would work on us—the men—one at a time with four hands. Both of them on each one of us, one after the other. Rowan was first. Murat and I decided to go for a walk and a swim on the next beach with the lagoon. He told me how fascinated he was with the camels, and that he had grown up with horses. I told him I was happy to hear this. In my head, I was starting to think about the northern horse contingent, and I was thrilled that he and Kurdi would be part of the horse people.

We swam for a bit and lay in the sun drying out. Everything was shining that morning as the tiny drops of evaporating water sparkled on our skin. As we walked back, he gave me a few drops of potent organic grass oil. They were tasty! I told Murat to go ahead of me for the four-hand treatment. He left to get ready for the session and I dipped in the water again. After a while, I felt a rush of goodness in my brain as my muscles relaxed. Laughter came easy. I was happy just floating in the water. Stepping out, I realized I'd lost track of time.

It was my turn to dry up and go back to the women. When I got there, Murat was glowing and calm, having his special tea concoction. I joined him, as Kurdi poured me a cup. We were all smiles. Murat finished his tea, gave me one of his solid and warm older brother hugs, and said to me, "Now is your turn. Enjoy fully, brother." His words seemed special, like a premonition. Even though they made perfect logical sense, I had the feeling that a deep, auspicious breakthrough was imminent.

Kurdi and Mona had closed off the view to the outside with colorful saris and veils. Kurdi told me to take my wet bathing suit off, then lay down for a bit in the sun. After soaking in the sea, the temperature was perfect. I dozed off, and when I woke up, four sensual hands were spreading a delicious blend of sandalwood and arnica oil all over my body. I opened my eyes; Kurdi smiled at me and placed a velvet bandana soaked in lavender on my eyes. Mona spread a little silk *sarong* on my groin. I felt eros rising as the pleasure of their soft but firm hands stroked my limbs with oil.

They were both sensuous and grounded, and gorgeous in very different ways. Their body weight supported their hands with each stroke. As usual, on this beach, a musician was practicing in the background. It sounded like a lute accompanied by a frame drum. I felt both in heaven and very much of the earth. It was as if I'd been transported in time to a goddess temple where an elder priestess and a younger one were initiating my body into itself.

Together, they continued oiling my body. Four sensuous hands, covering every inch of me. First, they had me lie on my stomach, then on my back, then sideways. They went through my limbs gently but firmly, creating muscle independence with their moves. With each of their strokes, my body was becoming more alive. The initiation also included Mona whispering affirmations in my ear. It was wonderful. Then, at some point, Kurdi said softly, "Now is the time for Mona to be with you intimately. I will leave you two alone." Kurdi kissed me on the lips and then on my forehead. She gently slipped away my lavender bandana, closed my eyelids with her fingers, and was gone.

Mona gently unwrapped the *sarong* from my groin. Looking

straight into my eyes, she said, "I want to tell you something, sweet and spicy one. I'm really attracted to you. I see you in all your depth and beauty. I want to become intimate and touch you with my hands, breasts, and tongue. Do you agree for me to do my magic with you?"

"Yes," I said. "I'm yours." Mona helped me to turn over on my stomach. Of course, by now I had an erection, but it felt quite different than usual. All my body felt alive. Direct blood democracy was taking place. My blood wasn't all rushing to my penis, but rather was distributed through my body equally. I felt my vitality rising and thriving.

Mona began slowly to brush her tongue up and down my spine. She seemed to delight in my trembling and sounds of pleasure. My skin was tremoring gently, and I was breathing deeply. She continued massaging me with her nipples alongside my spine, crisscrossing my vertebrae. My skeleton was awakening with her every move. She told me to keep breathing, to enjoy with my whole body. Then, she helped me turn over. She looked into my eyes and lovingly kissed me on my mouth. I felt vulnerable and present. My throat was coming alive as she touched and brushed her nails softly on my neck, my chest, my arms, my hands, then my legs, then my toes. She then started fondling my testicles with her delicate feet, then grabbed my phallus with them. The entire time, she whispered in my ear, "I see your beauty, I see your depth, I see your prophet, I see your life."

I was getting very aroused, and my heart was in it. And as I began to make primal sounds, my manhood throbbed and my tongue curled out like a cobra. "Don't hold back, my love," Mona whispered gently. I roared like a lion, coming as I hadn't in a long time. I undulated up and down with my torso and my tongue, arching into the air, screaming with fury. Mona held me firmly between her beautiful breasts until I surrendered into her arms. She gently placed me back on the mattress and tapped me slightly on the tip of my nose. Then she kissed my third eye and finally placed a long wet kiss on the center of my heart. I just lay there, jaw and sphincter, hands and feet, everything open, throbbing and trembling. Eventually, I fell asleep. Mona cuddled into my body and followed my lead into dreamland.

When we awoke, it felt like we were two butterflies flapping their wings into each other's hearts, resting like panthers and lions in the most replenishing and revitalizing rest of the last six thousand years. It was as if Goddess and God were alive and pulsating in love through us. All my muscles were relaxed. Even my eyelids and eyeballs. I felt surprisingly light and very happy. We both started laughing from the belly. It was a joy to breathe. Our bodies fit perfectly, and our bones weren't bumping into each other. It felt like the amniotic fluid of our memories was in sync. She kissed me with her tongue, then gently and slowly played with my lips. I was so happy. And so was Mona.

I thought about asking about her orgasm. She seemed to read my mind, and put her index finger on my lips, kissing me again as if to say, *it's all good. No need for anything now.* I felt her service was her pleasure in this moment, and that there was nothing to ask—just to relish the breasts and arms of a wonderful lover-being who sees me and pleasures me fully.

Mona accompanied me to my *husha* and tucked me into bed. She said she was joining Kurdi in the water, who was frolicking like a cross between a seal, a dolphin, and a whale. As you can tell...very hard to describe. She also told me that Rowan was leaving the next morning, and that she was moving in with me. She kissed me one more time and my whole body responded, delighted with its share in the world. I fell asleep again, this time with an enormous smile.

We all met for dinner, and I told my friends that I had fallen in love. They smiled. "No," I said, "not just with Mona! With all of you!" I told them that the Big Vision was just the first of a series of axial healing events that would happen around the world. As Frank Sinatra said, "If you can make it there, you'll make it anywhere" (he'd just confused NYC with Jerusalem). After Jerusalem, I said, we would move on to other root knots of conflict, helping to heal relations between Hindus and Muslims in Kashmir, between China and Tibet, and between Mother Earth and predatory capitalist "extractivism" in the Amazon. First things first, though. I was getting carried away.

I felt the need to transmit my personal experiences in the Holy

Land to my friends, directly. The best way I knew how was through story.

West Bank – 1998

ELIYAHU—THE one from Tantur, remember? I had met him in Berkeley. Part Hawaiian Sufi, orthodox Jew, "deadhead," and above all, devoted interfaith and peace activist. He and I had planned an encounter with a Palestinian Sufi sheik, and Eliyahu was a bit concerned about it. He told me that I would be only the third Jewish Israeli the sheik had ever met. These were tough times in the West Bank. Eliyahu had asked me to go slow and to read my host and the situation before initiating anything.

Eliyahu and I met early at the Damascus Gate in the Old City of Jerusalem to get a Palestinian taxi with a green license plate. It was the Jewish holiday of Sukkot[88], so I had brought the four ritual species connected to it: the myrtle, the weeping willow, the palm branch, and the *etrog*[89] citrus. Eliyahu didn't know I was also bringing...ha-ha...a powerful African djembe I had brought back from Ghana. *Just in case,* I'd thought to myself. It felt like a commercial: "Don't leave home without it."

Arriving at the sheik's abode in the small West Bank village, we were immediately ushered into the living room where he received his guests. Mattresses, pillows, a small table, Middle Eastern hospitality...you get the picture. After the formal and customary *Salaam Alaikums* back and forth, we sat down. Eliyahu introduced me to the sheik, and I started to show and tell my Sukkot symbols, thinking nature could get us onto common ground. He mentioned the *Suras of Lokman*[90] in the Koran. Everyone was polite, though it felt we were

---

[88] Sukkot: Jewish feast of Tabernacles, or booths, according to the Hebrew Calendar. One of the three main pilgrimage festivals celebrating impermanence.
[89] *Etrog*: Ancient Citrus. One of the four ritual species of the Jewish festival of tabernacles.
[90] *Lokman*: A sura (verse) of the Koran is named after him. Sometimes connected to the healing wisdom of plants and nature.

being shortchanged, staying on the surface of things, in our intelligent and safe interfaith conversation. It was time to upgrade the encounter.

Suddenly, I went to the entrance door, brought my *djembe* into the room, and took it out of the case. Eliyahu wasn't happy about this at all, but I pretended not to notice him. As I started drumming and singing *Allah Hu* by Pakistani Sufi Qawwali king Nusrat Fateh Ali Khan, I could feel the ice melting inside me, and in the room. By the time the chorus came—"*Allah Hu Allah Hu Allah Hu Allah Hu Allah Hu Allah Hu*"—it was already too much for the Sheik to contain. He smiled, then joined in the singing. He made a sign to his son, who brought a frame drum and started playing. By then, everyone was clapping to the ecstatic rhythm of the famous Qawali. When the song ended, Sheik el Refa'i[91] made another sign to his son. We all rose to do zikr for most of the night. After this, his son went to the kitchen and brought food for us. We broke bread together, and it felt like family. We had traveled far from our polite intellectual interfaith starting point.

I had been mesmerized by the young, bountiful woman who was sitting upright, just in front of me. I was sure she was the sheik's daughter. As we waited for the taxi back to Damascus Gate in Jerusalem, suddenly, the sheik surprised me.

"She's from South America, like you," he said with a smile.
"*Mexico.*"

Eliyahu called us from the doorway to say the taxis had arrived. I rushed over to talk to the young woman.

"Are you really from Mexico?" I asked.
"Yes," she said. "My Dad is from there."
"Where are you staying?"
"In Bat Ayin.[92] I'm studying *Kabbalah.*"
"Hmm. Can I see you again?"
"Sure," she said.
"Great. I'll come to pick you up in a couple of days," I said.
She ended up living with me for a year. I was in love.

---

[91] Sheik el Refa'i: Refa'i is a Sufi order founded by Ahmed el Refa'i, born in Basra, Iraq. Its name comes from the root of the word for "healing" in Arabic.
[92] Bat Ayin: Jewish extreme Israeli settler town embedded in the beautiful nature of the occupied territories.

But the year ended in tragedy.

To this day, I haven't fallen in love as strongly.

"Or have I?" I looked at Mona. She reached out and tapped me on the nose like the good witch she was, spreading shivers through my body.

We all played lots of good songs that evening, and the mysterious but friendly musicians showed up at the fire with their lute and frame drum. We hit it off and jammed well into the night. In the morning, we went to say goodbye to Rowan, accompanying him all the way to the taxi. He promised to meet us in a couple of months in Greece. Mona and I ran after his departing taxi singing aloud in epic farewell mode, so that Rowan with his head sticking out the window could hear:

Salamat salamat salamat ya habibna ya baladiat!"[93]

The kitchen staff joined us, singing and clapping to the well-known Egyptian song. It was a happy and momentous morning.

The next day, it was time for Kurdi and Murat to leave as well. That same afternoon, a special group of kids arrived at the Ras. They were part of an international activist group who had left school to devote themselves fully to the planet, their future, and climate justice. There were five of them. The oldest was eighteen years old, and basically their chaperone. The youngest was seven years old and was the eldest's sister; they were Swedish. The others were eleven, thirteen, and sixteen years old, from Belgium, Germany, and Australia. For some good reason, they sat right next to us. All of them were beaming as they told us a bit of their story. They were traveling together and learning about the world. They had decided to start with the Middle East— Palestine to be precise, arriving through Israel.

"Sounds familiar!" I said, winking at my beloved new friends. The kids didn't look surprised. They told us they were trying to sue the United Nations, just like the Earth Guardians were doing against the US government. They were on fire!

Kurdi looked at me, laughing. "Looks like you found your east."

---

[93] *Salamat salamat salamat ya habibna ya baladiat*: "Peace upon you beloveds, our people." Recorded by Sheik el Tuni and the Musicians of the Nile.

"What?" said Julie, the seven-year-old. That's my favorite direction! Can I tell you my dream?" Without waiting for our answer, she continued. "I dreamed that we would come walking, a lot of people from the east…sounds a bit weird, but I think it was to Jerusalem. I've never been there. Is that a city?"

Murat hugged her warmly. "Yes," he said. "We shall *follow the young*." From then on, that's the name they went by: the *Follow the Young* troupe. It seemed as if Julie the dreamer was the leader and they were following her—and we, the older ones, were following them into the future dream of a more beautiful and just reality.

Murat acted as a good grandpa and went to get them all mango juices. Kurdi, as a good grandma, hugged each of them. Mona and I helped by taking their bags, which, for some, were bigger than they were.

"Can I tell them about the Big One?" Mona asked. "They seem absolutely ready!"

"Indeed," Kurdi said.

"And G., you tell me if I missed something," Mona added, looking at me. I agreed in delight. It was already her vision too.

Mona told the troupe this was the first of a planetary relay of healing ceremonies to cure the pain, find the jewels that lie dormant below the hurt, and surprise reality in its cracks. Through those cracks, we would do collective magic. Mona was a radiant and charismatic storyteller, and the kids were in awe of her.

"Yes, please tell us more," Marikia, the eldest, begged. Ana, who was eleven, and Julie, the little one, pulled at Mona's dress. "Come on!" they said. Mona sat Julie in her lap and held Ana's hand. Clemens the thirteen-year-old German exclaimed, "*Wunderbar*!" Kai, the Australian sixteen-year-old, said, "Come on, let her talk!"

Mona continued, "The first one will be in Jerusalem! And then we'll move on to wherever we are needed. Maybe to Kashmir, between India and Pakistan; maybe China and Tibet, Goree Island in West Africa, Wounded Knee, Uluru, and the Amazon jungle."

"Is that near here?" Julie asked.

"Which one? India or China?" Ana said.

"Uluru is in Australia, my home, and is super far away!" Kai said.

"China and India are also far," Clemens said.

"Africa is right here to the south," Marikia replied, "but please, can we let Mona continue her story?"

"So back to Jerusalem!" Mona continued. "We will come from the four directions: camels from the south, right here from Sinai—the southern camel caravan."

"What is a caravan?" Ana asked.

"A kind of traveling group," Julie said.

"And how did you know that?" Kurdi asked Julie, stroking her hair.

"I saw it in a movie," Julie replied nonchalantly.

"Okay, so, hocus focus!" Mona said, bringing everyone back to the story. "Camels from the south…"

"A thousand camels," I added.

"Yes," Mona said. "A thousand boats sailing from the west, probably from Crete, in Greece. My brother, Captain Rowan, went to get them. He'll have them ready in a few months."

"Your brother is a captain?" Clemens asked.

"Most surely he is," Murat said reassuringly. Kurdi and I giggled.

"Can you stop interrupting her story?" Marikia pleaded.

"Yes. It's hard to follow like this," Ana added.

"A thousand horses coming from the north, near Kurdi and Murat's home," Mona pointed at them. "And finally, this is where you guys, the *Follow the Young* troupe, come in: a thousand children walkers leading from the east, probably from Bethlehem."

"That's where Jesus was born, right?" Clemens asked.

"Right," Mona answered.

"It is also part of Palestine, where we want to go next," Little Julie said.

"And how do you know that, sweet Julie?" Murat asked.

"Because my big sister Marikia told me," Julie answered. Kurdi let loose her famous laugh and we all followed, even the kids. Now we had real proof that her laughter was contagious—and that it worked intergenerationally!

"But actually, we would all come together in Hebron," I interjected.

"That's also in Palestine, and in Israel," Kai added.

"It's where Abraham and the ancestors of Arabs and Jews are buried," Mona said. "And after a very special healing ceremony there, we will all walk to Jerusalem!" After making the sweetest prayer for all waters, Mona sipped slowly from her water bottle. The kids said, "Amen." We were all moved once again by the Big Vision.

Murat got up and said, "It's time for the kids to take some rest, before dinner. We'll all meet at sunset here."

Sayed came from the camp to ask how many *hushas* the kids needed. All in unison, they said, "One!"

"We'll sleep together," Little Julie confirmed. Sayed smiled.

At dinner, right after sunset, Murat and Kurdi said they would be leaving us in the morning as they had a flight to Istanbul from Cairo. From there, they would go to Urfa and start recruiting horses and riders for the northern horse caravan. We would all meet in Crete that summer.

"I already started learning Arabic," Clemens said proudly.

"We want to join you!" the other kids said.

"Can we learn Arabic too?" asked Ana.

"Of course, tomorrow morning!" Clemens answered. We all started playing a happy song with Mona, and the kids danced, ran, and played around the fire. As it got late, and they got tired, Kurdi and Murat volunteered to take them to bed. Marikia stayed with us, though; she was an especially good dancer, and was uplifting the music with her movement. Around midnight we decided to call it a night so we could be up in time to say goodbye to our beloved elders, the Kurds. We walked Marikia to the kids' *husha* and said goodnight. Mona surprised me by suddenly running, racing me to our *husha*. The moon was out, and the night was luminous. We wrapped our arms and legs around each other and fell asleep. The way we fit together, it seemed like our bodies had met centuries ago.

In the morning, it was just Mona and I who bid farewell to Kurdi and Murat. "See you in a few months," I said.

"Five cosmic minutes," Kurdi answered. We hugged. We were all good huggers, but Murat's hugs were next level; it was such a nurturing experience and gift to be embraced by him. As the taxi set off, Mona and I waved goodbye, praising the nourishment of Murat's embrace.

After breakfast, we were in for a surprise. Musallem showed up at the beach with two of his youngest kids—a rare sight, as he usually preferred to stay in the desert, in the mountains. He said he had a day off and wanted to see us before we left back to Israel. "*Ya hara betak!*" he said to me as I met him. "You are together with Mona! So happy for you." The kids came "downtown" to the cafeteria for breakfast, and immediately hit it off with Musallem's young sons. They all ran to see some crabs on the shore while we waited for the food.

"This is the oldest of the *Follow the Young* group—her name is Marikia," I said, introducing her to Musallem. "And this is Musallem. He has been a friend of mine for twenty-five years, and knows and loves the desert very much!"

"That is true," He said, wearing his million-dollar smile.

"Hey, Musallem," Mona said, "maybe you can take us for a day trip with Marikia, the kids, and your sons?"

"Why not?" he answered.

"Even just across the road? Or to Wadi Thmile in front of *Maagana*, to the red dune?" I suggested.

"Good idea!" Musallem agreed.

"Let's go after breakfast. We can have dinner at Ahmed's tent on the other side of the road when we come back at sunset."

"*Mumtaz!*"[94] I said excitedly.

After breakfast, we gathered some drinking water and warm clothes for the evening, and crossed the road. It was the first time "the troupe" had been in the desert. Once we were far enough from the road that we couldn't hear it anymore, we stopped and sat down. It was powerful.

"Let's listen to Sinai," Musallem said.

After a couple minutes of silence, a beautiful flock of partridges came our way, very close to us. Ana was about to say something, but

---

[94] *Mumtaz*: "Perfect" in Arabic.

Marikia lovingly told her to just be quiet. We could hear the birds as they ran on the sand then took to a very low flight, flapping their short wings as is their custom.

After we broke the silence, I told the others that partridges appear in the Bible, when the Israelites were in Sinai for forty years.

"That's older than you?" Julie asked me.

"Not quite, Little Julie," I said, as Mona and Musallem laughed.

We kept walking until we got to a breathtaking narrow passage, which we had to cross one by one. The sandstone was pink, then yellow, then purple, and finally white. The kids stopped and painted themselves with it, then found an empty bottle and began pouring the different colored sands into it. When we got to the other side of the narrow passage, lo and behold, we saw a huge, beautiful sand dune in front of us. Immediately, Musallem and his sons started showing off their somersaults and rolling down the dune like masterful Bedouin acrobats. The kids followed. Clemens was first, then Kai, Ana, Julie and even Marikia. Delighting in the scene, I stayed behind with Mona, who took some photos and a video. Mona sang a beautiful Czech Roma song. I got goosebumps and she kissed me. Then we heard a voice from down below:

"Come on, guys!" Musallem shouted. "We are making tea!"

Mona and I decided to roll down the dune sideways, holding hands. We ate a bit of sand—actually a lot of sand—but laughed all the way down. When we reached the bottom, everyone was busy looking for twigs for the fire. Musallem had found a pot in a nook of the mountain hideaway—the traditional hidden "shelves" where Bedouins leave things. That's how a desert community works: you always have a pot, even if you didn't carry one.

Between all of us, we had enough water to fill up the pot. The fire was lit and Musallem took some tea and sugar out of his knapsack. The kids were proud of their fire production, and we were proud of them too. We had some wonderful tea with a few local herbs that Musallem had collected with the kids. He also taught them about the plants' medicinal uses. Marikia took out some delicious high percentage cacao with maca and salt, and we all had a sweet moment sharing it. Like most Bedouins, Musallem was a master with children and took the kids for a hike to explore some more. Mona and I stayed next to the fire. It was quiet and tranquil as the blue and orange flames danced in the bright sunlight.

We sat in silence, taking in the power of *yin*.[95] "*Dolce far niente*": the masterful sweet art of doing nothing. We simply sat, just receiving the desert's wisdom. It felt deeply sacred to be in the presence of Sinai with a gorgeous, wise, talented, magnificent woman, who I was falling more in love with by the minute.

The sun was still high, and the kids and Musallem wouldn't be back for a while. I wanted Mona to know about my Hebrew roots and lineage. Each new story I shared felt like another layer of myself revealed: a biographical striptease, designed just for her.

Philadelphia – 1995

I WAS anxious when I called, but when I said I was Rabbi Marshall Meyer's son, Rabbi Zalman scheduled me for an immediate appointment with him. I had met him briefly with my father at a *Havdalah*[96] workshop Rabbi Zalman had taught in NYC, years before. In our three-hour meeting at his home in Mt. Airy, we covered a lot of ground. As a starter, he simply asked, "What do you have in mind?"

Those were the wholly-holistic-holy '90s. Although Prime Minister Rabin had just been killed by a fanatic settler, the Israel I had arrived in was still bubbling with spirit. It was the era of the great "rehydration" of the culture of the Fertile Crescent: new wines, goat cheeses, architecture, healing arts, and a renewal of Middle Eastern music and dance. It was a blooming rebirth—though its spirit would wane, and soon after utterly collapse. A few years later, a threatening right-wing authoritarian and racist wave again took over the mood of the country—and has lasted until this day, subverting the democratic soul and prophetic spirit of Israel.

---

[95] *Yin*: The feminine and receptive aspect of the Tao in Chinese philosophy, complementing the *yang* masculine energy.
[96] *Havdalah*: Multi-sensorial Hebrew ceremony celebrating the end of the Sabbath and the beginning of the week.

Most of the players in the Israeli counterculture, who were later to surface as cultural pioneers and respected anchors of a new Israeli culture, were directly connected to the best of those three hundred participants at the first few Israeli Rainbow Gatherings. I had seen firsthand the profound liberation that Jewish Israelis feel when they encounter Hindu Gods, *Bhajans*,[97] *kirtan*,[98] and yoga culture. I had seen how singing Jewish devotional songs seemed to shrink their souls compared to how I saw them blossom singing Hindu devotional songs. I guess it's the detachment from monotheism, Israeli mono-Jewish culture, conflict, victimhood—and for many, most surely, a distraction from the hard reality of post-army trauma. I hadn't had the "Mama India" baptism yet. But all around me, in my circles of friends, it seemed like a requirement. My journey to India was imminent.

Back to my question to Reb Zalman:

"You know I'm now living in Israel. The tribe I'm surrounded with sings Hindu *Bhajans* freely for hours, but when they must sing *Lecha Dodi*[99] they get self-conscious and judgmental, and stop singing after five minutes. It's as if dwelling on Jewish content brings up all the constricting family, cultural, and national conditioning, even in the freest of environments. It makes me feel really uncomfortable. I also don't feel good about all the images and little statues of the divine Hindu pantheon."

Zalman gave me a good look, then took a big deep breath in. On his out-breath, he chanted an eloquent *Om Namah Shivaya*.

"Do you believe in one God?" he asked.

I didn't know what to answer. It sounded like a trick question. "Yes," I finally said.

"Are you sure?" he insisted.

Shit...what should I say? I doubted for another moment, then doubled down.

"Yes!"

---

[97] *Bhajan*: Hindu religious devotional chant.
[98] *Kirtan*: repetitive Hindu call and response devotional chant.
[99] *Lecha Dodi*: The Jewish Sabbath's main anthem, written by Rabbi Shlomo Alkabetz in the city of Safed in Israel in the 16th century to welcome the Sabbath on Friday evenings.

"So then, why are you concerned with what we call the One or how we sing to the One? If there's only One, then it must be the same One that everyone praises, right? So why does it matter which religious language you choose to pray in? Each way has its own uniqueness, power, and beauty, but they all point to the same One."

For a few more hours, I told Zalman of my visit to New Mexico and my incursion into medicine work with the Native American Peyote[100] church. I had met a medicine man there, the late Uncle Jimmy Reyna, and was bringing him to Israel. With peyote as a sacrament, we would do a dress rehearsal for our Metatron "Celestial Wedding" production on Yom Kippur.[101]

"Interesting. Maybe you should do it in *Shabbat Shuvah*?[102] Hmmm. Have you tried ayahuasca?" the white-bearded deeply ecumenical revolutionary inquired. With this empowering question, our three-hour meeting ended in a high vibration.

Mona looked at me with a deep love. I felt hugged by her eyes.

"A ritual theater collective experimenting with peyote?" she said. "That sounds great! What was the name of it? Metatron?"

"Yes," I replied. "It's the story based on Enoch, a character who appears in Genesis. He's called the Prince of Presence. There are a couple of apocryphal[103] texts dedicated to him: "The Book of Enoch" and "The Secrets of Enoch." They were both saved by the Ethiopian Church. Anyway, they tell the story of a scribe of truth who was seduced on Mount Hermon into becoming a heavenly spokesperson for the giants who had fallen from heaven to earth."

"Did he come back to earth?" Mona asked.

"They say he went through an initiation into 'angelhood,' and became the angel Metatron. That was the name of our group and the source of our first ritual theater production." "Fascinating!" Mona

---

[100] Peyote: a psychedelic and medicinal cactus plant originating in the Mexican desert. Contains mescaline. Sometimes called "Grandfather."
[101] Yom Kippur: Day of Atonement or "at one-ment." Part of the Days of Awe according to the Hebrew Calendar.
[102] *Shabbat Shuvah*: The Sabbath before Yom Kippur. A time of reckoning.
[103] Apocryphal: Books that didn't make it into the Bible for political and other reasons.

said. I tended to the fire and moved some of the *ratam*[104] twigs. As the ashes became more visible, the fire was turning gray. It was a gray mixed with shades of black and white, soft as velvet. I lay down on my back and Mona did the same. Then she leaned over and kissed my eyes, saying, "I love what you see." She started kissing my ears. "I also love what you hear."

She held my head with both her hands. It was as if the *Shechinah*[105] herself was cradling me with her kisses. I gazed at the sky, following a cloud passing by. "Shepherd of clouds," I said.

Mona gave an exquisite laugh. "Hunter-gatherer of winds," she answered, laughing again. We marveled at the mountain shapes and how they transformed before our eyes. The shade reached our spot and it started to get chilly, so we stood to put more twigs on the fire. Musallem came back with the kids, just in time for tea and a surprise: we had fried some bananas on the fire with the rest of Marikia's chocolate.

"How do you like the bananas, *jamaa*?"[106] Mona asked.

"Mmm," Kai said, with a mouth full of banana and chocolate. "Good on ya, mate!"

"The best ever!" Little Julie added.

Everyone, Musallem included, delighted in our choco-bananas. They made funny sounds as they ate them, and we all laughed together as everyone's face became painted in chocolate. Afterwards, Musallem—good dad that he was—went around with a water bottle and washed their sticky chocolate faces. We cleaned the fireplace, left it spotless, packed what little stuff we had, and went down to Maagana beach where a jeep was waiting for Musallem. Before he left, he told us that he'd started talking to his camel-people friends from different southern Sinai tribes: the Muzzeina,[107] the Jabaliya, and his own Tarabin tribe. He also mentioned he had a new connection from the western desert

---

[104] *Ratam*: Arabic for Retama, a genus of flowering bushes in the legume family found prominently in Sinai and the Levant.
[105] *Shechinah*: Divine immanent feminine in the sacred Hebrew pantheon. From the Hebrew root "dwells."
[106] *Jamaa*: Arabic term of endearment for "my group."
[107] Muzzeina: One of the eight Bedouin tribes of southern Sinai, supposedly originating from Saudi Arabia.

oasis in Siwa who wanted to join. "Stay in touch! Life is goood!" he called as the jeep drove off, blessing us with his joy.

We decided to walk back on the shore all the way to the Ras. On the way back to our haven, we passed the beach camps of Rock Sea and Moon Island. It was our last night, though the kids would stay a bit longer on their own. I gave them the contacts of my friends in Bethlehem, and surprise surprise, Marikia said they had already contacted those very people by mail. In fact, my friends were expecting them. I also gave them a few other Israeli contacts on the way north from Eilat, some friends in communities in southern Israel and all the way to Jerusalem. I asked the kids to please tell us when they reached Bethlehem, and said that we would meet them there in the spring.

That night, although we were exhausted, we stayed up late. Mona and I held hands by the fire. All the Bedouins were winking at me, and other old friends who had arrived at the beach were happy to see us together. We were too. The kids stayed up late and danced around the fire until they collapsed and fell asleep. We helped Marikia and Kai to carry them to bed. The next morning, we woke up nice and early and packed all our things, and went on our way. The kids were still sleeping.

CHAPTER 4

DUE NORTH

WE LEFT Bedouin-style, without announcing our departure. After some unnerving questioning of Mona by the Israeli police, we crossed the border. We decided to stop for breakfast at a friend's beach in Eilat just ten minutes from the border, and make an organic, slow transition into civilization. After a nice breakfast and a beer, I told Mona about my time as an Argentinian poet.

Paris – 1989

As a young Argentinian poet in Paris, my days generally consisted of one good film a day, great endless walks, crossing beautiful bridges, and getting drunk in French every night. My nights were the usual lonely poet stunt at the neighborhood bar near the Metro Voltaire in the 11th *arrondissement* next to the Bastille. My essential props were a notebook, a pen, and many drinks.

One night, I decided to write only after finishing each drink I ordered. In the presence of the muses, words were pouring out. On the third cup, I wrote that after the seventh cup I would meet nobility. When I got to my seventh cup, someone tapped me on my shoulder from behind. I turned around to see a short African man with long dreadlocks. He told me his name was Badu, and passed me a joint. As soon as I took a hit, I started feeling very emotional. Crying, I got up and ran to the bathroom, embarrassed and overwhelmed.

Badu knocked on the toilet door. "Brother, come out," he said. "We wanna be with you. What happened? Why are you crying?"

"I'm coming," I said, still sniffing my tears up my nose.

I got out of the tiny bar toilet, still a bit wet on my cheeks. Badu gave me a hug and told me, "Come, let's sit together with my friends." As I walked towards their table, I saw that they had invited the whole bar to a round of champagne. The French are usually overwhelmed by Senegalese generosity, seeming like greedy paupers compared to the elegant West Africans. There was a sassy French woman sitting with them. The other Senegalese at the table was a tall, fiery-looking man.

"*Comment tu t'appelle?*" he asked me. I told him my name. "Like me," he said. "Djibril is my name." I later learned he was a very famous Senegalese movie director who has since passed away. After another *petard*, a few laughs and champagne, Djibril and Alice left. Badu asked me to move to the bar next to him, and invited me for a last beer. We were both pretty drunk by then, though our hearts were fully open, awake, and with the ease of an after-party. "Where are you from?" he asked me.

"Argentina."

"Ah," he said, "my ex-girlfriend is from Argentina…she's still my good friend."

"Really?"

"Yes. Her uncle is a famous actor, a comedian there. I think he's Jewish."

"What's your ex's name?" I asked.

"Mariana. Mariana Briski."

"Wow!" I yelled, jumping off my barstool. "Norman Briski!"

"Who?" Badu asked.

"Norman Briski, the famous actor! He was my theater teacher for a few years in Buenos Aires. Amazing! And his niece was your girlfriend right here in Paris?!"

"Yes," he said. "I just saw her last month." Badu made me promise I wouldn't sit in the bar alone ever again when he and his friends were there, then invited me to a very cool-sounding Senegalese party that weekend. We also made a date to meet at my home before the party. When he arrived, Badu climbed up the five flights of stairs to my humble palace at 23 bis Rue Popincourt at Metro Voltaire. He took off his coat, and out of his pocket pulled a bunch of tapes of African music—*kora* music, to be precise.

"You are like a spiritual orphan," Badu told me. "This music will be a balm for your heart. The angel spirits came down to the forest with the kora to soothe people's hearts. I think you'll like it." As he clicked play while I was making both of us some tea, I felt the plucking of the harp in the center of my heart as a soul ointment. It was my direct and personal introduction to a remedy that served me well for many years: the medicine of African kora music. I became good friends with Badu, and now had a Senegalese posse, right in my own neighborhood in Paris. I never sat alone in that bar again.

At every mention of the word kora, Mona smiled, closing her eyes in delight. I could see she enjoyed hearing of her father's Senegalese culture and music.

We had decided to reach the north slowly. We would make stops at friends' homes along the way. It was also an opportunity for her to see Israel on her first visit. Our next stop would be Shaharut. I had some old friends there.

Shaharut – 2006

I TOLD Mona that my old friends, a couple, were the angels who took care of me on my 40-day retreat for my fortieth birthday, about a kilometer from their legendary open desert home. During my retreat, they came to visit me once a week just to check that I hadn't gone crazy. On Fridays, they would bring me candles, organic wine, and goat cheese—my only cooked meal of the week.

"What did you do in your retreat for forty days?" Mona asked as we started driving out of Eilat through the desert.

"I was very busy," I answered. Mona laughed. "I had quite a few chores in the morning. A good body cleanse, some running, yoga, and prayers. Did my three Jewish daily prayers in the morning, afternoon, and evening. I read the whole Old Testament, The Gospels, and the

Koran, and had an hour of Zohar studies every day, which is the main Kabbalistic text.

"In terms of food, I had quite a strict daily organic diet consisting of one or two raw vegetables and a bit of tahini each meal. Breakfast was just one or two walnuts, one date, and tahini. I had some free time once a day when I went for a walk in the desert.

"However, the main thrust of the intense schedule was my diary. Each day, I wrote down all the memories I could muster about each year of my life, represented chronologically by the relevant day in the retreat."

"What?" Mona asked. "Could you explain that one?"

"Ha-ha...so, for example, if it was day four in the retreat, I wrote about my memories of when I was four years old. I continued writing each day in my diary until age (and day) forty.

"Every three days or so, I would recapitulate and review my notes and burn some sage with the pages which weren't relevant to my life, stuff that didn't serve me anymore, and that I wanted to let go of.

"On Friday nights, I allowed my benefactor friends to bring with them one extra guest for dinner. Saturdays, it was me alone again, but it was a feast. I had the leftovers from Friday's meal, plus red wine and goat cheese."

"Brave man," she said, massaging my neck while I drove. We got to Shaharut an hour later, where we said hi to Liat, left our bag in their home, and went for a walk. They would be back in the evening, but of course, we were welcome to stay overnight. I showed Mona where my retreat had happened. After our walk, we went back to our host's place and had a nice long bath together. Their bathroom was fun and very artsy, as bathrooms should be. We lovingly soaped and scrubbed each other which brought me sweet memories of playing "scuba divers" with my dad in the bathtub in Buenos Aires. Mona remembered playing underwater with her brother Rowan with real scuba gear at Goree Island in Senegal.

"Isn't that from where most of the slave ships left for the Americas?"

"*Oui*," Mona said. "*Tu parles Français? Non?*"

"*Oui, je me débrouille,*"[1] I said proudly. "But not Wolof,"[2] I added.

Mona smiled. We had a friendly talk and nourishing homey meal with our hosts in their famous and cozy kitchen, then played some music. A couple of neighboring musicians joined and jammed with us. It was a sweet night. In the morning, we decided to buy some delicious local groceries at Neot Smadar's organic store. "The same wine and goat yogurt from my retreat," I said. We continued on our way, stopping an hour later at Mitzpe Ramon for a walk in the crater. We also spotted an amazing natural pool in the desert which was full of rainwater, and dipped in. It was a warm beginning of a winter day. No one was there, so we dried in the sun naked and made morning love. As we moved on, I told her of my times in New York.

New York – 1990

Cincuenta D'estos Para Empezar,[3] my first poetry book, had gone to print. I had begun writing it after too much anguish and an excruciating yearning for poetry. Starting in Greece and continuing in Paris, the fifty short poems were ready by the time I got to NYC.

When I looked at the first five hundred copies from the printer, I saw a couple minuscule mistakes. Like a new father worried about the health of my firstborn baby, I immediately called Paula from the printing house. "Oh, that's awful!" Paula said, apologizing. "We're sending you another five hundred copies, corrected and free of charge." I was elated, and started sending my first book to writers, critics, Spanish literature university departments, and other people I respected.

The book received a couple of good reviews and an invitation for a reading at the Latin American Book Fair at NYU, where I would be reading with the irreverent and wonderful Puerto Rican poet Giannina Braschi (who had also written a great review of my book). Following

---

[1] *Oui, je me débrouille*: "I get by" in French.
[2] Wolof: the main Senegalese tribal language.
[3] *Cincuenta D'estos Para Empezar*: "Fifty of These to Start With."

us on the schedule was a never-to-be talk by Octavio Paz. He had just received the Nobel Prize in literature, and wouldn't be coming to the conference as he had to go receive his prize in Stockholm.

I had about seven hundred copies left at my parents' home on the Upper West Side of Manhattan, where I lived for six months, regrouping after six years of not living on the same continent as them. I decided I was going to sell my books myself." There are lots of potential customers who read Spanish in New York City," I thought. I packed my big African Kente bag from my Ghanaen journey, filled it with *Cincuenta D'Estos Para Empezar*, and left for the Bronx Zoo.

It was summer, and after a few failed attempts at sitting somewhere shady with my books and a sign reading "Spanish Poetry," waiting for customers, I realized I had to be more proactive. The drill went as follows:

I started walking up to people.

"Do you read Spanish?"

If they said yes, then I switched to Spanish.

"Do you like poetry?"

If they answered yes:

"Are you interested in checking out my first book of poetry?"

Once they agreed, I would choose a poem and read it out loud to them. Then came the pitch:

"The book costs $5."

And so, I made my first sales. Every day, I went back home and counted my money in my parents' king-size bed. My mom was amazed at my success. In the beginning, I sold about twenty books a day, hitting at least two different Latino-prone locations in each borough, then the Spanish departments of universities. I did parks, Spanish libraries, the whole lot. By then, customers were either paying $5, a beer, or both. Some even paid $10 to show their support for an "entrepreneurial" young poet from Argentina.

My most successful day came when I discovered the Spanish Shakespeare Festival in Central Park. Literally hundreds of Latinos who liked Shakespeare in Spanish were standing in line, where they had arrived hours before, waiting to get into the free festival. Tickets were first come, first served, and the Central Park auditorium had a limited capacity. Yes, you guessed it! I pitched my book to every single person in the line. I was already quite confident about approaching my potential buyers, reading them poems and answering their questions about my adventures in Greece and Paris. When I returned home, my big bag was empty of books but full of dollar bills. I had sold two hundred fifty books in three hours, and poured all of the money onto my mom's bed. She had worked all her life since she was twelve and had a deep respect for making money; she'd been a successful businesswoman and was very proud of that.

"So, a poetry entrepreneur in New York," she said, delighted." Beautiful!"

Mona and I drove all the way to Tel Aviv and parked at Neve Tsedek, then walked to Jaffa and through the flea market, and back through Neve Tsedek. None of my friends were home, and we wanted to get to Galilee before dark. It was time to continue.

The day was unusually warm, and Mona wanted to go to the sea. We stopped at Bet Yanai beach, where I had lived for five years, for a dip. We continued to Pardes Hanna, where we stopped at Urvot Haomanim[4] for a delicious natural shake and healthy salad. It was almost sunset, so we decided to drive to my home. We finally arrived at the *reches*[5] and drove up the mountain to see, through our windshield, some of the brightest colors we had ever seen emerging from the sky.

It felt like we'd been invited to a divine vernissage. As we arrived in my little village, we heard the Muslim call to prayer coming up from the valley in canon. It felt majestic, and Mona's presence made it feel brand new for me, too.

"So beautiful," she said. She told me she was remembering her dad, who took them sometimes to a Sufi *Zawiya*[6] in Saint Louis, in

---

[4] Urvot Haomanim: A cultural market in the popular and mostly alternative town of Pardes Hanna in Israel.
[5] *Reches*: Local name for the mountain in Misgav where the villages of Yodfat, Avtalion, Yachad and Hararit are situated.
[6] *Zawiya*: "corner" in Arabic. Sufi sacred space for devotional gatherings at a corner of the mosque, outside the main prayer room.

Senegal. She said he had followed an amazing Sufi sheik called Abdulai Jai, or Sheik Jai, for short.

"Wow!" I said. "I met him briefly at the Waldorf Astoria in New York for the Millennium Peace Summit of Religious and Interfaith Leaders, in 2001. He was a beautiful and joyous being. When I met him, Sheik Abdulai Jai was in bed, already quite sick. I came in with my *djembe* and played an African song for him, which made him happy (as his disciple Fara Gaye told me when we were leaving the hotel room)."

"Who else was at the summit?" Mona asked.

"Pir Vilayat Khan, Goenka, and Amma Ji were there…but the most riveting moment was when Chief Oren Lyons and Indigenous leaders from Alaska to Africa and from Lapland to Tierra del Fuego went up the stage together as one group. They prayed and declared that the ice was melting in the North. They said they had been there before the UN building was built and would still be here after the building would be gone, and they got a standing ovation from everyone—rabbis, Christian and Shinto priests, Hindu Babas, Buddhist monks, Muslim sheiks, and nuns. I was, funnily enough, part of the Palestinian delegation of three as a translator for the Palestinian Sufi Sheik, and his son. The irony was that I translated for him from English into Hebrew!"

As we arrived in our mountain village, the wind was blowing strongly, as usual. We got our luggage out of the car and went into my house. I still felt like I was seeing everything through Mona's eyes. Mona had gotten a message from the Captain, and I had emails waiting to be answered from the new allies I had met in Lisbon. It was "office" time. Mona stopped me with both hands on my way to the computer, kissed me on the mouth, and said, "If we're gonna do office, let's make it fun!" She asked me for the Wi-Fi password and started playing a happy, tranquil playlist from her phone—kind of a cross between Grappelli and Bobby McFerrin. Somehow, it was perfect for the moment.

"Let's clean a bit first?" she said with a smile, while gently grabbing my butt. While she did some laundry, I did the dishes. "Listen,"

Mona said, "I'm not always Mary Poppins. But I do try not to lose my magic when I can help it." I cleaned the counter, even the *shmutz*[7] under the drying dishes—the whole fuckin' thing. I felt so happy that I continued with the gas stove, all five burners. When I was loved, there was nothing I couldn't do. I felt invincible.

Mona cranked the music up a bit more and started sweeping the kitchen floor before moving on to the living room. "Love your dome," Mona said as she tried some operatic voices under it. "What acoustics!" She approached me, dancing sexy and slow, kissed me, then cleaned the rest of the floor. It felt like a party.

After we finished our chores, Mona made one of her special tea concoctions, served us cups, and opened her laptop. I did the same. She winked at me, and we started to answer piles of emails and messages from those out-of-the-loop weeks in Sinai. Mona told me that the Captain's trip to Africa would be shorter than he thought. His partner there had done most of the wrapping-up for the refugee program, and when Rowan put out the word to his "nomadic skippers and sailors," he had gotten quite a response. He would be landing in Greece in three weeks. I continued with the online stuff until I saw a message from Ibrahim, our retired soccer star. He mentioned something that caught my attention: he had met legendary Brazilian ex-soccer player and activist Ronaldo and mentioned our "Big One" very briefly. Ronaldo had told him to keep him in the loop! I stopped instantly and screamed, "Ronaldo is in! Ronaldo is in!"

"What?" said Mona. "Who is Ronaldo? And why are you screaming?"

"Ronaldo, the Brazilian soccer star!" I said, exhilarated.

"You gotta explain, Spicy Honey." That was a new one. I liked it. But I didn't have time to indulge my new nickname now.

"Ronaldo is in," I repeated.

"You said that three times. 'In' what?!"

"In our 'Big One!'"

"What does soccer have to do with it?" Mona asked.

"It's our security, our protection. But I'll tell you more later."

---

[7] *Shmutz*: "filth" in Yiddish.

"Ooookaaay..." said Mona, looking at me a bit bemused. She stepped into the house from her makeshift office on my winter patio, next to the olive tree near the entrance. Walking into my studio, she said, "So, this is where you work?"

"Yup," I said. "Unfortunately, it's a bomb shelter, required by Israeli law. Every time I think of this, my mind drifts to moving my life next to a river in Portugal or Costa Rica... maybe when we are done with the Big One in Jerusalem. Who knows? Anyway, let me explain to you about the connection to soccer stars."

"I'm getting hungry, aren't you? Mona said.

"A bit," I answered.

"Let me fix something up for us and you can tell me over dinner." Mona kissed me on the nape, sneaking from the back, and left for the kitchen. I kept reading my emails and saw that Vasilis, our Greek media maverick brother, had also reached out. He had met with his five-person team, and they were into it. He mentioned that he had free access to an amazing piece of land that held a retreat center next to a river in southern Crete. It could easily fit thirty people inside and at least thirty tents comfortably outside. It was also a twenty-minute walk from the sea. It was ready for us, and could be available by the end of winter.

I replied immediately, introducing Rowan and Vasilis and telling them to please get the land ready for a big gathering in mid-March. They mentioned they had friends in common, as Vasilis had been a sailor. It was looking good! Then I got a recorded message from Musallem, who simply said:

"*Salamtak*, how are you? How is Mona? Life is gooood!"

I smiled wide as Mona called out from the kitchen, "Food is ready!" When I came in, a big candle was glowing on the table. A sweet music playlist was on, and she had also cooked a little dish of rice with vegetables called *kicheri*.[8] It was delicious. I opened the organic wine from the desert, and we toasted to our life on my

---

[8] *Kicheri*: South Indian-style dish with rice, vegetables, cumin seeds, coriander seeds, bay laurel leaves, black pepper, and salt, fried in ghee.

front porch just as the *moazin*[9] prayers were sounding out over Wadi Salame.

In the morning, we were meeting a friend who works with horses. "We need to start getting ready for the horses," I mused. "But first, how about an interspecies story?"

"What's that?" Mona asked.

Portugal – 2017

AFTER FINISHING another ten-day training at Tamera's Global Love School in southern Portugal, their horse instructor Marie invited me to come to check out the horses. There were four of us visiting; some had done Marie's horse course, and others had previous experience with horses. I could boast neither. I hadn't even been around horses since I was a little boy on summer vacations in Uruguay, and as an adult, I'd had a bit of a traumatic experience with a horse in Costa Rica.

I approached the horses very slowly at first. As I managed to touch one of them, my memory of overtoning with the elephants surfaced. I started toning, and one of the horses immediately stopped walking and looked at me intently. When the visit was over, Marie asked me if I would come to the course the next day to do overtones for the whole herd. I did. One of the horses who I later learned was sick with ovarian cancer really seemed to take it in. Marie told me that she'd never seen that horse so receptive.

The next year, I came as an "overtone" visitor again. This time, Tamera's horse woman was Freya, who remembered me and invited me to do my thing. First, we created a human overtone circle, then explored sounding with overtones directly on the horses. Mali, the mare with the tumor, stood still as Freya encouraged me to come closer and walk around her while overtoning. It seemed like all the horses made room for Mali's healing. What happened next moved me deeply. As I rested my hand on Mali's neck and kept toning, she kept completely still. After a couple of minutes, very slowly and taking care not to scare me, she moved one step forward, so my hand would be

---

[9] *Moazin*: The one who chants the Muslim call to prayer.

directly on her wound, at her uterus. Then Mali stood still again, as if to say this was calming and healing for her.

Freya was excited. She told me that if I was up for it, she would take me to her mentor's community next door, to visit her horses. I happily agreed, and did a one-hour session with those horses too. We agreed that the next year, I would plan a daylong workshop experience with humans, horses, and sound.

I also told Mona about my Galilean friend, Maya. I had been connected with Maya's family for three generations; my parents were friends of her grandparents, and babysat her father. I was Maya's counselor at a peace project in Europe when she was a teenager. Now, she worked one-on-one with kids and horses therapeutically, and had just opened a horse sanctuary to help people of all ages with trauma.

Unlike me, Mona was a horse person. She actually *rode* them. Knowing that, I had arranged for Mona to go on a three-day riding trip, without me. It started first thing in the morning. When I dropped her off, I was surprised to see that Maya had conjured an entire crew of equestrian Amazons. Including Mona, there were thirteen of them. I hadn't told Maya much yet, only that I wanted her to connect with Mona and that we had a big global peace project in mind and heart, culminating in Jerusalem. I added that I needed to pull together a real team of horses and riders. The first step for her was to meet Mona. I would join them upon their return, and we would talk some more.

In those three days, I heard news from my friend Stacy in Uruguay. She lived in a community that worked with horses, organic wine, and a recording studio, and she was in charge of the horses. I had reached out to her about the Big Vision, and her response simply said, "When are we meeting?" Such was her fire, blended with her practical European ways.

Freya, Juuna, and Marie, with whom I had that first sounding, overtoning, horse "intra-vaganza" in Portugal, were also keen on learning more. I decided I would wait to meet with Maya, then put them all in touch. When I met Maya, she told me she had recently started working with horses and Bedouins in the Galilee. The northern horse contingent was becoming a clearer reality. I was also waiting to hear from our Urfa ambassadors, Kurdi and Murat. They were connected with an old Kurdish friend of theirs who had a big horse ranch in Urfa, near the Syrian border.

Three days later, I met Mona and Maya. They looked like they had become friends, and seemed extremely happy with their thirteen-horse goddess crew. The other women were leaving when I arrived, but I could sense the deep bond of sisterhood as I walked into Maya's home. We had some mint tea. Maya said, "Can she stay with me?"

"No way!" I said, "I miss her already!"

Mona laughed. "We had a blast! The horses are so incredible and the women too! We'll create a great team," she added.

I started describing the Big Vision to Maya, but Mona interrupted, saying, "I already told her everything. Maya and her troupe—including the Bedouins we met on our second day of riding, just in time for our talk about the Big One—they're all in!"

I shared the news about the horse people from Urfa, Portugal, and Uruguay, and that afternoon, we all had a very successful and fun Zoom call. The goal was to get a thousand horses and riders to form the northern horse caravan. Maya agreed to coordinate from Galilee. Juuna, Stacy, Freya, Murat, Kurdi, and one person from the Bedouin group would each be responsible for a big herd of horses, their riders, and a team to coordinate them. The horses would be locally provided by our Middle East anchors.

"That's a lot of work!" Maya said.

"And a lot of horses," Mona added.

"But we'll do it!" Maya declared.

That week we got news from Captain Rowan. His work was done in Africa; he'd arrived in Greece and had landed at Vasilis's friend's property on the river, close to the beach. Mona and I started feeling excited about the prospect of our journey to Greece. She convinced me to keep it simple and just focus on creating the western boat caravan. In a very short time, Rowan needed to find twenty leaders to deal with fifty boats each.

"What about Vasilis and the media team?" I asked.

"Let's get the team together after our Eastern group begins creating its caravan—though if Vasilis himself can make it, let him come too," Mona said.

"We also need a big production team to put all of this together," I said, "and we still don't have that in place either...it's one of the crucial pieces of the puzzle."

Mona took both of my hands in hers. "Step by step," she said. "Stress and worries won't help us." Mona oozed a liberating practicality: a gift for my convoluted Piscean self. She then gave me a prolonged kiss on my belly button, and while pulling out invisible monsters from my stomach with her hands, invoked a magical spell: "I shall extract all fear from your belly!" That made me laugh quite hard.

"So, who's coming to Crete then?" I asked, once I'd recovered. "You tell me, fierce belly-stress extractor!"

"That's easy," Mona answered. "You, me, Vasilis, and Rowan."

"We'll probably need to return with the production team at least to Sinai," I said. "The Bedouins won't come to Jerusalem for a meeting...ha-ha."

"Yup," agreed Mona. "I'd love to go back to Sinai."

The next step was to call Captain Rowan and tell him it would be just us, so there was no need to prepare much. We told him about our plan to meet the entire crew only after all four caravans had coordinators and a production team was in place. Rowan asked us to give him another week or so.

The festival of Purim[10] was happening in Israel, so Mona and I decided to pay our respects to the wild spring fever and take that week off to party. It felt good to stop talking "serious plans" for an entire week. Our savings were enough to last until after Crete, so we thought about staying there for a couple of weeks. In those days of strategizing, for our own sustainability we came up with the brilliant

---

[10] Purim: The Jewish carnival, according to the Hebrew calendar. The last of the holidays before the spiritual reset at Passover. Based on the biblical Book of Esther, a farcical story which takes place in old Persia where the Jews were saved en masse after almost being massacred.

idea to organize a weekend retreat in Crete before Carnival took over. We had a week to promote the retreat, but if we had even fifteen participants, it would be a success financially, artistically, and spiritually. It would also give Mona and me a chance to teach a "playshop" together. We even had a free location: the big estate on the river where Rowan would host us. Rowan knew quite a few people in Crete and would help us promote.

I wasn't counting on what happened next. It changed everything. As the fire horse with five stars in Pisces that I am, what happened next would keep me swirling like a washing machine on a roller coaster ride for some time.

What happened next was this: at the first party we went to together for Purim, Mona met someone and fell in love with him. This time it wasn't her half-brother, but the real thing: a truly wonderful man I had always admired. I saw them making out at the party. It hurt like hell.

Mona disappeared with him for a few days. She didn't contact me or answer my calls, there was no trace of her online. I was a total mess. It felt like the longest week of my life. The first day, I was still answering emails about the workshops and the Big One… until fierce flashes of grief, desperation, and jealousy erupted. I became angry. This then upgraded to furious. In between, I felt attacked by waves of frustration.

Why doesn't she call me? How can she disappear like this? Was it all just a fling until the real thing came along for her? Or is this also a fling, and this is just who she is?

I couldn't stop my terrible inner roller coaster. After the rage, the tears moved in. They poured. I stopped eating. I started smoking joints compulsively again. I drank a lot of alcohol that week. I stopped feeling. The world felt numb, and I couldn't get out of bed. Once a day, I tried to answer emails about the workshops and some messages from the kids, from the horse team, even from Kurdi, Murat, and the Captain himself. It was too hard, though. "I'll write to you next week," I responded to all of them. My skin malaise and boils came back. My eyes hurt again. On the third day of excruciating pain, I had an awful dream—actually, a nightmare.

This guy comes to me as Don Quijote de la Mancha[11] *dressed in full gear: spear, armor, helmet, and shield. He takes off his armor and helmet, and it turns out it is actually me, riding on Rocinante, the horse.*

He then becomes Sancho Panza,[12] *and when I start looking at his face, he de-materializes and just his belly rides on top of his donkey. No head, no person inside. Just a belly, laughing at me full force. It's not funny, it's terrifying. The belly laughs at me and says, "So you think you're fucking Don Quijote? You're gonna save the world, huh?"*

I look at him, terribly perplexed and scared, and say in a very low voice, "I'm trying to be authentic."

The belly laughs even louder. "So, you have the savior syndrome?

"You've been alternating as victim and perpetrator, and now you're the fucking world hero? Who the hell do you think you are?"

I freeze, and my lips, throat, eyes, everywhere, is puffing up and getting red, exactly like the time a bee stung me and my allergy wouldn't even let me scream for help. My voice just won't come out. I am reliving the one and only bee sting I got at age forty, the one where they took me to the hospital in an ambulance.

I fall on the ground and start crawling towards the figure who is now towering over me and tell him, "I'm trying my best. I'm trying."

At this point, I am panicking that I might not make it and I'll die.

Suddenly, the laughing belly riding the donkey becomes the shadow...which becomes the towering figure over me...and finally turns into the face of the man that I admire, who Mona left with at the party...in love, or so I think.

As his face gets clearer, I wake up from the dream. I'm sweating. Everything is wet: my sheets, my blankets, my shorts, my T-shirt, my body, my bed, my cheeks. I get up, exhausted, and realizing it was a nightmare, take a few deep breaths.

It remains vivid. I go take a shower. Mona is still not back. No news from her at all. We are on the fifth day since her disappearing act. I sleep for hours, intermittently watching movies and drinking

---

[11] *Don Quijote De la Mancha*: The most important work by Miguel de Cervantes, one of the most famous Spanish writers of all time.
[12] Sancho Panza: The loyal shield carrier. Fat and funny companion of Don Quijote.

red wine. No end in sight. No energy, not even to get up to go shopping. Yellow lentils and the last bottle of red are all I have left. The old soup has been there sitting on the gas for five days now, and I just keep adding water. The house is a mess. I don't even have the energy to change my sheets.

Another day goes by the same way.

I finally get out of bed to go to the bathroom. I look at myself in the mirror. I look like a ghost. Deformed and pale. I get scared. Now it's been six days. The phone rings. It cuts off. And rings again…

"Hey?" says a familiar voice.

"Yes!" I answer, recognizing Mona's exquisite accent. The pain in the core of my stomach becomes even more acute. The phone gets disconnected again. I'm exasperated. It rings a third time. This time I yell, "Mona, what's your number? Please text me your number!" I breathe deeply, waiting for her message, but it doesn't arrive. I walk around like a crazed lion in a cage. I try my emotional release exercises. I punch my pillow. I do the silent scream. I have no more wine. I can't watch any more TV or even movies. My eyes hurt too much. I try playing the guitar, singing a song, even masturbating, all to no avail. Who am I kidding? I'm useless.

After a few hours of active impotence and existential despair, I give up, vanquished on the carpet of my living room, and finally fall asleep. I wake up the next day to a message on my phone: "I'm coming back tomorrow morning."

I start making coffee, but I'm too excited and the coffee spills all over the place. It was also the end of my coffee. "That's it!" I say. I shower and go out to the health food store down the mountain road, where I buy five liters of coconut water, coffee, and a whole bunch of good stuff to fill up my fridge. The world seems strange after a week of not being in it. My eyes slowly open again. I feel the vitamin D of the sun kissing my eyelids. It's as if I'm coming back from the dead. Luckily, no one is in the shop except for the guy at the cash register, busy with the inventory. So, I just pay and leave. Thank God, not a word is exchanged but the price. A direct glance or a "how are you?" would have been too much of a social challenge for me.

I get back home and start cleaning up the mess. After an hour, I stop for a break and decide to go for a walk. Yes! A bit of sun penetrating through the clouds of winter. My legs can move again.

But when I return to my house, every doubt in my universe comes gushing at me at once. Not just Mona and my love for her, but the whole big dream, the vision, the nightmare. I've only known her for a couple of weeks, but it still hurts like hell. It's the trauma of every rejection I ever experienced from women. The women who I wanted and who never chose me. *Bald, fat, old, and tired...* I catch my internal chatter and stop it. "Nothing good can come out of that," I tell myself. I eat some broccoli, rice with garlic, butter and spices. I have some chocolate for dessert. I find a good happy movie to watch and fall asleep at 9 PM after drinking a whole bottle of coconut water.

Of course, before dawn I'm up again. I drink my coffee, take a long walk through the olive groves, and am bombarded by a million terrible thoughts a minute. I breathe heavily and walk faster. I get home and take a shower, and as I'm drying off, I hear a knock.

"Hey, it's me...can I come in?" Mona asks in a shy voice that I've never heard from her before.

"It's open," I say from the bathroom.

I don't know whether to laugh or cry. As I come out of the bathroom wrapped in my *sarong* I see her sitting on the floor of the hallway.

(The story is so current that I can't help but write in the present. Did this happen? Is it happening now? Is this autobiographical or fiction? The present takes over.)

I'm feeling really weird. I feel numb and simultaneously about to explode at any time. My jaws are tight. My face muscles are frozen. Mona gets up and holds my hands. I shiver. I let go of her hands, turn around, and try to focus on making coffee. We both remain in awkward silence.

When the coffee is ready, I manage to say, "Let's talk outside. There's some sun on the front porch." We both go out and sit. I pour the coffee. We both sip at it. Neither of us wants to be the first to break the silence.

Mona finally says, "You know I care for you very much."

I try to take in her words and not respond immediately. I can't help myself, though, and lash out.

"So why didn't you call me? You disappeared. I went crazy for a week."

"I know. I'm really sorry. I thought of calling but didn't know what to say. I got carried away with Xavier. I felt the rush of freedom, just following my desire, the sex, the newness…"

"Listen," I said, "I really don't want to go into victim mode. I'm trying really hard to avoid that pattern. I just want to share that your disappearance made me question everything —even the Big Vision. I had an awful nightmare in which a shamanic Don Quixote accused me of megalomania and having a savior complex. I stopped looking at the computer, afraid I would have to answer emails, even those from our new closest friends. I was drunk for a week. I finished six wine bottles."

Mona came closer and whispered, "Can I hug you?" As she hugged me tightly, I started crying profusely. "My sweet and spicy baby," she crooned as she cradled me.

I composed myself and said, "I thought what we had together was real and went both ways."

"*Had…thought?* Of course, silly. I love you!"

I smiled and said, "But it could happen again with someone else, right?"

"Right," Mona answered. "It could happen to either of us."

"So…" I asked timidly, "do you want to be with him?"

"No, now I want to be with you! That's why I came back. The two of us together are bigger than either one of us alone. I started thinking of my brother, the Captain! Remember? The camels, the horses, the kids! Hebron, Jerusalem…even the Amazonas. Musallem! I feel an urge to get back to our project. With you!" As she mentioned Musallem's name, color returned to my face, to my skin. The tone was coming back to my body. With each of Mona's words, I felt my life returning to me in a real, physical way. And still, I wanted to know. "How was your time with Xavier?" I asked.

"I had an amazing time with him. It was a short-lived romance.

An adventure, an escapade, like in a movie when you are swept out of the plot into romantic dreamland.

"And today, I woke up and really missed you. You and our work for Mama Planet. And your laugh, and your voice, your big prophetic heart, and your spice. You! It feels strong that you are my crazy partner. No matter how many escapades I allow myself to go on, I will always come back. Anyway, that's my feeling now."

"And with Xavier did you feel that way too?"

"No, honestly, I didn't. It always felt like a side thing." I cried some more, this time mixed with a smile. "Come here," Mona said, and kissed me all over my face, licking and sucking my neck playfully, my nose, my eyes, until she tickled me and made me laugh with joy.

My body started shaking, then moving into a dance. Mona followed. She put a deep ethnic beat on, and we embarked on a radical improvisation all around the house. We danced with the books in the library. With the pots in the kitchen. With chairs on our heads. With pillows on our asses. It felt like a wake for the house. Everything became alive. Our bodies, the furniture—even the TV was exorcised through our moves. She really made me laugh. We went wild together. In the bathroom, in the shower, in the garden, dancing with every tree—the pear, the cherry, the olive, the palm, the grapefruit, the tangerine, the lemon, the walnut, the pomegranate, the bay laurel, even the macadamia. It felt like a wild spring festival dance—awakening every corner of the house, the garden, and ourselves. Then we came back to the bedroom and lay down with our feet up, clapping them together. It felt so good to move. Life was flowing through us, and it was wild, and it was brilliant.

We made love and dozed off. Suddenly, Mona jumped out of bed, woke me up, and said, "I'm starving! I haven't eaten since yesterday noon. Let's go out for breakfast! I'll drive! I'll pay! I'll be the yang today. Will you let me drive and be the pilot?"

"Yes, please!" I said.

We came back and finished all the arrangements for our trip. All of them! We answered all the emails! We set everything up. Then I looked at her and told her how much I loved dancing with her.

Buenos Aires – 1976

THE FAMOUS *kidushito*[13] happened on Saturday at noon. In our luminous living room in Belgrano R, nearly fifty congregants of my fathers' community gathered after the Shabbat morning services at the synagogue. Drinks, lots of vodka, appetizers, and conversation—mostly crossover realpolitik and liberation theology. These were the horrendous times of dictatorship, and my dad had begun visiting jails, getting more and more involved in human rights, and trying to save the lives of the "disappeared."

For the upper-middle class and established Argentinian Jews, it wasn't an easy sell. Carrying trauma—from the Holocaust, the Inquisition, the pogroms, you name it—and afraid of anti-Semitism, they feared coming out in public against the military. Most of these Argentinian Jews had a status to uphold—one which they had fought hard to achieve. They didn't want my father to make waves, rock the boat, or risk their social and economic privilege.

Meanwhile, in my room, it was a whole other story. I kept my door tightly closed, and if anyone ventured in there without knocking on a Saturday afternoon, they would find an astonishing scene. I was ten at the time, and had received a good pair of bongos as a gift. They were too big and heavy for me, though, and I couldn't play them. I had come out of my mom's womb at seven months, and was always the shortest, smallest, and frailest throughout grade school and even into high school. My friend Dario was much older than me; he could play bongos well, so I would call him away from adults' social mingling into my room, give him the bongos, and close the door. His instructions were simple: "Start playing and don't stop!"

Since I was three, I had been addicted to a TV show called "Daktari". It was filmed in Africa, about a veterinarian who healed all sorts of wild animals, and the backdrops showed giraffes, elephants,

---

[13] *Kidushito*: Spanish slang for "little Kiddush," an endearing play of words on the Hebrew word "Kiddush," the celebratory blessing of the wine. They used to happen at my home growing up in Buenos Aires every Saturday after the prayers at the synagogue, with many guests, cocktails, dips, and a theme of conversation relevant to the moment.

hippos, zebras, and antelopes galloping through the African savannas. My favorite, though, was when they showed tribal Indigenous Africans dancing in ceremony. It seemed to be a déjà vu, something I had experienced before. As Dario played the bongos in my room, I would dance like a wild animal, imagining stories traveling within my body as I moved into a trance, sometimes for almost an hour. It was thrilling to sweat my imagination and dance it away.

"I do love dancing with you," Mona said. "One day we'll go to South America together."

"When all this is over," I said, "we'll find a good clean river, clean air, and a nice juicy community of friends who grow food and are compassionate to climate and war refugees…maybe in Costa Rica."

"Agreed. But first, let's get our ferry tickets to Crete!" Mona said.

"Yup," I replied. "The sea seems the perfect way to go west."

So we did. Efficiency and clarity become easy when you play, when you laugh, when you dance, when you love—when you are not waiting or yearning to be rescued or loved, but when you actively *love*. As our beloved poet Jalaluddin Rumi says, "Be the Source and not its consequence."[14]

I ran all the way to the roof, pulling Mona by the hand. Standing above the dome, I cried at the top of my lungs, "Have you heard the latest news, Monaaaa?"

"Whaaaat?" she asked, mimicking my loud theatrics.

"It's been officially confirmed: there is life before death!"

We both laughed hard.

---

[14] "Be the Source, not its consequence": Rumi, translated by Coleman Barks.

CHAPTER 5

DUE WEST

Mona and I took a taxi to Haifa Port and caught the ferry. It seemed appropriate to go by ship. On the way to Crete, we met an amazing traveler. With her big afro and even bigger smile, she looked like no other on the boat. She later told us that she had just quit her position at Instagram, where she had managed many people as a top creative. She oversaw global special events and marketing and had a reputation as a social media wizard, but she'd gotten tired of working for a company that had no ethical values and put profit as their bottom line. Social media, in her words, was constricting human consciousness into loneliness, competition, and bullying, and was furthering the destruction of the planet as a tool of the virus called capitalism. When we met her on the deck of the ferry, we still had a long journey ahead of us aboard the ship.

"Hey, I couldn't resist your smile," Mona asked her. "What's your name?"

"Gena," she answered joyfully.

"I'm Mona."

She looked at us and we all smiled. It was obvious we clicked at first sight. Gena said she was taking a sabbatical from her normal life, then told us of her brief passage through Israel and her stay in Palestine, where she'd been in a session with a mixed Israeli-Palestinian group of friends who were experimenting with psychedelics and peace in Bethlehem.

"What a small world," I said.

"Yeah!" Gena replied. "Now I know why you look so familiar...I saw you at Jivana's!"

"Hmmm. I don't remember," I said.

"It was brief," Gena said. "You were singing with your guitar, and I was sitting with some Palestinian friends at another table. So what brings you to Crete?"

"We are on our Western journey..." Mona said cryptically.

Gena laughed. "What is that supposed to mean?"

"We're involved in a global healing project, focused on Hebron and Jerusalem," Mona answered.

"I like it already!" Gena said.

"We're on our way to create the western fleet of boats from Greece," Mona continued. "We have several caravans coming: a thousand camels from the south, a thousand horses from the north, and a thousand children from the east, from Bethlehem! First we'll make a pilgrimage to the "below," at the cave in Hebron, and then we'll anchor in the skies 'above,' finally arriving at the Heart of Jerusalem." Gena didn't miss a beat., "So, seven directions, camels, horses, boats, children, above, below and heart center...just missing the women!"

"We could add them to the circle in Hebron. Great idea! Sarah and Hagar get reconciled!" I said, excited.

"Wow—sounds like an amazing movie! *Lord of the Rings* in the Middle East," Gena said. "Where's Gandalf?"

"Well, that's Melchizedek, the first King of Jerusalem," I said, beginning my Kabbalistic rap. "*Melech*: King, *Tsedek*: Justice. He was also called the Priest of on High,[1] and for our purposes, Abraham's Mentor, or The King of Salem, *Shalom*, *Salam*. Abraham met him after his wars against the four Kings. Together in Jerusalem, they broke bread and drank wine together. The wine is the truth and the justice; the bread is the love and the peace.

"The instructions are that justice and peace intertwine as the eternal life elixir—as a moral compass and a matrix from which all sacred

---

[1] Priest of on High: Melchizedek, the first king of Jerusalem, serving El the Highest of the Canaanite Pantheon. Seminal mentor of Abraham, the Patriarch.

action is conceived. Love and truth go together as an eternal sacred bundle.

"*Chesed ve Emet Tzedek ve Shalom.*"[2]

That evening we stayed up late. We were both blown away by Gena's swift and impeccable rendering of everything that we'd said since we met her. There was a joy of immediate recognition of someone who palpitates and celebrates reality with a similar groove. Both Mona and I had the gut feeling that we'd found our production team chiefess on that ferry to Crete. We fell asleep happy as the boat rowed our dreams gently through the night, merrily to the syncopated beat of life.

The next afternoon on the deck, Mona popped the million-dollar question to Gena. "Could you put together a team to bring this amazing design into reality?" Gena didn't hesitate for a second. "Yes," she affirmed. Looking us both straight in the eyes, she continued. "It would be my honor and my pleasure…once I get the download of the whole plan. Hopefully in some quiet place in Crete?" she smiled. "I'm thinking it would be good for me to go to Athens and connect with my network there. I used to work with yacht fleets on the islands."

"Terrific!" Mona said, "My brother Rowan is waiting for us in Crete, together with Vasilis, our Greek media friend. They found an amazing home next to a river which we can make our base for a couple of weeks." We decided there and then to ignite a party and dance. It was our second night on the boat, and we could all use some movement. Gena opened her magic bag and pulled out the perfect mini speakers. "These sound good!" she said. Mona and I went down to our shared cabin to get some warmer clothes. The stars were out in full bloom. When we came back up, Gena had started a ruckus. There were about thirty people dancing on deck. The vibe was a cross between funk, hip hop, Senegalese Sabar, Dancehall, and some new kind of Motown trap. We danced for a couple of hours. At a certain point, Gena let her playlist lead and joined us in the dancing. We were quite the trio. I felt protected by joy. The vitality of two goddesses, the shine of our meeting; my own bliss, rooted in beautiful purpose; and

---

[2] "Unconditional love and truth, justice and peace," from Psalm 85:10.

the assuring feeling that with this level of trust and wild fun, anything coming out of us would be embodying our ethics.

We landed in Crete the next day. Rowan arrived in his pickup truck, which was cluttered with sails, pieces of a boat, a fishing net, and life vests, among other stuff. We squeezed into the crowded seats full of yacht paraphernalia as best we could. It was a happy quartet. The Captain looked good. He told us happily that his western fleet of boats was growing considerably, and that it had connected with a Sicilian fleet and some major NGOs, like Greenpeace, who were interested to hear more about us and would probably join our Big Story. It all sounded promising.

On the other hand, I had just heard before landing from an Israeli traveler about the horrible results of Israel's elections, adding to the devastating state of Palestinian human rights, government, and the complete absence of any prospect of a better Middle East. I had a hard-pressing issue with depression about the political and climate reality's devastating effects on animal species we would never see again. It all came back in a rush, penetrating my lungs, affecting my breath. I felt the need to tell my trusted companions what I was going through.

"Fascism is spreading all over the world," I ranted. "Israeli fascism is just the tip of the iceberg. There are talks about another war to save Israeli's prime minister from jail and to continue reaping profit for the global military-industrial complex. Beloved animal species are disappearing, the Amazon is being destroyed, and the massacre of Indigenous peoples continues unabated. World leaders and global corporations are trying to dig up our Pachamama for all remaining 'resources'…the planet, and human ethics, are in a dire emergency."

Mona put her hand on my belly and kissed my neck. Gena was having none of my litanies, and from the back interrupted, "Surfers!"

"Surfers!" Mona echoed.

"Yup! And kayaks and canoes—maybe even swimmers. Climate warriors fighting with canoes for the sinking Pacific Islands, just like in Australia. Maybe they could come too?" Gena suggested. She'd lived in Samoa, had worked for Amnesty International there, and had contact with frontline climate warriors from the Pacific Islands. She was also a surfing instructor, and had been doing healing work through surfing.

"Wow, amazing!" Rowan said. "The west is starting to glow!" There is a right time and space for grief and mourning, and according to the consensus of our vehicle's population, this wasn't it. My gloom and doom went ignored, dispelled by images of surfers, canoes, little boats, medium boats, and big ships all coming from the sea into the port of Haifa!

After winding up the mountain road, Rowan stopped at a small village. It was all white houses, blue doors and windows, and the crystalline turquoise sea, with old men sipping their *raki* on a little table outside the only taverna in town.

"Greek island—we are here!" Gena announced. We waited for Rowan to do some shopping and ordered some coffee, then drove on. After twenty minutes, we finally arrived at our destination. We unpacked our bags at the main house, an old traditional Greek stone home which had been renovated and expanded. It was a simple and aesthetic combination of stone, wood, and big glass windows, with two floors and a few rooms on each of them. The Captain showed us into our rooms. Gena and Rowan each took their own room, and Mona and I decided to share one. We got settled and checked out the bathroom, where the shower and toilet were half in the open, surrounded by thick bamboo walls.

I lay down for a power nap. When I woke up, I went down to join them. After we'd all been nourished by a delicious shake, Rowan said, "Follow me...this way." We began walking and saw that the roof of the house had solar panels. The kitchen ran on biogas[3], recycled from the toilet and composted. As we journeyed further into the luscious garden full of organic vegetables, herbs, and fruit trees, we passed a couple of small yurts, a tipi, and a few geodesic domes. They were all set up with shaded wooden decks as porches. Further ahead, we came upon an enormous, majestic yurt, big enough for eighty people to

---

[3] Biogas: Sustainable waste management solution; a bio-digester that converts organic kitchen waste into clean cooking gas and liquid bio-fertilizer onsite.

fit in comfortably. Naturally, we went in. Inside, there were wooden floors, an altar, a little stage, a sound system, and a screen. Amazing!

"This is usually used as the retreat center's main hub," Rowan explained. "This space should fit us all, right?"

"It's more than perfect," I said.

The captain signaled for us to move along. A few steps after the big yurt, Mona made us stop in our tracks when she said, "Listen to the water!"

Listening to the sound of the water, we all felt a rush of joy. It was somewhere close. Then we saw the sparkling creek meandering through the stones. Mona and Gena immediately stripped and went in. "Come on, us too!" the captain encouraged me. We jumped in and joined Gena's and Mona's giggles in the water. The river reached our shoulders. At Gena's signal—a snap of her fingers—all four of us took a deep breath and plunged underwater, holding hands in a spontaneous underwater circle. It was so good to be together under fresh water in that delicious moment.

We emerged from the water and dried in the sun. Then Mona said, "How far is the sea from here?"

"Not too far, about a thirty-minute walk," Rowan answered.

"Let's go," Gena said, "so we can see the sunset—it's almost time."

Along our walk, we noticed an opening in the fields close to the creek and saw a shepherd herding his sheep.

"This is his grazing land. He's our neighbor," said Rowan proudly.

"Wow! Our nearest neighbor is a shepherd, only twenty minutes away...cool!" Gena said.

We finally got to a fantastic small beach, hidden by a few big boulders. It was just us, and oops! A local fisherman. As we ran into the sea, we caught a glimpse of him pulling out his net full of fish and octopus.

We had a swim and each took some frolicking time to ourselves. We finally came close to each other; then, before coming out of the water, Gena snapped her fingers again and the four of us submerged and joined hands in our salty underwater initiation circle. It seemed as if the "underwater circle" was becoming part of our language.

It felt great to dry out in the Minoan heat, in the cradle of the magical and matriarchal civilization of the ancient West. The piercing light of the sun in full splendor on the white sandy beach blended with the smell of grilled fish coming from a mysteriously hidden spot. Following the scent, we found the abode of a local fisherman. His name, we learned, was Yorgos.

"*Yasus*,"[4] Yorgos said. "*Apodo*,"[5] he called to us.

His shack looked better than we thought. He pulled out four wooden stools from his donkey cart, a bottle of *raki*, and five glasses. "*Katse*,"[6] he said, showing us the stools. Then he gave each of us a shot of *raki* and offered a toast in Greek. "*Yamas*!" We all answered with a smile, "*Yamas*, Yorgos!" He shared his food with us, and it was delicious. Yorgos didn't speak a word of English—only Greek. He communicated loudly with his hands and laughed a lot during the meal, and we savored his fish, *raki*, and beautiful hospitality. His laugh reminded us of our beloved Kurdi. The Captain, who understood a bit of Greek, had met the fisherman once before. He told us that Yorgos was the twin brother of the shepherd, Yanis. Neither of them had gotten married, and they lived together at the end of the village near the cemetery.

We bowed in gratitude to Yorgos and thanked him profusely. Before we left, Rowan made arrangements for Gena to leave the island the next day. It was time for her to get up to speed with the Big Vision, talk to her people in Athens, and return with the other crew members to the land in a few days.

Checking the internet again, I saw terrible news from Israel and Palestine: there was another round of Hamas missiles and Israeli planes bombing Gaza. I took a deep breath into my heart.

As we started beautifying the living room and making it cozy, we all knew the time was ripe to meet formally that evening. For us, this

---

[4] *Yasus*: "Your health" in Greek. Also used as a casual greeting.
[5] *Apodo*: "Come here." Literally, "here" in Greek.
[6] *Katse*: "Sit" in Greek.

clear call to sit together literally meant getting the vision rolling—and for Gena to then bring that excitement to Athens and build the perfect team including Vasilis, our media man, who had confirmed he would be coming back with her.

I started reading parts of an old, shelved project we had worked on with brother Sami and friends from the "We Refuse to Be Enemies" and Bethlehem crew:

"We recognize that global conflicts continue to spread and that the Middle East is one of the most contentious areas of such violence today. We understand the need for a paradigm leap in how we perceive and engage in conflict. We, individuals who live in the Holy Land, who seek peace and justice in this land with allies from around the world, call for direct global engagement at a mass scale for a successful and healing impact at the root causes of collective Palestinian and Israeli trauma, pain, fear, and oppression.

"We draw upon the resources available from our Earth's global wisdom to infuse the Fertile Crescent with a collective radical experience to midwife a new story. We invite internationally accomplished individuals to become part of a worldwide initiative that focuses our energy and action on healing one stress point of the planet at a time, starting with the conflict in the Middle East. These individuals are leaders of global spiritual and religious communities, sports personalities, artists, scientists, Nobel laureates, and other guilds of humanity.

"We call upon these 'sacred agents' to come together and declare a united and uncompromising stand for peace, equality, and justice in the Holy Land through a radical and creative surprise healing intervention for collective trauma. We know we will encounter voices of hopelessness, hatred, and fear, as we intend this initiative to be multidimensional in its scope, piercing in its depth, and creative of a long-lasting effect that begins disengaging the root blocks in our cultural, religious, and national conditioning."

"Can I keep going?" I asked.

Gena nodded.

"Rationale: Poetry of Surprise & Healing.

"'It always seems impossible until it is done' (Nelson Mandela).

"Despite the enormous task at hand and the common perception that it is impossible, we believe that there are cracks in the collective Palestinian and Israeli hatred and fear.

"These cracks will gradually open from a deep-rooted and innate desire by all to live in freedom, peace, justice, and equality. Our intention is to zoom into these cracks and create breakthroughs in the defense systems of collective, national, ethnic, and religious assumptions, loops, and stereotypes.

"We believe it is possible to forge an evolving grammar and understanding of activism that will surprise the narrative of despair and hopelessness. This new paradigm and story will no longer fuel the arguments of fear and victimhood. It will ultimately make irrelevant all those who perpetuate such a disconnected story.

"Global leaders, the international community, Palestinians, Israelis, Jews, Muslims, Christians, and representatives of other religions, traditions, and beliefs will converge together in creative nonviolent and healing action in two locations in the Holy Land: Hebron and Jerusalem.

"Our globally focused initiative will include the acknowledgment of injustice, reconciliation ceremonies, music, and creative nonviolence. The action will also seed a process of further work to flourish. It won't end with a one-time event; instead, we will create clear channels of action on and offline for people to partake in after the event."

I continued to flow, adding spontaneous images:

"Palestinians and Israelis form a spiral, facing each other in silence, sharing their truths, hopes and pains. Prayers. Music will be an integral part of the ceremony, both from the participants and invited musicians from around the world. It will include humming, clapping, and soloists voicing their collective historical traumas, fears, and healed dreams."

"Enough for now," Gena interjected, with her excellent timing. "I get the big picture and I'm excited. You'll get to articulate and unpack some more once I'm back with Vasilis, so we can start designing a strategy for all this." I was relieved. My visionary juices were drying up. My eloquence was fading, and I couldn't see myself going further at that moment. We decided to take a break until Gena and Vasilis returned. What was simmering inside me was something I felt I couldn't yet share with Gena. I wasn't sure about the Captain either, or even Mona. I would keep it to myself for now.

The next day, the Captain brought Gena to the port. He had to stay in the village for the day. I decided that I finally needed to share my doubts, fears, and weaknesses with Mona; I couldn't contain them alone anymore. I asked her to come to the river with me. After we'd dipped into the water, we sat on top of a couple of massive and beautiful boulders. I went for it.

"I need to share with you the shadows of the Big Vision we are dreaming up. I can't keep it to myself anymore. I know you are strong enough in the vision to take in and digest all of this."

Mona looked into my eyes with a rare blend of penetrating nonchalance. She then proceeded to kiss me on the lips and hug me tightly, infusing me with life. I smiled, a bit baffled by the kiss, and tried to focus on my words. "I'm thinking of the ego trip of the hero, the 'super savior,' the 'super martyr,' the self-righteous triumphalist," I continued. "The archetypes which are still embedded in the old story of life-sucking competition, domination, personal success. You know what I mean? The way we feel about manifesting 'the' vision which will contribute to accelerating planetary healing.

"A 'new' paradigm?! A 'new' story?! Who the fuck are *we*? Who am I to design a surprising reality-bomb? Aren't there thousands of other people who think they too have the right answer that will save humans from conflict, save ourselves from isolation, from destroying other species, our home, our planet? Are we also playing into human supremacy?"

"How can an act that doesn't have the proper plans for sustainability for seven generations built into it work at all? Are we just on a major megalomaniac trip? Are birds into this? Are trees? Is Mother Earth with us? Do we just want to put it out there just to make a movie afterwards, to be famous? To be one of the good guys? Are we just in this so people respect us? Admire us? Am I doing this to prove my life is worth something? Am I just excited about this whole thing, because I'm in it? Because I'm its propeller?"

As soon as I pronounced the words, they hurt me deeply. I felt, for a cruel moment, the absence of gratifying answers. Mona kept listening with empathy. She didn't interrupt me once; simply let me release it all. Or at least what I thought was "all" once I'd exhausted myself, on the brink of tears. Mona took me in her arms with a warmth and ease that I hadn't felt before. She caressed parts of my body I didn't even remember as my own. Each stroke felt as if she was touching me for the very first time. She was venturing into new and groundbreaking discoveries through bone, muscle, skin, and beyond, making me feel part of thriving life again.

Unexpectedly, the second wave of my litany erupted:

"I'm even scared of what will happen in the next five years. I think of settling in Costa Rica, or Portugal, and then I'm afraid of what might happen climatically with food, water, and war refugees there. The fear of not seeing my blood family again. Getting stuck somewhere with the wrong people at the wrong time in some climate catastrophe. Getting older, body problems. What about the Middle East? Do I really want to do this? What if I spend the next couple of years trying to save the Holiness of the "Holy Land"? Do we need to focus on the Amazon instead now? Or after?

"Can we create these life-supporting alliances and ceremonies to untangle our sick reality, to dismantle the dying agreements which created the knots of global historical trauma throughout human history? I'm talking ethnic, racial, religious, gender, class, root conflicts between humans and with our Mama Earth and all its living creatures, including rivers, mountains, animals, trees, and all other beings."

Mona caressed my head with her fingernails, brushing them lightly on my arms, my legs…she knew what to do. I started crying, and she simply encouraged my weeping to flow by pressing on my solar plexus and holding my jaw firmly. It was a torrential stream of tears, and as she held me while I cried, she teared up a bit herself. This went on for a while. To me, it seemed as if I was crying for eternity with the intensity and desperation of an abandoned baby after his ancestors had gone extinct.

Finally, she helped me to lie prone on the ground and breathe everything out into the Earth. When I eventually calmed down, she helped me get into the creek and then joined me. We hugged in the water and, after snapping her fingers *à la* Gena, we went under and held hands. This third submersion worked like a charm. Our already-traditional subaquatic circle gave me strength and a big smile. I emerged from the water and started laughing. Though we hadn't found answers to any of this, nevertheless it felt like we had crossed through to the other side of Reality. We splashed and played with the water. We be-longed.

Mona held me floating on my back, "watsu-ing" me. With Mona next to me, I felt alive. Everything seemed possible. After resting a bit and catching our breath, she confessed, "I'm also afraid and in doubt sometimes. I'm in deep gratitude for your transparency. For showing me your vulnerability."

She didn't say much more, but instead took me by the hand. We realized we were hungry, and there was a beautiful little edible garden near the river. We collected some arugula, lettuce, parsley, mint, tomatoes, cucumber, beet, and a couple of carrots. When we got to the kitchen, we found three different kinds of sprouts that Rowan had been growing. We threw it all together with fresh lemon, olive oil, and Mona's goodies from her personal stash. This time, she carried hemp and pumpkin seeds, a rich assortment of spices and salts, and a little organic bottle of pomegranate concentrate, which she sprinkled on our magical salad. Our neighbor the shepherd had left us two dozen fresh free-range eggs from his own hens that morning. I cooked them softly with butter, scrambling them with mint and parsley, red peppers, chives, a bit of our neighbor's goat cheese, and tomatoes. We topped it off with a bottle of cold rosé.

After our meal, I was ready for a siesta. Mona decided to go for a walk. We got a call from Rowan, who said he wouldn't be coming for another couple of days. Vasilis's plane was delayed, which worked well for Gena, who needed more time. Though the prospects for our playshop had collapsed, the Captain had managed to pull off a private gig for us with a couple of millionaire Swiss tourists who were cruising on their yacht. It was a house concert at our place—or, as I called it then, a "PrayerFormance." The Swiss tourists would come the next day at sunset for drinks, music, and stories. Rowan said he closed the deal for €4,000, an exorbitant sum for us at the time. It basically set Mona and me up for the month. It was also enough for us to buy our airfare back to Jordan and rent a car for driving into Bethlehem—our eastern frontier, and the last of our four cardinal directions.

Laura and Max arrived with their small entourage, and turned out to be socially engaged Buddhists. They loved our "PrayerFormance" of sacred activism through story, prayer, and song and, overflowing with love, said that they wanted to spend more time with us and learn about what we were up to. After we concluded our last healing prayer, we sat with them for about an hour answering their questions. They tipped us another €1,000 for our time together, then sent their people away for the night, and their driver and private assistant went to sleep at the only bed and breakfast in the village. When our newly be-friended couple returned, Mona told them about our "Biggie" in a nutshell. Their mouths opened wide with a simultaneous "Wow!"

Laura immediately said, "We need to support you! Right, Max?"

"Absolutely," he agreed. They walked out onto the patio.

Five minutes later, they came back. "We have a family foundation," Max announced, "and have decided we want to take care of you as much as we can, financially at least. We were anxiously waiting for a sign of the next project in our lives. This is it! At this moment, we pledge €1 million for you to use as you see fit. We can open a new bank account in your name so you can administer it as needed."

It sounded inconceivable—but when the timing is ripe, miracles happen. I thought of great artists in the renaissance and the patrons who sustained them by funding their work. "Our company can help with lawyers, accountants, and all the bureaucracy, which you, as artists and visionaries, shouldn't have to deal with," Laura continued. "We will open all our contacts for you. We're acquainted with the Queen of Jordan and the King of Morocco. We are members of the

Board of Directors of the Cannes Film Festival and have major friends in Hollywood. Because I used to edit an international fashion and lifestyle magazine, we know plenty of influential people personally who owe us favors. In short—we are all in!" Mona and I looked at each other in awe, eyes brimming with tears. We hadn't even reconnected with Gena and Vasilis yet, and we already had €1 million for our budget!

Tiokasin's telepathic resonance suddenly pounded in my heart. "Peace with Earth, not on Earth," he had said. Tiokasin had grown up with Arvol Looking Horse at the Cheyenne River Reservation and they had remained close ever since. Without saying a word, I just began reading out loud from one of the documents in the Big Vision folder. It was time to go deeper.

From Chief Arvol Looking Horse, Nineteenth-Generation Keeper of the Sacred Pipe Bundle of White Buffalo Calf Woman:

"I, Chief Arvol Looking Horse, of the Lakota, Dakota, and Nakota Nations, ask you to understand an Indigenous perspective on what has happened in America, what we call 'Turtle Island.' My words seek to unite the global community through a message from our sacred ceremonies to unite spiritually, each in our ways of beliefs in the Creator.

"We have been warned from ancient prophecies of these times we live in today but have also been given a vital message about a solution to turn these terrible times.

"To understand the depth of this message, you must recognize the importance of Sacred Sites and realize the interconnectedness of what is happening today, in the reflection of the continued massacres that are occurring on other lands and our own Americas.

"I have been learning about these important issues since the age of twelve when I received the Sacred White Buffalo Calf Pipe Bundle and its teachings. Our people have strived to protect Sacred Sites from the beginning of time. These places have been violated for centuries and have brought us to the predicament that we are in at the global level.

"Look around you. Our Mother Earth is very ill from these violations, and we are on the brink of destroying the possibility of healthy and nurturing survival for generations to come, our children's children.

"Our ancestors have been trying to protect our Sacred Site called the Sacred Black Hills of South Dakota, "Heart of Everything That Is," from continued violations. Our ancestors never saw a satellite view of this site, but now that those pictures are available, we see that it is in the shape of a heart and, when fast-forwarded, it looks like a heart pumping.

"The Diné have been protecting Big Mountain, calling it the liver of the earth, and we are suffering and going to suffer more from the extraction of the coal there and the poisoning processes used in doing so.

"The Aborigines have warned of the contaminating effects of global warming on the Coral Reefs, which they see as Mother Earth's blood purifier.

"The Indigenous people of the rainforest say that the rainforests are the lungs of the planet and need protection.

"The Gwich'in Nation in Alaska has had to face oil drilling in the Arctic National Wildlife Refuge coastal plain, also known to the Gwich'in as "Where life begins."

"The coastal plain is the birthplace of many life forms of the animal nations. The death of these animal nations will destroy Indigenous nations in this territory.

"As these destructive developments continue all over the world, we will witness much more extinct animal, plant, and human nations, because of humankind's misuse of power and their lack of understanding of the "balance of life."

"The Indigenous people warn that these negative developments will cause havoc globally. There are many, many more original teachings and knowledge about Mother Earth's Sacred Sites, her chakras, and connections to our spirit that will surely affect our future generations.

"There needs to be a fast move toward other forms of energy that are safe for all Nations upon Mother Earth. We need to understand the types of minds that are continuing to destroy the spirit of our whole global community. Unless we do this, the powers of destruction will overwhelm us.

"Our Ancestors foretold that water would someday be for sale. This Prophecy was hard to believe! The water was plentiful, pure, full of energy, nutrition, and spirit. Today we have to buy clean water, and even then, the nutritional minerals have been taken out; it's just clear liquid. Someday water will be like gold, too expensive to afford.

"Not everyone will have the right to drink safe water. We fail to appreciate and honor our Sacred Sites, ripping out the minerals and gifts that lay underneath them as if Mother Earth were simply a resource, instead of the source of life itself.

"Attacking nations and using more resources to carry out destruction in the name of peace is not the answer! We need to understand how all these decisions affect the global nation; we will not be immune to its repercussions. Allowing continual contamination of our food and land is affecting the way we think.

"A 'disease of the mind' has set in for world leaders and many members of our global community, with their belief that a solution of retaliation and destruction of peoples will bring peace.

"In our Prophecies it is told that we are now at the crossroads: either we unite spiritually as a global nation, or we're faced with chaos, disasters, diseases, and tears from our relatives' eyes.

"We are the only species that is destroying the source of life, meaning Mother Earth, in the name of power, mineral resources, and ownership of land. Using chemicals and methods of warfare.

"Our vision is for the peoples of all continents, regardless of their beliefs in the Creator, to come together as one at their Sacred Site."

Max and Laura kept looking at each other and at us, bewildered and thrilled, as beautiful smiles plastered their faces. Laura was a stylish, attractive woman in her sixties and Max was a handsome, fit, and young sixty-year-old. He went deep into introspection, closing his eyes for what seemed forever. Then he said, "I used to be the head of new app design at Facebook, in its early days. Maybe we could design a holographic map of Earth's sacred sites and superimpose the human body and its organs on it."

"Yes!" I said. I couldn't believe my ears: he was quoting verbatim from yet another old, shelved project of mine called "The Game," in its first original vision.

"Can I read you one more relevant thing, from an old proposal for another project?" I asked, already knowing their answer. They were thrilled by all that had transpired, and they showed it. This was very rare for Swiss Buddhists.

"'Sacred Healing Ceremonies' around the globe, organized through intergenerational collaboration. Possible locations:

- India – Ayodhya – Babri Mosque
- South Africa – Robben Island
- Northern Ireland – Belfast
- USA – Wounded Knee
- Tibet – Lhasa
- Australia – Uluru
- Amazonia – Sarayaku, Ecuador
- Israel – Palestine – Hebron

"These sacred healing ceremonies are a way to access new information and embed it into our DNA as a physical, emotional, intellectual, and spiritual reality. They serve as a 'blueprint' towards a new paradigm of consciousness. They will encompass a public witnessing of humanity's historical pain-body, collective trauma, and their 'healed image' at key global stress points. These collective experiences might surprise the defense mechanisms of our constructed reality and contribute to 'midwifing' a new story for humankind.

"That's it. Enough. I think you get the point," I concluded.

"I'm all in," said Max, without missing a beat. "We've been dreaming of a project to give all our energy to. This is it!"

"We want in! Would you have us?" said Laura softly. Mona reacted with a warm and spontaneous hug to both. And I followed.

"Is this a yes?" Max said.

"Hell yes! I hereby name you both CEOs of this project," I announced.

"Wow!" Max said. "You've known us for about five hours."

"And you just gave us €1 million," Mona replied.

"That's true," Laura smiled. Surprising us all, she began giggling and then laughing out loud. We joined her. This reminded us again, of course, of our sweet Kurdi. Max was completely transformed, and in a frenzied leap of trust, unexpectedly started tickling Mona. It was as if a wild leprechaun had possessed him. We all exploded in laughter because Max wouldn't let go; Mona tried to escape, but he had her by her legs, which were apparently her most ticklish point. Max was bonding in an extremely original way and celebrating it! *The best I can do here*, I thought to myself, *is to go with the joyous flow and put some music on*. I pressed play on "Duke's Place" by Satchmo and Duke Ellington himself, as Mona opened another iced bottle of rosé—it was spring, after all. It seemed as if this whole enterprise had a secret password: LAUGHTER, all in capital letters.

Laura started moving her hips with me, and proved quite the dancer. Max took Mona on, and all four of us ended up hugging and giggling on the floor. We lay down there on the floor for quite a while, making fun of everything and everyone, being as silly as we could: first with strange movements, copying each other, then with funny faces and ridiculous sounds. Screaming at the top of our lungs, we competed to see who could be more out of tune. At a certain point, we laughingly decided to go to sleep to get an early start in the morning. There was so much to do! Mona and I could still hear some giggling through the staircase when we finally got up to our room.

We all woke up at 6 AM, and met in the kitchen for coffee. We hugged like we hadn't seen each other for years, although we had met just a few hours ago and had slept a door apart. After that, we went to the river and formed our underwater circle, holding hands. It felt as if Laura and Max were already an integral part of our crew. They were officially initiated.

Then we got word from Gena that they were coming back the next day. We decided to contact the kids, our friend Sami in Bethlehem, and our dear Murat and Kurdi, who had apparently gotten all the way to Kobani in Rojava and were now back in Urfa, at their friend's horse ranch on the Turkish side. We wanted everyone to be present, at least by video, at our first official crew meeting. Max volunteered to set up the Zoom call and the other technical aspects. Mona, Laura, and I decided to create a temple in one of the cozy domes to set the space for each of us at our first meeting: Vasilis, Gena, Rowan, Max, Laura, Mona, and me—and on video, Murat, Kurdi, Ibrahim the retired soccer star, Sami, and the *Follow the Young* troupe: Marikia, Kai, Clemens, Ana, and Little Julie.

We all had to work on our presentations, and decided together that we would go into 24 hours of silence, from sunset till the next sunset when everyone else arrived. We would also each sleep alone that night, and planned to have our auspicious Zoom call the next morning. For the second time, Max got hold of his "peeps" and told them they would be delaying their departure and staying at least another night with us. He encouraged them to have fun at the taverna with the locals and their famous *raki*.

Enchantment was taking over, and my dreams were exploding with questions, ideas, doubts, and visions. Eventually, the next day and its sunset arrived—and with it, the thrill of seeing our friends climb down from Rowan's pickup truck. There they were: sassy and spunky Gena, good old Vasilis (whom I hadn't seen since Lisbon at Bruno's in the summer), and of course, our dear Captain Rowan. We were delighted to see each other. Some were meeting for the very first time. We unloaded the truck and set up everyone in their rooms with enough time to shower, chill after their long journeys, and get ready for dinner.

The Zoom was set up for 9 AM. When we walked into the dome after breakfast, it looked, smelled, and sounded like a living temple. It was our first official crew meeting, and there was a palpable feeling of exhilaration in the room. Gena volunteered to facilitate the meeting, which made me happy. Max made sure that the kids, Ibrahim, Sami, and the Kurds (Murat and Kurdi) were online, and after a song I led with Mona and a one-by-one check-in, Gena asked me to share the news. I looked at Max, Laura, and Mona. We all giggled a bit before I started talking.

"How fun and exciting is this...we're all together! The first bit of small news is that we have a starting budget of €1 million, donated by Max and Laura's family foundation."

"Yes!" Gena said. "When did that happen?"

"Two nights ago!" Mona answered.

"I knew something good would come out of that gig," Rowan added.

"We're still here!" Laura said. "We couldn't leave. There's too much good stuff going on. This will become our life's priority for the next couple of years."

"Yes," I said. "Laura and Max offered to oversee the online platforms, special guests, and all the bureaucratic support we need: lawyers, visas, accountants, connections to royalty, and artists from Hollywood and the fashion world."

Max owned his new online role: "As for the big picture, we'll create a holographic map of the world's sacred sites corresponding to the human body." Max then proceeded to read Arvol Looking Horse's message, calling it a blueprint for the map. Vasilis and Gena were visibly impressed. Clemens, our thirteen-year-old German boy, spoke up, saying he was really into the online stuff and volunteering to join Max's team. He was currently learning coding, he said, and very much into the tech world. Murat said that we should add Rojava to the map, especially for the future of Kobani in Syria, close to the Turkish border from where he and Kurdi had just returned. Then Kurdi broke the good news: they had recruited a hundred riders and horses, from Urfa and even Rojava! They had also contacted the horse leaders from Uruguay and Portugal.

We were thrilled but not surprised when, ten minutes into the meeting, Gena recognized Max from their time working at Facebook. They agreed that the production and media team would set up their own meeting later that day over Zoom, including Clemens, the "young coder." Gena said they would come up with a timeline with Laura, who was in charge of the celebrity guests. That meant that no one in the meeting was going anywhere until we had set our timeline.

Gena had scooped her amazing five-person production team

from Athens, Istanbul, Vietnam, Colombia, and France. They would be ready to begin working as soon as we'd finished our scouting in Bethlehem. Vasilis had also concocted teams of video editors for each of the four directions. This added up to a crew of twenty, ready to go, after our meeting in Bethlehem. Vasilis's four teams would all converge in Hebron, and finally Jerusalem. Gena concluded with the certainty, calm, and poise of a benevolent queen:

"We are still missing confirmation from the northern horse leader from the Galilee who will coordinate the horse caravan together with Kurdi and Murat, and from Musallem, our southern camel leader. This calls for another trip south and yet another one north. We will include this in our timeline."

"Rowan? How is the western caravan doing?" Gena asked.

"We've recruited to our fleet not only boats, yachts, and catamarans, but also swimmers, surfers, and paddle boats. We have about seven hundred units, and only need three hundred more."

"Beautiful!" Gena said.

"Don't worry, Ibrahim," I said. "The ball is coming to you. I'll probably be in Portugal this summer—will you be there?"

"Aiwa!" Ibrahim answered. "And I also have good news for you. I mentioned all this to Ronaldo, the Brazilian, and Zanetti, the Argentinian, both of them well-known soccer activists—and they are both in!

"As I understand it, soccer will be a big part of the Jerusalem ceremony—a kind of protection at the time of the ceremony. Soccer stars as outer guards at the eight gates of the Old City. The goal is to bring as many stars as possible—Messi, Zidane, Ronaldinho—to serve as 'popular and beloved shields' for what will be happening in the ceremony's inner circles. Ronaldo suggested we should add stars from other sports to our outer circle too."

"*Iiwa*!" I said, trying out my rusty Moroccan accent.

"We should also add our famous friends from the film and fashion industries to this outer circle of protection." Laura pitched in.

I continued, "The second concentric circle will be other guilds of humanity: astronauts, doctors, shoemakers, artisans, chefs, engineers, garbage collectors, etc." This was inspired by the guild and color brigades of Extinction Rebellion's direct creative action movement, which came from the UK and had spread around the world.

I was on a roll. "The ring inside of that will be the internationals. Within that circle we'll have Nobel Peace laureates, Indigenous elders, and Spirit Holders of different sacred traditions, including representatives from all three local Abrahamic paths. Further in will be the local people. And at the epicenter of the spiral, we'll have the 'soloists' voicing the collective trauma for the healing ceremony. Finally, floating as free agents around and about the spiral will be the 'sound guides' and musicians.

"It's all still a work in progress," I added. "But you get the idea."

Vasilis took notes, looking enthralled by the prospect of capturing all of this on film and in stills.

"Hey, when do you all come to *Beit Lahem*? We miss you!" Little Julie asked, pronouncing it like a local Palestinian.

"We'll get back to you, sweet Julie, as soon as we get the timeline set," Gena answered.

"Marikia," Mona asked, like a caring big sister, "how is it going in Bethlehem?"

"It's been great! We met amazing people, and we are helping in the Deheishe refugee camp with puppet shows, music, and skateboarding, or anything on wheels… right, Ana?"

"Right!" Ana said.

Australian Kai didn't sound happy, which surprised us. "Did you really say Nobel laureates?" he asked. "Why are they part of this?"

Mona and I looked at each other, in premonition mode. "Kai, can you tell us more?" Gena asked. "We want to hear you out."

"Not yet," Kai said. "It's a very sensitive subject. Let me think about it some more. We'll talk live once we meet in Bethlehem." We all agreed, and left it at that. Trying to diffuse the mood, Marikia intervened. "We have been meeting with the Bethlehem activists and some youth from the Deheishe refugee camp," she said, "and they are super into the non-violent children's march from Bethlehem to

Hebron and then into Jerusalem. They also mentioned including Gaza in some way, maybe via video?"

"It all sounds great! *Follow the Young*!" Murat said from the Turkish side of the screen. All the kids waved and blew kisses to Murat and Kurdi. Little Julie spoke for all five of them: "The coolest and sweetest grandpa and grandma in the whole world." We all laughed, except for Kurdi and Murat, who started crying with joy. Gena decided that was enough for now, and handed the meeting's closure to me. I signaled to Mona and told everyone in the dome, "Bring what you need and come to the river in ten minutes. I'll meet you there. Rowan and Mona will show you the way." I stayed with the others on Zoom and told them they would be with us in spirit in our customary underwater circle in the river. I double-checked on Kai and promised him we would talk some more about the celebrities' protective role. "Okay," said Kai, but he sounded apprehensive.

We went through our subaquatic ceremony and then told everyone to make their own lunch, at their own pace, in silence. There was free time to process, incorporate, rest, digest, and hang out. The media, map, and production teams of Vasilis, Gena, Max, and Laura met after that. Then we all gathered again for dinner. Laura was a good cook, and Rowan joined the cooking team. Vasilis offered to help them out. They decided to do a Mediterranean tapas meal, with fresh sardines and more of the delicious French rosé from the couple of crates that Max and Laura had brought with them from their yacht.

Over a sambuca digestif, Gena and Max updated us about the media and production meeting. Vasilis was on fire. He had made a rough budget for all the video and stills teams, including social media and press, coming from each direction, converging at Hebron and finally in Jerusalem. We would synchronize the timing for the holographic map's online release with the southern camel caravan's departure from Ethiopia; Max, Laura, and Clemens were on it, and would go back to Europe and set it up. The plan was to simultaneously launch in Bethlehem, the Galilee, Greece, Urfa, Portugal, Switzerland, Hebron, Gush Etzion, Jerusalem, Costa Rica, Brazil, India, China,

New Zealand, Slovenia, and Egypt. All were places where we had people who would join with some sort of delegation for the ceremonies.

Laura and Max finally announced, in tears, that they had to leave the next day. It was clear now that our encounter with them had had a critical impact, and that their life had radically changed direction. For their farewell, we decided to hold a dance party. Vasilis would be the DJ this time. We decided that everyone would play somebody else from the group, exchange wardrobes, and get dressed in each other's clothes. As preparation, we would consult with each other for the next two hours, while Vasilis arranged his playlists. I decided to become Mona, and Mona wanted to be me. Laura became Rowan, Gena became Max, and Vasilis was the joker, dressing up as a little bit of each one of us. Max remained himself. It was so much fun to meet later at the party and see each other with different identities, clothes, movements, accents, gestures, and jokes. We danced, played with each other, and melted into bliss throughout the night.

The next morning, Rowan took us to the airport. This time, Mona and I were flying with Gena and Vasilis to Tel Aviv. We were at last on our way to meet the *Follow the Young* troupe and Sami—our dear family in Bethlehem. At Ben Gurion Airport, Vasilis was stopped and taken out of the normal line for interrogation. This lasted for about two hours, and it was ugly. Increasingly, we were hearing stories like these about the Israeli airport. Even Jewish Americans were being detained for ridiculous reasons. It was clearly a fear-mongering campaign designed to scare anyone connected to any kind of human rights, especially Palestinian rights. It reminded me of the darkest hours of the Argentinian dictatorship. After we finally left the airport, we had to calm Vasilis down—though we were all quite affected, which was understandable. Thankfully, we had an amazing rental house in Jaffa waiting for us where we could indulge in two days of laundry, rest, communications, and city life. Next stop: Bethlehem.

CHAPTER 6

DUE EAST

WE RENTED a car in Jaffa and arrived at brother Sami's home in Beit Jala. "*Habibi*, how are you?" Sami said, as usual. Even though he said it every time I saw him, he somehow managed to make it feel special and new every time he called me *habibi*. I introduced him as my dear brother to Mona, Gena, and Vasilis. As it turned out, he had already met Gena in their work with medicinal psychedelics for trauma healing—and, no surprise, they liked each other. Vasilis had met Sami briefly at the Sacred Activism gathering in Portugal.

"Where are the kids?" Mona asked.

"Oh! They are super busy in the Deheishe refugee camp today," Sami answered. "They are making a puppet show for the children. Oh my god! Those kids…everyone in Bethlehem loves them." We all smiled wide and proud.

But first things first: Sami had prepared a sumptuous Palestinian breakfast for us. After breakfast, we decided to crash our kids' last puppet show as we waited for the day to cool off a bit. Like Jerusalem, Bethlehem gets chilly at night. We were all relieved when the heat receded, and the winds started to blow. We hopped into Sami's car and went to the refugee camp, which was packed with youth trying to get the best peek at the puppet show of our one and only *Follow the Young* troupe.

The show was deep and spiced with humor. The troupe had worked intimately with some of the locals' grandmothers to create the puppets, while other new friends from the refugee camp were helping them with the sound system. They had devised their own soundtrack, of course, including a song in Arabic which they'd learned in Sinai and a Palestinian one they'd learned in Bethlehem. The play featured living water and air flowing clean again; they showed the puppets regenerating healthy soil and planting trees. The finale of their act was a real tree-planting ceremony in the refugee camp—and that day they planted three trees, one for each performance. The kids looked beautiful, blooming in their power. We felt so inspired by them; it was as if the youth were igniting the last candle of hope for human initiation. (As the Dalai Lama told us at our private audience in Dharamsala, "the youth will make you feel as if you have multiple hands and legs.")

We managed to get really close to the stage, and when they came out for a bow to a standing ovation, Little Julie recognized us and immediately hopped off the stage and came running towards us. First, she jumped on Mona, then on me. She led us by our hands to the stage and didn't let go until we'd hugged each one of the kids. Vasilis and Gena did the same. We were all in heaven with our brilliant youth, and decided to take everyone to have something to drink with the "other" Sami, the tea man who had an iconic *baladi*[1] stand near the market. It was shady and cool there, and felt homey, with little old-school stools and a simple bench made of wood. We were received warmly by the legendary host. It seemed as if people had been having tea there for hundreds of years in the same manner. It was a whole different world at a completely different pace from the market and the hustle and bustle of the tourist shops around the corner.

After that, we took the kids to eat at the Aftim restaurant, which of course they knew and loved by now. The falafel, humus and traditional dishes were top quality, as usual. Then we went to Sami's office and waited for him there while he finished up some business. Mona told the kids a bit about Crete. Clemens was super excited about the online hologram map. By then, Julie was already in Gena's lap—that didn't take long, I thought to myself—and Kai was playing soccer with Vasilis and Adnan the caretaker in the patio. Marikia was

---

[1] *Baladi*: From the word balad, "village" in Arabic. Used colloquially to mean "local and authentic."

showing me some new *Dhehyeh*² dance steps she'd learned as Ana flipped through her phone showing off her new Palestinian tunes. She could sing the Arabic lyrics with a fairly good accent too.

When we arrived at Sami's home and settled in our rooms, we realized that Clemens was struggling with his emotions. He was German-Jewish, and one of the kids had accidentally revealed Clemens' identity to one of the refugee kids, which had brought the indignation of the other kids in Deheishe. Sami told Clemens that he was a proud Palestinian peace activist and had taken a DNA test which had shown him to be 80% Jewish, genetically. That made Clemens listen and pay attention.

"Wow," said Mona, "what an opportunity to break these stereotypes—for the Palestinians, for these kids, but mostly for you, Clemens."

It felt appropriate to tell them my initiation story at my Bar Mitzvah in Argentina. I doubted if even my close brother Sami had heard this one.

Buenos Aires – 1979

IMAGINE THE military, the police, and the 1 percent against the Argentinian people—the leaders, the organizers, the thinkers, the visionaries, the courageous—basically, anyone who could potentially threaten them. This wasn't imaginary, though. The regime made these people disappear, imprisoning them in clandestine concentration camps beneath the streets, literally under the "civilized" culture of Argentina.

Since early in the dictatorship, my father had taken the theology of liberation, the teachings of his mentor Heschel, and the prophetic tradition of justice seriously. As a rabbi, he felt a duty to be an active part of the incipient human rights movement. At first, he worked with the *Asamblea Permanente por los Derechos Humanos* (APDH)³ and with

---

² *Dhehyeh*: Traditional Bedouin wedding dance.
³ APDH: *Asamblea Permanente por los Derechos Humanos*. One of the first Argentinian human rights organizations, founded in 1975.

the *Madres de la Plaza de Mayo*,[4] with the names of their beloved "disappeared" ones written on their white handkerchiefs. ("Disappeared" usually meant they were killed, and their bodies never found.) Later on, my father began visiting "political" prisoners, regardless of if they were Jewish or not, trying to get them released from jail and out of the country. He also helped a few brave lawyers to create the *Centro de Estudios Legales y Sociales* (CELS)[5] and supported the *Abuelas de la Plaza de Mayo*,[6] the grandmothers of the disappeared, whose children had been killed and grandchildren secretly sold or given to military families for adoption.

1979 was the year Maradona rose as a star in Japan at the soccer youth World Cup. At that same time, the Inter-American Court of Human Rights—the justice-seeking judges based in Costa Rica—were visiting my home, investigating the Argentinian dictatorship's crimes against humanity. That day, our building in the *barrio*[7] of Belgrano R – Zapiola and Avenida de los Incas was surrounded by police in civilian clothes driving the infamous Ford Falcons of the paramilitary secret services. My father pointed them out to the judges and me from our home's fifth-floor living room window, right next to the piano.

It was also the year of my *Bar Mitzvah*.[8] I was thirteen years old, and uncomfortable about my height, my small body, and my small penis. Every one of my friends seemed to be growing, except for me. I even went to an endocrinologist who had recommended some pills for growth. Soon after that, I stopped taking them. (I'm still short.) However, my charisma, audacity, being "in" with the cool girls, and soccer skills made me very popular—this was Argentina, after all. By high school, though, things fundamentally changed. I was already the

---

[4] *Madres de la Plaza de Mayo*: Most emblematic Argentinian human rights group opposing the dictatorship. Mothers of those who were "disappeared" during the horrendous military dictatorship. They wore the names of their children on their white headdresses.

[5] CELS: *Centro de Estudios Legales y Sociales*. An Argentinian lawyers' organization who championed human rights in the times of the dictatorship, founded in 1979.

[6] *Abuelas de la Plaza de Mayo*: Like the "Mothers," they looked for their disappeared grandchildren who were robbed and adopted by military families after being born in secret jails. The grandchildren are still being found as adults, up to this day.

[7] *Barrio*: "Neighborhood" in Spanish.

[8] *Bar Mitzvah*: Jewish ceremony of initiation into manhood at age thirteen.

weird son of a "Yankee" rabbi. Almost all my classmates had a private tutor and were working hard in mathematics and physics to get into a good Argentinian non-Jewish high school, whereas I was terrible at (and hated) those subjects and would be staying in the Jewish school. The other kids, even the ones who used to be my friends, started avoiding me at breaks. Soccer wasn't that much of a deal anymore, and for the growing girls, I was very short and tiny. I began to feel seriously ostracized, and experienced a deep feeling of rejection and isolation.

The Argentine military dictatorship was at its apex and was "disappearing"—torturing and killing—youth by the thousands. In those days, my father used to co-lead the weekly walk led by the *Madres de la Plaza de Mayo* to the Casa Rosada, the main government house in Buenos Aires. He did this with Alicia Moreau de Justo, an old-school socialist, Adolfo Perez Esquivel, the Nobel Peace Laureate, and the president of the *Madres*. Every Thursday, they would circle around the *Plaza de Mayo* demanding to see the dictator of the military junta, and that he bring back alive thousands of "disappeared" citizens.

I was in the midst of the preparations for my bar mitzvah: the long practices for my Torah reading,[9] the anticipated thrill of slow dancing at the Saturday night party with that sexy girl from my class I had a crush on, and the news of a *Torah* speech by my maternal grandfather at my ceremony. My only living grandfather was a quite-learned American rabbi who I hardly knew. He lived in Israel by then, and was quite conservative in his worldviews, though an innovator in religious law. My fond memories of him, when he visited Argentina, were of his fun stories of Ichel, Michel and Pichel.[10]

There's a Jewish tradition in which the Thursday before you are called up to be blessed and read from the *Torah* at your bar mitzvah on Shabbat morning, you put on your *tefillin*[11] for the first time. That

---

[9] Torah reading: The Torah is divided into portions and each week has its own portion which is read on Mondays, Thursdays, and the Sabbath, according to rabbinic tradition. Mine was the first chapter of the book of Leviticus, or "Vayikra" in Hebrew.

[10] Ichel, Michel, and Pichel: Well-known characters in Yiddish funny folk stories for children.

[11] *Tefillin*: Phylacteries. Ancient biblical prayer ties made of hide and biblical "totafot" in Hebrew. They are worn on the left arm near the heart, and on the third eye,

Thursday morning—March 29, 1979—my dad, or "Ata," as my sisters and I had called him since childhood, told me that we would go to visit a Jewish political prisoner under house arrest and wrap my *tefillin* for the first time together with him. The news gave me the shivers. I knew deep down that this would be a cardinal and sacred moment. As it turned out, the experience would move me to my core, and make a radical imprint on who I am today.

My father had visited the political prisoner, Jacobo Timerman, in jail in the aftermath of his disappearance. He had been tortured in solitary confinement, and was now under house arrest and waiting to get out of the country. He was one of the lucky ones who survived, maybe because he was a pioneering famous journalist. He was also a self-declared atheist and a cultural Jew. Jacobo would later dedicate his book, *Prisoner without a Name, Cell without a Number*, to my father. The book told of the atrocities he went through since he'd been arrested, and the dedication read "To MARSHALL MEYER, a rabbi who brought comfort to Jewish, Christian, and atheist prisoners in Argentine jails."

When we entered Jacobo's building, we were required to go through a full police security check. Then, upstairs in his apartment, we were surrounded by three policemen with machine guns: his guards. We went into his study, and Jacobo hugged my father tightly. My father announced, "Today is my son's bar mitzvah. He's becoming a man, and I thought it would be appropriate for him to pray and put on his *tefillin* for the first time with you and me."

It was deeply emotional for all three of us. A sense of holy ceremony enveloped us, and we could see the policeman at the study's entrance holding his machine gun and looking completely disconcerted. We proceeded with the ceremony. It was intense, and by the time we got to the blessings and intentions for the middle finger wrappings of the *tefillin* with Prophet Hoshea's words *V'erastich li l'olam*,[12] the three of

---

reminding us to align thought with action. Used mostly in the morning while reciting the sunrise prayers.
[12] *V'erastich li l'olam*: "I shall be betrothed (to God) forever"—the phrase is recited as we wrap our straps of the Tefillin on the left hand's ring finger.

us were crying. We prayed, reciting the *shema*[13] for Oneness together. "Now you are a man," my father said. "You have experienced compassion and injustice firsthand." I knew this was a seminal moment, and my initiation into Sacred Activism—my trampoline into the courage to stand with the oppressed against injustice, with empathy, and rooted in heart-centered Spirit. I wore my heart and head phylacteries with pride that morning, embodying the best of our prophetic tradition. *Tefillin*, I learned, served as reminders of the sanctity of life: in thought, when worn on the forehead, and in action, when worn next to the heart on the left arm.

On Saturday night, after my bar mitzvah, the religious ceremonies, my readings, my speech, my grandfather's and father's blessings, and the big festive family meals, I finally had my slow dance with the girl I had a crush on. We became a thirteen-year-old "couple" for ten days.

Clemens, encouraged a bit by my story, asked me if I could tell him more about Buenos Aires. "Please!" Little Julie added enthusiastically.

So, I went on.

Buenos Aires: 1981–1983

BY 1981, I'd finally decided to leave the Jewish high school. My mother didn't take it lightly, to say the least. In choosing where to transfer, I looked hard for, and chose, the high school with the worst reputation in Buenos Aires at the time: Guido Spano.

That year, my fourth year of high school, I was absent from school a total of forty-five days. By the end of 1982, my last year of high school, I decided to drop out altogether and focus on my true passions: theater and life. My mom was distraught, but Ata made me promise I would finish the exams by myself and graduate. I took a tutor for math, physics, and chemistry, and eventually graduated

---

[13] *Shema*: One of the main prayers of the Jewish tradition. A proclamation of the Divine unity. An incantation of six words declaring that our particular God is the same as the universal One.

by the end of the year. I was seventeen years old. That same year, I became very active in the movement against the dictatorship to bring back the disappeared and fight for human rights and democracy. By 1983, I became part of the late Augusto Conte's campaign for congressman and helped found the Jewish Movement for Human Rights (MJDH), led by my dad and the journalist Herman Schiller. We organized a ten-thousand-person demonstration at the *obelisco*[14] in the heart of Buenos Aires against antisemitism and for the return of the disappeared, alive.

I remember going to visit different political parties to invite their pledge for support and their appearance at the demonstration. I reached out to the Peronist, Communist, Socialist, and Radical parties, and even the Argentinian Andean Indigenous Movement; upon hearing my father's name, they all said, "Of course we'll endorse the march. We'll be there." It made me proud. During one of Augusto Conte's campaign reach-outs, I decided to go to my old Jewish school and talk to my former classmates about voting for a human rights candidate in the first democratic elections of 1983. Though the dictatorship was slowly transitioning out of power and into democracy, the oppressive feeling was still very present. That same evening, an old classmate who had been present at my talk called me on the phone.

"After you left the classroom," she said, "the headmaster, Isabelinski, came to our class and told us directly that your proposal was dangerous and that we shouldn't listen to you. He continued, in a threatening tone, 'You know what happened to people like your old classmate and his loud father, just a couple of years ago.'" I finally understood: my troubles and unpopularity in school from the seventh grade through the third year of high school were rooted in something much bigger than my personality. My schoolmates' parents were afraid for their kids' safety and had told their children not to get involved with me.

My rebirth had begun. I was committed to art and theater, bringing down the murderous dictatorship, and stewarding the return of democracy. I was happy, alive and kicking. I had many non-Jewish

---

[14] *Obelisco*: Main monument in Buenos Aires's main avenue, 9 de Julio.

friends. I was out of the ghetto, this time on my own. I had finally encountered the "other" Argentina.

Clemens seemed moved, and everyone was listening attentively. The other kids didn't know much about Jewish rites of passage and were excited to learn about them, and balance out their experiences of Arabic and Palestinian culture.

The next morning, we all went to the Banksy Museum. By our third day together, we decided to start talking about our holy walk from Bethlehem to Hebron and then to Jerusalem. We met in the beautiful meditation room at the Holy Land Trust. Sami was happy that women, youth and children would be leading the walkers. His three daughters wanted to join and, committed to organizing youth in Bethlehem, walk with them. They were quite impressed with this colorful bunch of global climate justice activists their own age!

Kai said, "What about kids joining us from Jordan?"

"Yes!" Sami answered. "We can get a point person in Amman. Hopefully someone below the age of twenty. And maybe even in Iraq?"

I added that we could include Iran in the northern horse caravan, maybe even one rider from there. "It could also be on a donkey!" I said.

"I love donkeys!" Little Julie exclaimed. "Could I ride one, once we get to Jerusalem?"

"For sure!" Mona said, surprising us all. Sami said he would get back to Little Julie about the donkey. Then, as usual, he had to leave quickly for another meeting in his office upstairs. We decided to go back to Sami's home and make the "online hologram map" call to Switzerland. Mona and I were so happy that Gena and Vasilis were with us. Gena was now the pilot; everyone in the group had their special gifts, and luckily not everyone had to do everything. Laura took the call in Switzerland as Max was busy that night.

"First," she said, "we just transferred the first installment to you via Zelle, Gena. You can use this money for everyone's travel and a basic income for food, gas, and a little extra per day. Please administrate the budget from now on and pay each of the members of 'the Biggie' accordingly."

"Right on!" Gena said.

"As for the hologram," Laura continued, "Max is in full design mode. He's busy tonight with a coder friend of his, figuring it all out. He said he expects to launch soon, if everything goes well. Max said that they are developing phase one and opening online traffic for all the interactive links on the map, representing all the stations of our journey: South—Sinai and Egypt; North—Galilee, Israel, Rojava, Syria, Urfa, Turkey; West- Crete, Greece; East—Bethlehem, Palestine, Amman, Jordan; Below—Hebron; and Above and Heart of the Matter—Jerusalem." Laura added that countries like Portugal, Costa Rica, Scotland, Iceland, and New Zealand would probably be included in phase two. Phase three, about two weeks before the Hebron ceremony, would include the US, China, Russia, Brazil, and India.

Vasilis interjected, "Can I get a map with dates on it, Laura? I want to plan press and social media events at each of the location launches."

"You got it, Vasilis. I'll communicate with Max about this. It shouldn't be a problem."

Gena had printed a little booklet with all the inspirational texts we'd mentioned, in different colors that were easy to identify. It even included Arvol Looking Horse's transmission and the basis for the hologram, as well as the stories of the Cave at Machpelah/Ibrahimi Mosque, King Melchizedek, and Hagar and Sarah, all of which had inspired our greater vision. She'd been collecting and editing the booklet with Mona since we met on the boat to Crete. I wasn't aware of this at all, and it made me extremely happy! Gena was so discreet, and such a pro. Infused with joy by Gena, Mona, and the emerging timeline of the sacred action, I said, "Let's rent some bicycles and ride to Hebron, and then Jerusalem! Maybe Julie can ride her donkey?"

"Yeah!" everyone answered in unison. The meeting was short, efficient, and over. It was a good strategy to finish when all of us were still excited.

The following day was all about getting ready for the journey. We needed at least ten bikes, and Sami and his staff delivered. They even surprised Little Julie with her own donkey. She was in bliss when she heard the news!

CHAPTER 7

SCOUTING

Below

WE NEEDED to get an early start for our journey to Hebron. Though electricity filled the air, something wasn't right. Kai, our young Aussie friend, approached Mona and told her the time had come for us to talk about something that was boiling in his heart, before we left. It was 6 AM.

Kai came from a radical activist family and had always been deeply embedded in the social justice movement. He was very inspired by Occupy Wall Street and had been part of commando actions for Greenpeace with his parents since he was a very young child. His words came out loud and clear. He was very disappointed that we'd decided to include the Dalai Lama and other Nobel laureates and celebrities in our big ceremonies. He called them sell-outs to capitalism and its disgusting system. He went on to attack Mandela as another traitor who did nothing against corporations, leaving big business in South Africa intact. We listened to him with some pain. After he'd finished, Gena took it on herself to tell our young friend that she respected his passion and agreed with his views on hierarchy and anti-capitalism.

"In one way or another," she said, "we are all embedded in this terrible and unjust system." Sami mentioned the added value of strategy in our actions, and the context for accepting allies. Vasilis talked about their security value for the safety of the events, and the potentially massive coverage in the media. He reminded us of how some of them had really helped to amplify Standing Rock's global visibility.

Through each round of the conversation, Kai was calming down. His face was relaxing as his frustration seemed to melt. Finally, I said, "Kai, I hear you. However, we might need these people to birth our dream. Even if they all have their shadows, just like each one of us, maybe we can see them as strategic bridges from the old system. They are symbols of the possible transition from the old western mainstream story towards the memory of our original story. They will protect us and amplify the reach of our action.

"A critical mass of people around the globe trusts and looks up to them. The laureates, the famous sports figures, the fashion and movie stars probably won't be attacked violently. They will be our first line of physical defense, as they are an intrinsic part of the language, luster, and pride of the ruling and dying system. They might come in very handy. We might really need them in the frontlines."

"Hmm," Kai said, still not fully convinced.

"Could you please sleep on it, and we'll talk more later?" Mona requested. Kai had a big crush on Mona. It was obvious from the way he looked at and interacted with her. Just then, in perfect timing for Kai's emotional breakthrough, Little Julie—whom Kai adored—asked him to help her mount her donkey. It worked as an irresistible spell, and Kai beamed.

"Okay," he finally said. "I get your point. Let me digest this."

At our first rest stop, I told everyone a story about Sarah and Hagar. Sami then told them a different story of the two brothers, descendants of Isaac and Ishmael, who raped the same woman—a metaphor for raping the same land.

Our practical goal for this bike trip was to scout the graves of our ancestors to find locations for all the guests and ceremonies, find proper lodging for horses and walkers, and locate parking for bicycles and the general public. At our last stop with the bikes before arriving at the double cave, a few elements of the action became clear. The soccer game would only happen upon everyone's arrival to Jerusalem.

For Hebron, we decided to have four thousand people in concentric circles, representing all sides of the conflict, with the Spirit Holders and the different guilds of humankind supporting the safety of the ceremony. Inside the circle, we would have four hundred people, representing the four hundred shekels with which Abraham bought the Cave of Machpelah. Naturally, there would be a live stream of the healing ceremony at Hebron so that it could be witnessed online globally.

After two hours of biking, still early in the morning, we made it to the outskirts of the cave in Hebron, the "umbilical cord of the universe." Our unique ancestral healing ceremony between Palestinians and Jews would happen exactly where Isaac and Ishmael left off at their father Abraham's burial on the fifteenth of Sivan, according to the apocryphal Book of Jubilees, some 3,500 years ago.

As we rode the final stretch of the journey before the checkpoint, we went into deep silence, penetrating the marvelous. Everyone seemed to be feeling the power of the ancestors, the double cave, and our common mission. At El Chalil, we sat down under a big olive tree, where I felt compelled to tell my companions about my father's death.

New York – 1993

I WAS living in Sinai amidst magnificent, beautiful sandstone mountains. While writing my second Spanish book of poetry, *Tribus de Pura Temperatura (Tribes of Pure Temperature)*, I was yearning for a visit from my father. I dreamed of writing a play with him about our father-son relationship, and eventually touring the world with it. I had it all figured out and was hoping my dad would take a sabbatical from his rabbinic life in NYC.

On one of my routine visa missions to the Egyptian consulate in Tel Aviv, a dear and old friend of my father's called me long distance and said, "Please take a taxi to the airport now and find the earliest flight tonight to New York. Don't worry about the cost. Your father is having an operation on Monday." It was early afternoon on Saturday.

"It's very serious," my father's friend said. "You should be here in New York tomorrow before it happens."

I was staying at a close friend's home in Tel Aviv, so I got my passport and toothbrush and left for the airport. By Sunday morning I was on the Upper West Side. I had the key to my parents' apartment, so I let myself in, and realizing my parents were still sleeping, decided to sleep a few more hours. (Wow! I haven't said the words "my parents" in a long time.)

As we woke up, and after the effusive hellos and a little breakfast, my father proclaimed dramatically, "We are having a big party tonight! Let's get the house ready." By noon, my sisters had arrived to help beautify the house. My big sister Anita, the visual artist, oversaw the aesthetic details and flower arrangements. Dodi, my middle sister, cooked some delicious food. My mom laid the tables, supervising the whole enterprise. I hadn't seen my family in a while, but nobody really had time to catch up as we were expecting guests by early evening for cocktails. The piano had just been tuned and was looking good. I made sure the CD player and stereo were working. Soon enough, the guests started showing up: a few cousins from my father's side, my mom's brother and family who lived in the same building, some close colleagues of my dad, and a handful of dear friends.

Anyone who's been at my family's home can attest to the quality of our hosting. Plenty of tasty food, beauty all around, music and dance—and yes, except for my non-drinking sisters, alcohol in abundance. That night was special, to say the least, and my father sang quite a few of his favorite tunes, accompanied by a friend at the piano. We also sang a few old Argentinian folk and rock songs we grew up with. I was asked to sing a couple of Israeli Hebrew songs and a Bedouin one from Sinai. The night also called for champagne, which wasn't a regular drink of choice at our home. As my dad tapped his champagne glass gently with a spoon, we knew a speech was imminent.

"Tomorrow," my father announced, "I'm going to go through a big operation."

My sisters, my mom, and most of us started tearing up. Just before the mood in the room turned somber, Ata continued, "So tonight we celebrate! Turn the music up!"

So we did. We got drunk, danced, and celebrated till midnight. One by one, the guests hugged my father, holding back their tears, full of emotion, each one in their own style. We cleared the living room and took all the dirty cups and plates to the kitchen. It was 1:30 AM when we went to bed.

At 7 AM, we left for the hospital. After all the paperwork, Ata lay on a gurney in his hospital pajamas. I was his companion into the operating room, and pushed the stretcher for him as we sang together, inspired by the prophet Amos:

"*Al tira Israel al tira*
ki gur aryeh lo ata
ukshe aryeh ishag mi lo ira, mi lo ira."[1]

Then it was time for me to go back to the waiting room to join my family. Ata never came out, though. He never regained consciousness after the surgery, and it took almost two days for him to die. My pain was physically unbearable. I remember the complete constriction of my solar plexus and stomach, and the excruciating anguish inside my chest. My tears were loud and endless. It felt like I couldn't go on.

We went home, and while my father's rabbi colleague and his close friend went to do *tachrichim*,[2] I stayed with my sisters and mother. In the midst of our torrential weeping, we got dressed with great difficulty and went to the funeral at B'nai Jeshurun Congregation[3] on West 88th Street. The whole block surrounding the synagogue was full of people: multi-faith clergy, congregants, friends, family, homeless people, Latinos, African Americans. Not that I noticed any of them as we walked in with my family. I was in a daze, sobbing and hurting deeply. I couldn't see anything at all.

We made it to the pulpit, where one of my sisters spoke, and the

---

[1] *Al tira Israel al tira, ki gur aryeh lo ata, ukshe aryeh ishag mi lo ira, mi lo ira*: This popular Israeli song is based on the words of the prophet Amos, "Don't fear oh Israel, because you are a lion's cub. And when a lion roars, who shall but not fear?"

[2] *Tachrichim*: Wrapping of the body for burial in the Jewish tradition.

[3] Congregation B'nai Jeshurun: One of the oldest Ashkenazi synagogues in Manhattan. My father became its rabbi in 1985. There were eight people during services when he took over. Nowadays, a few thousand families are members.

other one read a text. Finally, my mom whispered in my ear, "You have to say something." I couldn't imagine saying anything. Still crying, barely able to get the words out, I told my mom, "I can't."

"You have to do it," she said.

Slowly, I moved forward to the pulpit and started banging the table with all my strength in a steady rhythm. I didn't say a word. Nobody did. There was an absolute and electrifying silence blasting from the crowd. My voice burst out from within the excruciating pain and tears:

"*Al tira Israel al tira,*
ki gur aryeh lo ira,
ukshe aryeh ishag mi lo ira, mi lo ira."

It was prophet Amos, and my last blissful memory of ecstatic singing around the fire in Israel. It was also my last moment with my father on the stretcher as he entered the operation before his death.

We drove to the cemetery in Norwich, Connecticut and buried my father later that morning. The grieving was so loud that nobody could hear the rabbi's prayers. After lowering my father's casket into the ground, I got on all fours and started throwing earth to cover the casket with my bare hands. I couldn't and didn't want to use the shovel they were passing around. Amidst fistfuls of soil, I wept and wailed from my guts.

We went back home and started *shiva*[4] right away. Hundreds of people passed by my parents' home: family, friends, students, rabbis, colleagues, interfaith clergy, activists of all sorts, homeless people, and artists. I learned that week that for the past month, Ata had been teaching a special course on death and dying. The second day of the *shiva*, a young *Paulista*[5] arrived. He had worked assisting my father in the last couple of years, and knew me from my time in New York before I left to travel through East Africa and eventually settle in Sinai. He simply gave me a hug and, through my tears, passed me a small bag. I went into my father's study, opened it, and discovered

---

[4] *Shiva*: The seven days of mourning in the Jewish tradition. The immediate family observes it by staying at home and not doing anything, and are instead visited, consoled, and served by the community.

[5] *Paulista*: Someone coming from São Paulo, Brazil.

to my surprise it was ganja. Enough for the whole week. Enough for whoever wanted. The sacred plant medicine brought part of my rebellious countercultural identity into the shiva, independent of my father and family. At my most vulnerable and desolate moment, it empowered my sense of worth and desire to stay alive.

The next day, one of my father's congregants brought a bunch of drums and shakers and taught us all a Zulu funeral song. "*Baye saku sasa bayeza*," we sang, which translates as, "They are coming." That week we sang many songs, cried many tears, and laughed many laughs. Some of the people and students who came to pay their respect joined the circle. Others thought to themselves, the son of the rabbi has gone mad! Look at him playing drums, smoking marijuana, and even laughing at Rabbi Marshall T. Meyer's *shiva*!

The ebb and flow of our time together begat the hit song of our mourning which sustained us as our anthem for the week. We sang it often:

"*Amor, amor, amor, amor el mensaje es el amor*
ama a tu prójimo como a ti mismo el es tu amor."[6]

I had heard it first in Ireland, from an Israeli brother who had heard it in Mexico. I had already tweaked the Spanish words a bit. The Hebrew words followed:

"*Hareini mekabel alai et mitzvat haboreh Veahavta lereacha camocha.*"[7]

The words were the blending of a prayer by the great Arizal, Rabbi Isaac Luria,[8] with the most important mantra of the Bible: "Love your neighbor as yourself." Throughout the week, we kept changing the

---

[6] *Amor, amor, amor, amor, el mensaje es el amor, ama a tu prójimo como a ti mismo, el es tu amor*: Spanish for, "Love, love, love, love, the message is love, love your neighbor as yourself. They are your love."

[7] *Hareini mekabel alai et mitzvat haboreh, veahavta lereacha camocha*: "Here I take upon me the commitment to love my neighbor as myself." From Leviticus and then embellished by Rabbi Isaac Luria in the Shabbat morning prayers.

[8] Arizal, Rabbi Isaac Luria: Most important Kabbalist from the sixteenth century who arrived in Zafed from Egypt. He had lived for seven years as a hermit on an island in the Nile, until he dreamed he had to come and teach Rabbi Chayyim Vital, his elder, then the great Kabbalist of Zafed, who later became his main disciple. His son, Shmuel Vital, was the one who delivered all the extant works of the Arizal in written form.

word "neighbor" for the names of the people present in the room, singing each of their names one by one.[9]

Back at the Cave of the Machpelah, Mona was sitting next to me and massaging my heart from behind. She used her two fingers, piercing my heart open from both sides of my spine. Intuitively, everyone paired up and started to heart massage each other, first from the back, then from the front. We kneaded each other's chest muscles to penetrate and open the heart, communicating through sign language.

We intended to make a circle to encompass the whole cave from both sides of the fence. Before that, we had divided into two groups and gone inside for our own ancestral shrine moment. Both groups emerged slowly, and we physically surrounded Abraham's grave with our circle. For the circle to be complete, though, the two-armed soldiers had to join hands with us—and they did! For a moment, we all sang "Love Your Neighbor as Yourself" and "I'm a Mirror to You and You Are a Mirror unto Me."[10] Sami and I led a prayer for Abraham in Ishmael and Isaac's name. Mona and Gena completed the worship, paying homage to the sisterhood of Sarah and Hagar, and we asked Little Julie to add a few words for the future generations. All our words were a blessing for the release of the conflict between the two brothers, the two matriarchs, and our two peoples.

Afterwards, we went back to the old olive tree where we had sat before the ceremony. We realized that we could only fit about a hundred people around the grave, so we decided the ceremony would have to take place at the Ibrahimi Mosque, or "The Hall of Isaac." The rest of the walking crowd would have to participate from behind the military checkpoint.

We then began our ride to the old city of Jerusalem in silence and stopped only after forty-five minutes. Julie's donkey wouldn't move anymore, so we decided to make a stop right there and then.

---

[9] To listen to "Veahavta," go to page 227.
[10] To listen to "Rei - I'm a Mirror to You and You Are a Mirror Unto Me," go to page 251.

Above

As we approached the outskirts of Jerusalem, we knew that the "above" direction would include freed white doves, hot air and edible balloons, and our virtual hologram map projected on the sky, all above the one square kilometer of the three sacred sites of the Old City of Jerusalem.

We dismounted from our bikes and donkey to see Jerusalem from above as we kept "heartstorming." The four caravans would arrive at the eight gates of the Old City of Jerusalem, and needed space to park hundreds of horses, camels, and up to a million people all around the Old City. The Sultan's Pool was one of the possible areas; Tantur Monastery, King David's Tower, Liberty Bell Park, Hutzot Hayotser, Abu Tor, Gethsemane, the Mount of Olives and other sacred sites surrounding the Old City would also serve as encampments to host the massive numbers of people. At sunset, we went to visit Daniel, an elder friend who had developed a hologram for a light show about "Heavenly Jerusalem" as a city of peace for all its visitors. We concurred with him: the old city of Jerusalem would be an international safe haven to celebrate the inheritance of peace, for all peoples of the Earth.

On To Jerusalem

We decided that the soccer game would include a fashion show with a catwalk and famous models during halftime to attract worldwide media. After the game, the soccer players would parade out of the stadium to hold guard at their gate posts in the outer circle and serve as extra security for the ceremony happening inside. Participants would surround the Old City of Jerusalem, and the Nobel laureates and Spirit Holders would complete the concentric circle by surrounding the Holy Sepulcher Church, the Wailing Wall, and Haram al-Sharif/Al Aqsa Mosque.

As we passed each of the eight gates of the Old City with our bikes and our little donkey, we could feel our hearts pumping faster.

Gena and Vasilis kept taking notes on their phones, and the rest of us, deeply moved, could hardly talk. We did mention some elements of the Jerusalem healing ceremony, though: it would include finger snapping, clapping, humming, and simple choruses and movements by the masses. Soloists would voice crucial blind spots and traumas from both peoples, at both the individual and collective levels.

When we arrived on the north side of Jerusalem, close to Abu Tor, we saw the silhouettes of a group of riders on horseback. As they got closer, I recognized Maya, two of her horse rider friends, and her brother—all from the Galilee—gallantly approaching us on their horses. They dismounted, and after warm hellos and introductions, Maya told us she was coming to scout the area for where they could tie up their horses for the big event. They had ridden the trail all the way from the Galilee and had designed a good itinerary with proper stops along the way. It would take them ten days at a moderate pace.

Musallem had come up with the idea of swapping and planting seeds: each camel or horse rider, boat person, and walker would bring a seed to Jerusalem to plant there and take a local seed from Jerusalem to plant a tree wherever the camel or horse was coming from. He had talked with Murat and Kurdi, who had in turn transmitted this great idea to their Turkish, Kobani, Iranian, and Lebanese riders. There were about three hundred horses all together from those areas. So between camels and horses, boats, and walkers, we would plant four thousand trees in Jerusalem. In turn, the caravans would take back new seeds to plant in Jordan and all the way to Iraq and Iran if possible. The boat and sea people would bring seeds back west to Crete.

Later in the evening we Zoomed with Ibrahim, Kurdi and Murat, and Max and Laura. Max told us with great enthusiasm that they'd hired an amazing team of four people—for the four directions and four caravans—who would take care of all communication with the authorities. That would be our permit ministry, linked directly to our mastermind, Gena. The most incredible news of all was that Pope Francis himself was apparently considering publicly supporting the event. This was wonderful to hear, as permits through the Vatican would be much easier to get with the Pope's endorsement. I whispered to Mona with a sarcastic smile that we would have to explain the Pope to our young warrior, Kai.

Ibrahim gave us an encouraging briefing, saying that the soccer stars were adding up. Ronaldo had already talked with Ronaldinho, and he was in! Zanetti was still talking to Messi's people, but he had recruited Mohamed Salah, and Zidane. Megan Rapinoe and Mia Hamm, the US soccer stars, were in as well. Ibrahim had connections with a basketball All-Star, and through him had recruited Kareem Abdul-Jabbar and Larry Bird. The sports names kept coming, including tennis legends Martina Navratilova, the Williams sisters, Federer, and Björn Borg. The American football star activist Colin Kaepernick was fresh on the list. We decided that we had to place at least four stars at each of the eight gates of Jerusalem, and ten more for the all-star soccer match. Ibrahim said that his goal was for the five-versus-five game to be live streamed worldwide. Ibrahim was on fire! Max was too: he said he was already in consultation with Mark Ruffalo, Shailene Woodley, Harrison Ford, Spike Lee, Danny DeVito, Richard Gere, Frances Fisher, Jane Fonda, and more.

For music before and after the soccer game, we had enlisted Baaba Maal and a Pakistani Sufi Qawwali singer, a Christian Armenian Palestinian singer, and a Jewish Israeli liturgical singer with Iraqi ancestry. Laura had gotten in touch with Catherine Deneuve and was adding a couple of big names from the fashion industry as well. They were trying hard to get big stars from Africa and the East, including China, India, and Russia.

The call went on for a while. At one point, Max said with excitement, "I just got a Whatsapp message from the Nobel laureate conference. They are meeting in the Vatican at the beginning of the summer, and we're invited to present our plan there. There will be many crucial people present."

Mona checked in on our young Ozzy revolutionary, Kai. "Are you okay with all this?" she asked.

Kai smiled and said, "Thanks for challenging me. I understand now that being right and succeeding in our purpose isn't the same. I'm all in." We were deeply impressed by Kai's maturity and flexibility. It was amazing to witness such a quick shift in his strategic perception, though we all knew that his heart was malleable and huge.

Gena kept taking notes a mile a minute as her joy increased visibly. Kurdi mentioned that Stacy, the horse woman from the Uruguayan community, had been in touch with the horse caravan people of Argentina and Mexico; they would be joining the caravan from Urfa, once they got to Turkey.

It was getting late, so we got an Airbnb big enough for all of us in beautiful and quiet Ein Karem,[11] a fifteen-minute drive from Jerusalem. The next morning, we all went to visit our dear cheese-wizard baba at Sataf. Jeremiah was our good friend and hosted us for breakfast with his legendary hospitality, white hair, beard, clothes, amazing cheeses, good olives, and fine red wine. I always thought he looked like Geppetto. Later on, I thought he was more like Gandalf. After a great meal, It was clear to us: we would regroup again in Rome.

The next morning, a small contingent of us left for Sinai. We had decided to spend time in the mountains to prepare for the Vatican meeting. The best choice for us would be to stay at Jebel el Bargha, at Musallem's mountain desert haven. At my request, we would pass by Wadi Meliches.

"Very good reason to return to Sinai," Mona remarked.

"We also want to get Gena's vision about women marching into the picture," said Marikia. "The natural choice seems to be "Women Wage Peace."

"I'm already on it," Sami said. "I'm connecting Gena to the women leaders of the movement. They will be coming with the children from the east, with Palestinian women on the Palestinian side and Israeli women meeting them as soon as they cross the green line."

We rented a big van to return south to Eilat. It was big enough to fit all of us, and even our luggage—mostly Mona's viola, my guitar, and Vasilis's camera and tripod. Our new satellite telephone was waiting to be picked up in Eilat.

---

[11] Ein Karem: Old residential and now touristic neighborhood in the outskirts of Jerusalem. The birthplace of John the Baptist and his mother. Home to some beautiful churches.

CHAPTER 8

BACK TO SINAI

WE REACHED the border and an old-school Bedouin taxi driver who I've known for years was waiting for us at the Egyptian side—this time with a big van. We went straight to Wadi Zamri,[1] crossing through the desert mountains. Our dearest Musallem and his friend Suleiman were waiting for us with two jeeps. Musallem decided we would sleep at Jebel Barga, his home in the mountains, for a couple of nights. As Bedouin travel goes, though, we would make countless stops along the way. Gena, Vasilis and Sami were the only ones who hadn't yet been to Sinai. They were "wowing" one moment and diving into deep silence the next. They eventually transitioned into singing, laughing, and ecstatic joy for the rest of the journey. I marveled at their transformation.

We finally arrived at our destination and parked at the enormous dune on the other side of the mountain. Musallem and his son showed off, indulging us again with their famous Bedouin father-son acrobatics at high speed all the way down—this time, at their own backyard sand dune. Vasilis got amazing stills and video footage of their antics, already thinking of the presentation at the Vatican. I peeked at Vasilis and Gena, who were taking copious notes and excitedly consulting with each other. As for me, I was thrilled to be with my brother Sami for the first time in Sinai—and to have Mona with me too. It was hard to concentrate on anything else.

When we arrived at Musallem's land, he treated us to a tour,

[1] Wadi Zamri: A Bedouin village in the middle of the desert. It has its own school.

showing us his rainwater retention pool, solar panels, and regenerative agriculture soil and land project. We plunged into the pool's cold water—a joyous delight in the middle of a very hot desert day. After our customary subaquatic circle, presided over by water priestess Gena, Suleiman and Musallem went to cook us dinner. Around the pool and under a big siyala[2] tree, Gena said, "It's clear from the amount of beautiful footage Vasilis is getting that Musallem will be profiled on video with his camels, so there's no need for him to come to the Vatican." Mona added, "The same could happen with Rowan on a boat from the west and the northern horse caravan led by Murat, Kurdi and Maya." Kurdi said, "Yes, I agree. The effect of having us riding our horses through Urfa would be more powerful." Marikia volunteered to accompany Little Julie in some kind of movement routine and audience interaction during the presentation.

"We could also profile the other kids and the eastern caravan on video," Vasilis added.

Sami summarized, "So that leaves me, G., Mona, Marikia and Little Julie. Gena and Vasilis can serve as backup, production managers, and general guidance for the presentation. Max will function as the MC and help Vasilis and Gena with sorting out the budget, itinerary and the hologram map."

Musallem's voice reverberated in the desert mountains: "Dinner is ready!"

The skies flushed orange and pink as the sun disappeared like a big bald head behind the mountain. After dinner, we made our first satellite conference call. The call's first issue was the camels. "I can put together a hundred camels," Musallem said. "Maybe fifty more could come from Siwa and Farafra. I will talk to my friends in the western desert."

"What about Ethiopia and Somalia, the biggest camel population in the world?" Rowan asked. "I worked there, and I know an amazing camel herder trying his luck with new camel milk products. He's the only one making it all fair trade and organic. He's married to a Danish woman. They're based outside of Mogadishu."

---

[2] Siyala: Typical desert acacia tree indigenous to Sinai.

"Wow!" Max interjected. "That will be a long, long way, getting from Somalia to Jerusalem. Permits for a fifty-camel caravan through all those borders. Ethiopia, not a problem. Then Sudan, Egypt, and finally Israel—the most difficult border to cross, and with a hundred and fifty camels!"

"The journey by land would take about two and a half months," Rowan said.

"It's great to have Africa in!" Mona exclaimed. "Africa unite!" Gena and Mona both shouted with joy.

"All continents will be represented," Gena concluded. "The 'Spirit Holder' circle of the ceremony is a planetary effort, with one stress conflict of the Earth in focus: Jerusalem! It's like acupuncture." Kurdi echoed Sinatra's words as she started singing, "If we can make it there, we'll make it anywhere, it's up to you: Je - Ru - Salem!"

Gena was on a roll, adding, "We should re-confirm with the Pacific Island warriors and get them to meet us in Crete with their fleet! It will take them about six months to get there from the Pacific Islands."

"*Ne!*"[3] Vasilis chimed in. "And each caravan will have their own documenting team, streaming live to the world on their journey to Jerusalem."

Marikia and Little Julie had so far been quiet on the call. "Hey," Marikia said, "is the head of the UN coming to Rome?"

"I saw Greta from Sweden talking to him," said Little Julie, "and I think I can convince him about Jerusalem too!" Musallem couldn't contain himself and gave Julie and Marikia high fives. Kurdi went for the grandma hug. They really were friends, Kurdi and Little Julie. It's as if they had known and empowered each other for thousands of years. It was never clear who was mentoring who, and maybe that was the point.

Max, intuiting the end of the call, said from the other side of the screen, "I'll try my best!" And with that, the meeting was over. A beautiful virtue of our team was that we all felt a similar pulse of time which synchronized our attention and let us feel when to end our meetings. We, a spontaneous community that had met each other

---

[3] *Ne*: "Yes" in Greek.

on the road very recently, were already attuned to the precious intelligence of timing. We were a collective of holy weirdos and celestial rascals—a group of sacred agents who had found a common mission with the Earth, as Tiokasin always reminded us. Through the richness of our diversity, we embodied many of the roles of an archetypal village.

I asked Mona to come with me to our sleeping quarters. We set up our space on the soft and cozy Bedouin rug on top of the silky white sand. I felt I needed some intimacy and private time with Mona, and some grounding. I felt a sudden rush of vital joy as I realized I was alone with her. Out of nowhere, and feeling tickled in my soul, I said, "Rojava Amazonas."

"Are you calling me that?" Mona started laughing. We were in a very narrow canyon, our voices generating a multifaceted echo which was still reverberating tenfold. *Onas, onas, onas...*

"You know the Onas?" I asked. "They are one of the original peoples, a tribe from Tierra Del Fuego[4] in my native Argentina." I shouted even louder into the canyon: "Ama-zonas, Ama-zonas... Ama-zonas..."

"Yes," Mona said, "love the zones...I got that one."

"Which one?" I asked.

"All of them!" she answered. "All the planetary zones, all the directions, all the beings, and all the parts of your brain and your body too." She started scratching my head with her fingernails nonchalantly, and said, "I will give you a brain shampoo, but right now, let's start with a heart bath. Ready?"

"Of course," I said.

Mona began massaging my heart from behind. She had done it before in the double cave, and knew I loved it. She sat behind me and pierced through my personality, shield by shield. I was tearing up and then laughing, feeling deeply held by this amazing healing woman. After a while, I started weeping inconsolably. Mona held me from my solar plexus with one hand and from the back of my heart with the other. Then, she rolled me into a fetus position and embraced me

---

[4] Tierra Del Fuego: The most southern province of Argentina's twenty-two provinces.

strongly, encompassing me from all directions. She locked me into her bosom with her legs and arms. I felt like I was in a butterfly cocoon in the womb of a mama whale, utterly safe and lovingly cared for. Eventually, I fell asleep.

At dinner, we had decided that the next day would be "Vatican presentation day" prep. Musallem felt otherwise, and after breakfast, he announced, "All aboard! We're going to Meliches[5] for the night." We drove down the bumpy and beautiful road. Each stop was more stunning than the one before. Musallem showed us some massive retention spaces for rainwater. It was impressive to see the Bedouins getting ready for future unpredictable times, and it would definitely be part of Vasilis's video presentation. Around noon, we reached Wadi Ruahbiya and stopped briefly for a tea, this time at the Bedouin tents. As before, Musallem told me to lead the others to Wadi Meliches, where we would all meet. He and Suleiman would drive the long way with the jeeps and get a meal ready for us.

It felt so good to go down to Meliches with my "beloved enemy" *habibi* Sami and the entire sacred crew. As we skipped down through the colorful sandstone, we caught a glimpse of a cute and very quick *arnab,* or desert rabbit. When we finally made our way down to my house of dreams at Meliches, Gena, Sami, and Vasilis were awestruck.

"This is where you lived, prophetic rabbit?" Sami said to me. "Here you stayed four months without moving? Wow!"

"What he said!" Gena added.

While Suleiman and Musallem finished cooking dinner, we went to set up our beds for the night: a rug on top of powdered sand, a blanket below us, and two blankets on top to protect us from the night's desert cold. After a delicious dinner, we began discussing our appointment at the Vatican.

"How long is the presentation? Sami asked.

"Twenty minutes," Marikia answered.

Vasilis broke it down for us. "Screen divided in four: South, Musallem riding on a camel and leading nine more camels. North:

---

[5] Meliches: The mountain and the valley got its name from the verb "to lick." Fresh water drips from the mountain.

Murat and Kurdi riding and leading ten horses. West: Captain Rowan sailing, leading ten boats, surfers, and swimmers. East: the kids and the women, a group of fifty people walking from Bethlehem."

"Wow, I can see it!" Kurdi said excitedly.

"Actually, there's more," Vasilis continued. "Above: hot air balloon, white doves, edible balloons, and holographic animation. Below: animation for the cave ceremony—I already requested this from a friend of mine and he's on it. Heart of the Matter: animation of the Old City, mapping of the soccer game, the stars as guards at the eight gates. Concentric circles reaching the center of the spiral with the Nobel laureates, local elders, and those of different sacred traditions. Movements, clapping and humming choir, with Palestinian and Israeli soloists expressing crystallized 'collective trauma songlines' in the center."

"*Ekfaristo*, Vasilis! So precise!" I said. "Beautiful!"

"What about Marikia and Little Julie's choreography?" Kurdi asked.

"We'll make all the laureates and guests dance at the Jerusalem part, at the end of the presentation, as a real celebration," Little Julie declared.

"Maybe I'll begin the presentation with a viola intro," Mona suggested, "then your guitar?" she said, looking at me. "And we can end by singing together. We can also support the girls with the dancing at the end."

"I will introduce the last concentric circles, and the soloist pieces," Sami offered.

"And I'll demonstrate, with your help, the clapping choir and humming before the girls dance at the end," I added.

"It all sounds amazing!" Gena said.

Vasilis was on a roll. "I want to start tomorrow," he declared.

"Musallem, can we get ten camels together and begin filming?" Gena asked.

"Of course!" he said. "I'm here for you." I knew It wasn't easy to get ten camels to show up on a day's notice, but hey, this was our legendary Musallem, who made things happen Bedouin style.

The presentation was fleshing out. After the wonderfully fun shoot with Musallem, Gena, Vasilis, Kurdi, Sami, and the kids got their things ready for departure. Musallem would give Mona and me a ride to the beach camp where we would stay for a few more days. We would then cross to Jordan, traveling from Akaba to Wadi Rom. We'd stay there a couple of nights and then meet Sami, Little Julie, Marikia, Gena, and Vasilis in Amman to fly together to Rome. Gena and Vasilis had ten days to pull off this intricate production. Max was on the hologram animation, and Clemens would assist him online from Bethlehem. Thankfully, Max had gotten us all satellite phones for better communication.

This time, Mona and I decided to go to a different beach camp, further north and closer to the border of Taba. It was more intimate. Our friend the Bedouin host told us that he was very happy we were coming, and that he would be waiting for us, adding that there were no other guests. As soon as we arrived, he announced nonchalantly he had to go to Cairo for some business. He showed us the workings of the kitchen, electricity, water, and other details; provided us with some veggies, fruit, and eggs; and left us alone to wander at our own private beach in Sinai!

That night, I woke up from a powerful dream. It took me a while to find a piece of paper and pen to write it down with (the batteries had gone dead on my phone, where I usually write my notes, and I had lost my charger on the desert journey). I searched frantically, trying not to wake Mona up, doing my best not to get distracted by the myriad of thoughts coming to me at the speed of dark. All in all, I remembered most of the dream. I have no idea what it all means, but for some reason, it feels important to share it:

I am received by a beautiful, young, dark-skinned Polynesian-looking woman who shows me where the best phone reception is. As I speak with my dear brother Amir in Australia, she waits from afar, and at a certain point in our deep conversation she says something which I can't hear and disappears.

Suddenly, I'm running away from the police in Costa Rica, along with a crowd of people. Among them I distinguish some downtrodden rebels who I'm connected to in some strange way. We keep bumping into each other as the police get closer. The police catch some of the rebels. I am scared and keep running for my life through a big park.

We land through a hole in the ground into a Far-Eastern-looking print shop run by geishas. They smile, half surprised, more by the style of our fall than by the fact that I am there. As I leave the shop, I gladly meet again the dark-skinned guide with short hair. I follow her into the dark, where we see greenish tubes dangling from the ceiling of a tunnel. She takes a few hits from enormous water pipes, which are filled with ganja and hashish.

"That's how we get ready as we pass through here," she says cryptically. "We're always ready."

We finally arrive at an ultra-underground space with a bar. There, I see some familiar faces from our rebel escape. They look different than they did before. Now, each one is individuated, unlike the other crowd of indistinguishable people. One of them is a rather tall, beautiful woman with medium-length black hair that she wears in pageboy style. She begins smiling at me, flirting, dancing, and then kissing me. It is clear she likes me. She is very attractive, and I really enjoy being courted and seduced by her.

My new guide and I keep walking while kissing until we get to an adjacent room, where someone recognizes me and says, "There goes the South American." It seems as if everyone is waiting for me on the other side, next to the wall. There is a well-tended king-size bed and I sit there alone. Someone asks me, as a formal invitation, who I want to be initiated by. As I quickly ponder the question, I see a little piece of paper with the name "Rangel" written on it. It would have been natural to point at my beautiful guide as my choice. But the name gets stuck in my head as a sign, and I say without thinking, "Rangel."

Rangel is brought from another room by a group of older, well-groomed and elegant wise women. She is in her sixties and has curly hair; I remember her as one of my teachers in an eros training I once attended. The older women escort her, and then help her ceremonially onto the bed. She speaks to me earnestly and softly, making me feel comfortable and safe. Suddenly, she takes off her curly wig and intricate mask. It reveals that "she" is really a "he"—a bearded man with short black hair.

As people around the bed gasp in awe, I remain surprisingly calm. Then Rangel asks me if I want to be initiated by him. He makes it clear I can say yes or no. Still fully present and calm, I say no. A ceremonial liquid gushes forth from a corner of the bed. He takes it in a small gourd-like container, climbs down from the bed, and disappears from the room.

I hear a murmur in praise of me and my tranquility as I get up from the bed and am taken back to the dancing bar. This time Maria, that is her name, is escorting me while dancing in what seems to be an official part of the ritual. Rangel has become the happy barman and starts serenading us with an operatic tenor voice to the song "Maria" from *West Side Story*. People are celebrating as if something has been achieved or resolved.

Then I once more find myself running away from some authorities following the rebel tribe. By now they feel like friends of mine. I get a bit carried away by my joy and naivete and make the mistake of sliding down the slope into the corner of the park. They all just look back at me as they cross the corner of a short bridge, directly above. I realize I am in danger. I must get out of there as soon as possible and follow them back to the bridge, except it is hard for me to climb back up. And then, unexpectedly, I see a man under the bridge, which is made of old junk and some pieces of wood. He is half man and half tree. He shows me a thick branch I can hold to pull myself up onto the bridge. I do so, and find my friends already at a big avenue full of trees which in turn becomes a forest.

I finally wake up, exhausted, at an alternative farm in rural Central Portugal…and then I realize I am really at the beach of my Bedouin friend in Sinai, and Mona is still sleeping.

The next day we were supposed to cross the border into Eilat, Israel and then into Jordan, making our way north to meet the others in Amman.

I went for my usual early morning dip in the calm Red Sea, before the winds began. It was the best way to start the day. No humans, pets, or even trees. Just rocks, water, coral, and fish. The same place where life started fourteen billion years ago. This personal custom helped me slowly transition to a "good morning" through admiration of more recently evolved ways of life—a date tree, a cat, a camel—before approaching any human beings. After coming out of the cold and salty water and worshiping the morning sun, it was fair to say I had earned my coffee. As usual, I was the only one awake. I sat sipping my coffee and looking at the sea of reeds as the tiny waves kept gently dancing with the shore: a soft sound massage for my arteries and veins. The waters seemed to be conspiring with me to live another day.

After my morning rituals, I went back to kiss my beloved Mona. I cuddled her, entangling myself in her delicious legs and bosom, blending with the morning sun and my sea-salt fresh sparkling skin.

"I feel sick," Mona confided in a sad tone.

"Oh really?" I said, caressing her warm forehead, realizing she might have a fever.

"Yeah, I have a sore throat, and my stomach is all crampy," Mona said.

"Hmm," I considered. "Better stay in bed, rest, and try to sleep it off. I'll bring you a pot of hot healing tea."

I mixed some *samua*[6] for the stomach, *habak*[7] for the throat, cinnamon, ginger, and a tiny spoon of St. Catherine's honey. By the time I came back with the healing brew, Mona was sleeping, and sweating profusely. I realized there was no way we were traveling the next day to Jordan. I assumed my role of healer and caregiver, making her drink plenty of healthy liquids. She couldn't eat anything, though, and her constipated cramps had by now become diarrhea. After the third day, thankfully, her fever had disappeared, and she started eating again, very lightly at first. She still wasn't ready to travel yet, though, so all our plans for journeying to the amazing Wadi Rom and Petra were

---

[6] *Samua*: A Sinai indigenous medicinal desert plant good for digestive problems.
[7] *Habak*: Sinai indigenous mint. Local to the high mountain area of St. Catherine.

canceled. However, we did have to be on time to meet our beloved crew in Amman for our flight to Rome.

The day before we left for the Israeli border, Mona was back to her beaming self. She thanked me sincerely for taking care of her. I said it wasn't over, and that I was going to give her a full body massage. I put some good Persian fusion music on and opened the two-hour session with some breathwork, placing my hands on different parts of her back and lungs. I asked Mona to breathe into my hands. We began blending beyond the confines of healer and healee (is that a word?). Then, with organic CBD and arnica oil blended with some sandalwood, I proceeded to greet her muscles. I played with her imagination while stroking her as deeply as her muscles were ready to allow. At times, I stayed on specific points, and at other times I glided through. The guided imagery I chose evoked her early childhood in Senegal, including antelopes running through her quadriceps, giraffes on her neck, and elephants stomping on her feet. She lay on her stomach for what seemed like an hour, then turned on her back for another full hour. I connected and played with her whole body, including kneading with my knees, elbows, hands, and even my head. I bit her heels and chin lovingly. We breathed together throughout, even during her belly and intestine massage.

I then suggested that she rest, and Mona fell into a deep sleep for about half an hour. When she got up, I was back at her side. She smiled with her open, relaxed, happy face as she said, "Was that shamanic or what?" We made love, then went into the sea together and floated, intertwined as dolphins in slow motion before emerging from the water, both inspired and happy to be alive and in love. My poet took over. "Birds are the fish of the sky, fish are the birds of the water," I proclaimed.

"Exactly!" Mona replied. "And birds are the fingernails of trees."

I kept frolicking inside my words, taken by the pleasure of the unknown, "When joy rides poetry like a magic horse, letters become trampolines of verbs and…"

"And we need to start packing to get to Jordan on time!" Mona said, finally breaking our trance. So we did, leaving our friends' empty beach cleaner than we found it. Our crossing to Eilat and into Aqaba was uneventful. We took the bus to Amman, and then a taxi to the airport. There, we had a long wait, and Mona asked me about my mom.

I told her about my mother's breast cancer, which had since disappeared. It had happened when I was traveling through New Mexico.

Taos – 1995

THESE WERE times of intense joy, learning, and empowerment. My father had died two years before, and I was becoming my own father.

I was traveling in between production breaks with my theater company, Metatron. Our group included an architect; a tarot reader; a seventy-six-year-old ex-professor and Holocaust survivor; a Palestinian dancer; some musicians, actors, and poets; a martial artist; a yoga teacher; and a couple of circus performers. We were all united in spirit through our diversity. Our work rhythm consisted of traveling around the world to learn, each in our own field—for example, the martial artist in China, the yoga teacher in India—and coming back together after our journeys to teach each other what we'd learned. Then we would co-create a new piece for the Acco Fringe Festival reflecting our newfound *in-formation*. This artistic process continued for three years.

This time around, I was searching for Native medicine. Everything in New Mexico felt welcoming and sweetly magical. I landed in a health food store in Taos, and had drunk their smoothie, eaten one of their delicious healthy sandwiches, and had been browsing through their books for the last couple of hours. It was getting late, and I was still there with my big knapsack. A friendly, smart, and conscious-seeming young woman, accompanied by her partner, saw me and asked, "Where are you from?"

"I live now in the Galilee," I said, "but I'm originally from Argentina."

"Are you looking for a place to stay? It's getting late. I'm Meredith, and this is Pete. We live here at the shop and can give you a free hammock for the night on the patio."

She seemed cool, and I didn't have the energy to go looking for a place to stay. "That sounds great!" I replied.

Our conversation lasted only a bit longer. They showed me my hammock and served us all some soothing herbal tea. "You know," I said, "I've read, or actually devoured, all the books of Castaneda since I left Argentina in 1988—and I've come here looking for medicine." They laughed. "Ha," Pete said. "You and countless others. We're used to it, people coming here looking for medicine and the stereotypical 'old Indian shaman.'"

"Listen," said Meredith, "for a taste of Indigenous culture, there's the *pueblo*, not far from here. It's beautiful. They hold a weekly tour, which is happening tomorrow."

In the morning, I got up before the store opened. While my hosts were in the shower, I took off for the *pueblo*. I was carrying a small bag with my poetry book *Tribes of Pure Temperature* to give away and sell. As soon as I got there, the fragrance of the sweet soil reminded me strongly of my beloved Sinai. I ate some of the *pueblo's* delicious fried bread, then asked around and found the visitors' center. There was a tour starting in ten minutes. I thought to myself, *this is not exactly "the old Indian," but what the heck, it's a sunny day.* The tour guide's name was Joanne, and she was a tribal member of the Tiwa Pueblo nation. She was an artist, radiant and very present. The tour was quite interesting, and at the end, I gathered my courage and asked her, "Do you have five minutes?"

"Sure," she said, warm and friendly.

"I really enjoyed your tour and want to gift you with my new book of poetry," I said. "It's a journey from fire, through air, water, and earth. I thought you might appreciate it, as you mentioned you were also an artist."

"Thank you so much!" Joanne said. "Where are you from?"

"Argentina, but I'm based in the Galilee, Israel," I replied. "Can I ask you a sensitive question? I really don't know if it's okay to ask."

"Sure, shoot," she said, smiling invitingly.

"Do you know where I can find 'medicine?'"

"Hmmm," she said. "There are a few options. Okay, you see that cemetery at the outskirts of the *pueblo*?" She pointed into the distance and continued. "There's a little stable after it, with two horses. Next to it, there's a caravan belonging to a man named Jimmy Reyna. You can ask him."

"Can I tell him you sent me?" I asked.

"Sure," she said. Then we hugged and parted ways.

That afternoon, after enjoying the *pueblo* for a few hours as a tourist, I decided to go look for Jimmy. Gathering my bravery, I walked past the cemetery. It was getting dark, and was very quiet. I spotted the little stable with the two horses, and next to it a little RV, just as Joanne told me. That had to be it. My heart pounding, I knocked on the door.

Nothing.

"Jimmy?" I called. "Is this Jimmy Reyna's home?"

Nothing.

More than five minutes had gone by as I began to walk away. Suddenly, the motorhome's window opened, and the firm voice of an old Tiwa Indian startled me, freezing my steps.

"Who's there?"

I turned around, quite afraid; the voice was loud and scary, or at least that's how I experienced it then. Nonetheless, I turned around, told him my name and said, "I was sent by Joanne the artist/tour guide, and..." As I was about to continue, the old Indian said sharply, "Come back tomorrow," and shut the window. I remained standing in front of his door for a full minute, then realized there was nothing to do but go back to Taos. It was getting dark, and I caught the last bus to town. When I came back to my hammock hotel, my hosts, who lived behind the shop in their lush garden and communal space, welcomed me with a tease. Meredith asked rhetorically, "So you found the old medicine man? Ha-ha!" Her housemates all laughed with her.

"Well, not exactly...but he told me to come see him tomorrow."

"Is this your subtle way of asking for hospitality? You want to stay with us for the weekend then?" Pete said, picking on me.

"Is it possible?" I asked.

"You're lucky!" he answered. "Molly is leaving today for a week, and you can have her room if you want...you just need to feed her cat once a day."

"Great! No problem," I said happily. Meredith insisted on making fun of me. "So the old Indian told you to come back?" Over dinner, I told them how my day went. They smiled with suspicion. "You shouldn't have too many expectations," Pete said. "Many like you come here to magical Taos and get really disappointed."

"Okay," I nodded, a bit tired of their sarcasm, and said, "I had a long day, and I want to talk to my family in New York. Can I use the phone in the other room? After that, I'm going to bed, so good night."

"Sure, you can use the phone," Meredith replied. "Good night."

I called my mom, and my dear sister Dodi answered the phone. She was a promising pediatrician, on her second marriage with three kids and living in a brownstone on the Upper West Side. "How is your trip going?" Dodi asked. "Are you in New Mexico?"

"Yup, in Taos. It's beautiful here. I'm staying in the garden at the back of a health food co-op. Nice people are hosting me."

"I have some bad news," my sister said.

"What?" I asked anxiously.

"Mami has breast cancer. She was just diagnosed, and they are operating on her next Tuesday. I think you'd better come back to New York as soon as possible."

"Oh no...shit. Is mom in pain?" I asked.

"Not really, just disconcerted and scared."

"Okay," I said. "I will check flights tomorrow and try to get there as quickly as possible."

"Please do!" my sister insisted. We ended the conversation. It took me quite a while to fall asleep, but I finally did.

On Friday morning, I got up early before anyone else and went to the *pueblo*. I ate the amazing fried bread again, then ventured directly to the RV beyond the cemetery. This time, I was ready. I had prepared a short and clear speech which I'd learned by heart. I knocked on Jimmy's door again.

"Who's there?" the old voice shouted from the window. I held my own, and said, "My name is...I come from Argentina, and..."

As I was about to continue, surprise, surprise! Suddenly, Jimmy opened his front door and said, "Argentina? Come inside." His voice sounded soft this time, and his demeanor was that of a compassionate grandpa as he proceeded to immediately show me an album with photos from Buenos Aires. "See," he said in a calm voice. "This was in El Tigre,[8] where we did a ceremony organized by a doctor, a Jewish doctor."

"Wow," I exclaimed, "El Tigre is where I used to train and play soccer. Amazing! I'm also Jewish and live in Israel now. I grew up in Buenos Aires!" He didn't seem at all surprised, and continued gently showing me more of the pictures. I recognized amongst them an *inipi*.[9] Then Jimmy prepared some coffee for us and asked me straight up, "What are you looking for?"

"I'm looking for medicine," I replied bluntly. I thought then that I was not supposed to use the actual word *peyote*, so simply said "medicine." That much I knew, or thought I knew.

"Aha," Jimmy said. "Why do you want medicine?" I told him that I'd spoken on the phone with my sister in New York last night and had learned that my mom had just been diagnosed with breast cancer and was getting operated on next Tuesday. My sister was a doctor, I said, and had suggested that I return to New York as soon as possible.

"Well," Jimmy said, "this Sunday is Mother's Day. You came in good time. A new roadman[10] will be initiated to lead the ceremony in honor of Mother's Day. His own mother, who is sick, will be there participating inside the *tipi*. You can come and pray for your Mom's healing."

"Really?" I asked, excited. "I can come?"

---

[8] El Tigre: A beautiful area on the outskirts of Buenos Aires. A wonderful river and an island. An area home to famous sports clubs, amongst them the Jewish club Hacoaj, for whom I played soccer.
[9] *Inipi*: Lakota heart and spirit cleansing ceremony. Sometimes called "sweat lodge" by white people. Going into the dark womb of the earth and coming out again reborn, midwifed by "ancestor" hot stones which have water poured on them. It is a praying circle which traditionally includes four rounds.
[10] *Roadman*: One of the names for the leader of a peyote ceremony in the Native American Church.

"Yup. Just get here early, around 2 PM, with warm clothes and a blanket, and we'll go together."

"Do I need to know anything beforehand?" I inquired, a bit apprehensive.

"No, don't worry," Jimmy reassured me. "I will be with you. Just don't be late. We'll have some driving to do."

"Okay," I said. "Thank you so much." I shook Jimmy's hand and left.

Now my brain was scrambling. I was thinking a mile a minute. I had to get back to my mother as soon as possible. I checked flights, and there was still one available seat that night, which was a Friday, and the next available seat wasn't until Tuesday. I felt the pressure to reach a decision before I got back to the gang at the co-op.

When have I ever been invited by an old Indian to attend a ceremony? I asked myself. Never! It's Mother's Day, and I can pray for her. My prayers will be more powerful than if I succumb to the worry patterns of my family life in New York and panic about my mother's cancer.

Finally reaching a decision, I passed by an internet cafe and booked my flight for Tuesday. Then I called my sister and told her with full confidence that I was coming back on Tuesday. She sounded surprised that I was delaying my return, but was too busy to keep talking. Dodi was in charge, helping my mom with preliminary tests at the hospital before the operation.

"Okay," she said, and hung up.

I went back to my kind but skeptical hosts. Pete asked, "What now, Castaneda boy? Has the old shaman told you to come again? Ha-ha...is there a ceremony on the way? I nodded, but didn't answer. "By the way," he continued, "you can move to Molly's room now. She's gone already, and it might rain today." I decided that I would say no more until after the ceremony. I simply told Pete that I had booked a flight to New York for Tuesday because my mom was sick.

On Sunday, I packed my blanket and warm clothes and went to Jimmy's. My fear this time wasn't because of sweet Jimmy, but because of the ceremony itself. I arrived on time as promised, and

Uncle Jimmy, as he was known by his people, was already packing his pick-up truck.

"I gotta feed the horses," he told me. "You can put your stuff in the truck meanwhile."

When he was done, we both hopped aboard, and he started driving.

"Where are we going?" I asked.

"To the sacred Blue Lake. It's only used for ceremonies. Don't worry—just stay close to me and you'll be fine."

We arrived after two hours, and Uncle Jimmy parked his truck next to the other cars. We joined the people with lots of "hellos." Everyone knew Jimmy there. I just nodded politely. We drank some water and Uncle Jimmy instructed me to get in line to enter the tipi. The sun was setting, and the Blue Lake skies were exquisite beyond description. About forty Indigenous and about five "whites" like me were about to enter the tipi. And I was terrified!

Just before I entered the tipi, I recited the *shema* prayer as I thought I might not come out of this one. Fortunately, Uncle Jimmy sat next to me. Then someone said, "Fred couldn't come. Uncle Jimmy, could you do the cedar?"[11] We were sitting in a circle inside the tipi, and it was pitch dark as the fire was still being lit. Jimmy said "Sure," and got up. Amid the confusion, I lost my blanket—and most importantly, Uncle Jimmy was no longer next to me. The fire was fully lit now, and I found myself sitting in a tipi full of Indians. To my left was a man mocking me. I was terrible at rolling the tobacco inside the corn husks, and it kept falling onto my lap.

"What are you doing here?" the man sneered. "Are you a policeman? CIA? FBI? Come on, tell me."

"What? I came with Uncle Jimmy," I said, very uncomfortably. I finally succeeded in rolling my tobacco, our first task of the ceremony. By then, we were all praying our intentions. Even as the peyote sacrament went around, the man to my left kept staring and making fun of me. I ingested some peyote and the mocking got worse. "CIA? FBI?

---

[11] Cedar: Used for cleansing and purifying through its smudging smoke and sweet fragrance.

What are you doing here, white man?" As I was about to answer him, the man sitting to my right spoke to me. "I'm a Lakota,"[12] he told me. "I will help you. The man to your left is Diné and will bother you all night, if you let him. Now open your mouth and swallow this."

My friendship with the Lakota people would continue to this day. Fast forward twenty-four years, to 2019 at the third "Defend the Sacred" gathering. I was triggered by someone in a challenging situation, and in a moment of rage, I began shouting. My traumas erupted like a volcano, and I lost it. Without saying a word, our beloved Lakota elder—one of the initiators of Standing Rock, the late Ladonna Bravebull Allard—stood up instantly and embraced me, interrupting my anger in a tight hug. Immediately following her with the velocity of the wind, Tiokasin, our friend and Lakota elder, placed his big arm around my shoulder and took me for a walk. Neither of them uttered a sound. It was clean technology: silent and exquisite peacemaking at its best.

Meanwhile, back in the Blue Lake medicine ceremony, the Lakota sitting to my right gave me an extra generous portion of peyote powder—and within twenty minutes, everything disappeared. No more Diné, no more Lakota, no more Uncle Jimmy, no more fear. I heard only the water drum[13] pulsating through the universe and the fire design glowing in its beauty. I felt more alive every instant. Someone passed me the rattle, and I began singing what came out from me. By then, the tipi was flying in song and spirit. The mom of the roadman and his children were sitting next to the altar. I was praying for my mother and started crying. The sunrise came as a balm with the water woman[14] offering us a chance to pray, and then drink, for the first time since sunset. I felt reborn. We got out of the tipi one by one and had a scrumptious communal buffalo meal. We now saw the sacred

---

[12] Lakota: These original people from Turtle Island were composed of seven nations, and their relatives are the Dakota and the Nakota. White people refer to them as the Sioux Nation. They were the last Indigenous nation to fight the US Army in the late 1800's.

[13] Water drum: ceremonial drum used in peyote ceremonies. Assembled and disassembled after each ceremony.

[14] Water woman: At the end of the peyote ceremony, there's usually a woman who brings and blesses the water before everyone drinks it at sunrise.

grounds in daylight. We gave a few hugs, shook some hands, and then Uncle Jimmy said, "It's time to go."

I returned late to the compound, and luckily my hosts were all out. I was exhausted and fell asleep till Monday afternoon. When I got up, to my surprise, there was a really nice farewell meal for me.

"So, what happened?" Meredith asked. "You slept a lot!" I told them about the ceremony as best I could. Pete said, "It must be the Native American Peyote Church. I'm surprised you found them so quickly." My plane was leaving early in the morning, so we said goodbye that night. When I landed, I took a taxi straight to the hospital where my mom was recovering from the operation. My sister said it all went well, and that they were just waiting a couple of weeks for some definite tests. After a few weeks in New York, I returned to my theater company in Israel and flew Uncle Jimmy there as our guest medicine man.[15] Our dress rehearsal was a peyote ceremony on Yom Kippur. Shortly before that, my mom's breast cancer went into full remission, until this day! As I write this, she has just turned eighty-seven.

As I finished the story, we realized we just had another hour before meeting our friends. We found ourselves involved once again in conversation about our Big Vision, and began enthusiastically planning for our twenty-minute presentation at the Nobel Peace Laureate Summit at the Vatican.

---

[15] Medicine man: Shaman, or the person who can eat the pain of the tribe and bring healing to the people.

CHAPTER 9

NOBEL LAUREATES

When Sami, Marikia, and Little Julie arrived at the airport cafe, Mona and I were just getting started. After our bubbly hugs and hellos, they told us that Gena, Vasilis, and Max were already in Rome, waiting for us at the hotel. A car would pick us up at the airport, whose chauffeur would be holding a sign reading "Nobel Peace Laureate Summit." Mona debriefed the others. "We only got to the opening music," she began. As she finished her sentence, we heard the last call for all passengers flying to Rome to please board immediately at gate 29. We ran as fast as we could, and just made it onto the airplane, sweating copiously, breathing, and laughing hard. Marikia and Little Julie had raced us all the way to the plane.

We only had two nights in Rome before our big presentation. In those days, there was a lot of talk about wild love, dark matter, black holes, and a big resurgence of the mysteries. We needed to include all of that in our presentation, for as mystical flexitarian anarchists say, "If I can't dance, it's not my revolution." We trusted our dear wizard Vasilis and our captain Gena's excellent, relaxed production overview and their ability to cover it all.

Our plane arrived in Rome, and the Laureates Summit had put us up in a five-star hotel. The first thing we did was turn in all our desert-dusted clothes to the hotel's laundry. Immediately after that, Mona and I got some well-deserved sleep in our room's soft and immaculate king-size bed. After all, we had journeyed from Sinai, then rushed through Israel, Jordan, and all the way to Rome. Marikia, Little Julie, and Sami went to the hotel pool. When we woke up, we had a message waiting for us at reception saying that Gena and Vasilis would meet us for dinner at the hotel at 8 PM. Max was busy, he would join us the next morning for breakfast. Ibrahim would be joining us on screen from Paris with Ronaldo from Brazil, announcing all the sports stars who had confirmed. Laura would pass to Ibrahim the list of famous artists who were coming to Jerusalem.

So there we were, at a five-star hotel in Rome. A colorful and diverse squad to say the least: Sami, our dear brother and Palestinian activist; Vasilis, our Greek hero; Gena, an Afro-American genius and cool queen supreme; Marikia, the brilliant and swift Swedish teenager; her little sister Julie, a cosmic crystal granddaughter; Mona the goddess; and me. While we waited for what turned out to be excellent Italian *gnocchi al pomodoro*, we sipped our Chianti. With Gena's help, Vasilis ran through the timeline of the presentation so we could understand the context, the stage setting, and our positions in the space. They had already created a tentative sequence which each of us simply had to flesh out with content. There would be four screens placed at the four directions, with sub-screens for all the traveling groups. Marikia would be coming from below the floor on an open elevator with her puppet and Little Julie would enter from above on an acrobatic aerial silk. They had figured all this out themselves and Max had convinced the Laureate Summit committee to go ahead with all of it (after donating a substantial amount of money for their next summit).

The next day, we had only one hour for our dress rehearsal in the actual space while our audience was having lunch at an adjacent dining room of the Vatican. I was busy with Mona on the music and Sami with his spoken word. We knew our exact stage coordinates and cues, thanks to the precise work of Vasilis and Gena, but the quality and content of our routines, music, and words were up to us.

The Presentation

THE BIG day had arrived. Max introduced us very briefly in just one tight minute. Like a good Swiss, he was extremely precise.

Reality suddenly sank in: there we were, at the lavishly luxurious, historic, though tragically corrupted Vatican, with so many larger-than-life characters in the room with us! Amongst them were ex-Irish president Mary Robinson, the Guatemalan Rigoberta Menchu, Malala from Afghanistan, and a couple of Nobel laureates I had met personally: Perez Esquivel from Argentina and His Holiness the Dalai Lama.

Vasilis, who was in charge at the media control cabin, converted the room into a black hole as if it were a planetarium. The laureates, plus a selected few invitees including Pope Francis, gasped audibly. As the Big Bang exploded, forming the galaxies and begetting life, a timeline appeared on the screen: fourteen billion years, from water and rock formations up to the appearance of human beings. The whole evolution of the universe in a nutshell. Then, cross-cultural celebrations from the sixth century BC filled the screen. There were animations and illustrations of Isaiah the Prophet in the Fertile Crescent; Lao Tzu in China; Gautama Buddha in India; Heraclitus in Greece; and the Mapuche, Aymara, and Lakota cultures from Turtle Island and the Condor lands.

Then the timeline fast-forwarded to the thirteenth century AD with the Sufis from Khorasan and Turkey, Rumi, Hafiz, Yunus Emre, and Bektashi; and the Kabbalists from Spain, France, Italy, Morocco, and Egypt. Fast images followed of Leonardo Da Vinci, Sor Juana Ines de la Cruz, Rabia al Adawiyya, Beethoven, Gandhi, Tesla, Albert Einstein, Buckminster Fuller, Etty Hillesum, Rosa Parks, Martin Luther King, John Lennon, Mother Teresa, and Bob Marley, and then the youth movements led by Greta Thunberg, Emma Gonzales, Youth for the Ganges, and the Earth Guardians. It all moved forward at a voracious pace. Vasilis' visual masterpiece was accompanied by Mona's haunting viola. At the end, four screens plus their sub-screens, synchronized to the second, popped down from the four cardinal directions and their sub-directions.

It was surreal to see our friends on site for the first time. There was our southern camel caravan: Somalia, Ethiopia and our own Musallem from Sinai. There was our northern horse caravan: Urfa (Murat and Kurdi), Uruguay (Stacy), Portugal (Freya), and Galilee

(Maya), all riding their horses. There was our western boat fleet: Crete (Rowan), and the Pacific Island warriors on boats and canoes, including surfers and swimmers. Finally, there was our eastern walking caravan: Boulder, Colorado (the Earth Guardians); the Standing Rock Lakota youth; the Ganges youth from India; and our own *Follow the Young* troupe (Kai, Clemens, and Ana) making their way towards the separation wall in Bethlehem. Each caravan's departure locations and estimated arrivals in Jerusalem appeared onscreen. A closeup of each caravan leader's glowing face closed the frame. They now appeared as animations, approaching Hebron from the four directions: camels, horses, boats, swimmers, walkers, and bicycles.

Following a sharp break into 3D slow motion, a hologram of the Double Cave of the Machpelah and Hebron emerged from below. In it, Marikia, in a hyper-fast dance with her puppets, told of the re-encounter of Ishmael and Isaac at the burial place of their father Abraham, and the healing meeting of Hagar and Sarah that we were praying for. Mona played the viola, and I joined in, tapping on my miniature Moroccan ceramic drum—which still sounded, after all those years, like a mix of tribal pagan Saharan and Berber trance. Out of an epic lighting transition came yet another 3D holographic animation of Palestinian and Israeli men and women, representing the three monotheistic religions, holding hands and surrounding the grave of their common ancestor Abraham.

I sang the first three verses of my song "Wholly One," corresponding to the three Abrahamic sacred paths:

"*Adonai Hoshia Hamelech Yaaneinu Beyom Koreinu*
Ya Rahim Ya Rahman Dul Jalali Uali Kram
Holy Father, Holy Son, Holy Spirit Three in One."[1] [2]

Mona joined with a viola solo. By then, all four directions and caravans merged into the different arrival areas at the outskirts of the

---

[1] *Oh, master redeemer and sovereign, Answer us when we call you, Oh merciful, oh compassionate, You're revealed through your generosity*
, Holy Father, Holy Son, Holy Spirit Three in One: This song of mine is called "Wholly One." It comes from my album, *The Human Project*. Each of these mantras represents a different sacred tradition which together complete the ONE puzzle of Creation. Here, they are translated into English.

[2] To listen to "Wholly One," go to page 227.

Old City of Jerusalem. As Ibrahim came up onscreen with Ronaldo and Zanetti in full soccer gear, spikes and all, he gave us a list of the sports stars, fashionistas, and Hollywood icons who'd already confirmed to guard the eight gates of the Old City. While bouncing the ball with their feet, knees, shoulders, necks, and heads the soccer players told us the names of the all-star lineup for the soccer game at the Sultan's Pool and the fashion show.

All of us were seeing this for the very first time. We had all been blown away by the first twelve minutes. Sami then began to speak, eloquent as ever, voicing the trauma of the children of Abraham—first as a Palestinian, then as an Israeli. I sang the last three verses of "Wholly One" with Mona adding a vocal solo in Uolof, and Little Julie came gliding down on a purple silk from the ceiling. Recorded claps, hums, and soloists singing of Palestinian and Israeli traumas of violence and massacres grew in volume, as Sami and I prostrated ourselves in prayer. Little Julie and Marikia helped us rise to our feet, and Mona joined us for our last circle. In slow motion, we posed in a short series of synchronized movements based on the prayer movements of the three Abrahamitic religions, then held each other's hearts. The presentation had ended in exactly twenty minutes. The laureates and special guests looked awe-stricken. The room was in absolute silence—until the Dalai Lama got up and started cheering. "Wonderful, that's wonderful!" he exclaimed. Mary Robinson and Pope Francis followed, until they all finally rose to give us a standing ovation. Vasilis the magician turned on the house lights—and we were back again, at the fucking Vatican!

It was time for the Q&A. According to the plan, we only had ten minutes left. Our mastermind Gena, our maverick Vasilis, and our benefactor Max joined us onstage. Max, now back in his MC role, didn't know whether to burst out crying or laughing. He stoically kept it together, and as we all hugged and congratulated each other, he asked the laureates and guests, "Any questions?" We all turned dead silent as assistants brought chairs, a table and a pitcher along with glasses of water for everyone. The Dalai Lama suggested a minute of silence before we all began talking again. Relieved, we all complied.

Malala, the youngest laureate, went first. "Thanks so much for this. You made me cry with hope! How can we get involved and help you? I definitely want to. And I feel many in this room do as well."

We were all way too excited to speak coherently. "Go *habibi*," Sami said to me. "You answer this one." Reassured by him, I answered, "We came here to invite you to take part in this healing ceremony in Hebron ending in Jerusalem, for the sake of the children of Abraham and all sentient beings."

"We will be very happy and honored to host any of you who want to participate," Max added.

"I'm not a Nobel Laureate," Pope Francis said, "but I would love to participate."

It was then that Little Julie burst forth, addressing Pope Francis directly. Pointing at me, she said, "He's Argentinian, you can speak to him in Spanish. You must know his father, the late Rabbi Marshall T. Meyer." Everyone laughed with love. No one could resist Little Julie's adorableness, courage, and dimples. Francisco came forward. "*¿Así que el hijo de Marshall Meyer? Mira vos... ¿Y dónde naciste?*"

"*En Córdoba, pero crecí en Buenos Aires*," I answered.[3]

The Dalai Lama said, "I know these two. I met them before. Right? Sami, I met you in Bethlehem? And you, looking at me? Didn't you come to my office in Dharamsala?" We both nodded, proud of his acknowledgment. "That's all wonderful! I want to participate!" said HH and laughed so hard that most everyone followed suit, until the whole room became an enormous laughing parlor—quite some healing for the Vatican. From the corner of my eye, I could see the Swiss guards trying to contain their laughter. It didn't take long until one of them lost it, and then they all joined in, dropping their funny colorful hats on the floor.

"*Ecole qua la risa e divina!*" Francis said. "*Avanti alegria!*"[4] Then

---

[3] *Así que es el hijo de Marshall Meyer?! Mira vos... ¿Y dónde naciste? En Córdoba, pero crecí en Buenos Aires*: In Spanish: "So you are the son of Marshall Meyer?! How about that... Where were you born?" "In Cordoba, but I grew up in Buenos Aires."
[4] *Ecole qua la risa e divina! Avanti alegria*: In Italian: "Laughter is divine, may joy prosper."

Adolfo Perez Esquivel got up and said, "*Gaby Meyer, el hijo de nuestro valiente y entrañable Marshall!*[5] Of course we'll support this!"

I whispered in Max's ear that I had something to add, and he gave me the mic. Tiokasin, my Lakota friend, showed up in my telepathic field as if helping me to spell it out. "In the ceremony," I said, "there will be youth, women, a council of elders, representatives of First Nations, and Indigenous and original peoples from all over the Earth."

"We will bring the Irish whistles, bagpipes and bodhrans if you want," announced Mary Robinson, joyfully.

"Could they come on the boats from Crete?" Mona asked.

"We could arrange that," Mary answered, humoring her. She turned to Sami. "Are Palestinians from Gaza involved in this?" He answered her immediately, as if ready for the question. "Not yet, but we are trying our best to have them be a part." And then, looking straight into the eyes of the Pope who he had met the year before, Sami said, "Remember, we came here with my Japanese peace-seeking friends, and you asked us to pray for you. We have indeed prayed for you. And now I would like to request His Holiness to intercede for our Israeli permits."

Gena handed Max a little note. He read it quickly, then added, "We also need your help for permits from the north, for Syria and Turkey, and for the southern camel caravan coming from Somalia, Sudan, and Egypt." Pope Francis, who was cornered from all directions, said, "I will try my best, for the peace of the Sacred City of Jerusalem and *Tierra Santa*."

Following protocol, Max was prompted to close. The Q&A had ended; the laureates would continue their closed session after a ten-minute break. Everyone had left the building except for Sami, Max, and me lingering in the hallway. Malala was still congratulating us and talking about bringing some Qawwali masters to Jerusalem for the ceremony. As we were leaving, an emissary of the pope told Max

---

[5] *Gaby Meyer, el hijo de nuestro valiente y entrañable Marshall*: In Spanish: "The son of our courageous and dear Marshall."

that before we left Rome in the morning, Francisco wanted to have a word with us.

We were walking on air when Max called us, skipping down the sumptuous steps. "Come on, sacred agents!" He took us to dinner, where we got tipsy, first on Campari with ice, soda, and a twist of orange, and then on a red Chianti with our meal. Even Marikia drank. Little Julie dug deep into the best mascarpone in the world. We ate at the hotel, which was convenient since we couldn't really walk in straight lines anymore. The next morning, Sami, Max, and I had to meet with the Pope at 9:30 AM sharp. The others were lucky enough to sleep late. The Vatican people knew we were flying at 1 PM. So, it was clear it wouldn't be a very long meeting—fifteen minutes tops!

"*La combinación del fútbol con la paz es algo que me alegra el corazón, y encima en la Santa Jerusalén! Una maravilla!*"[6] the Pope proclaimed as I walked in. A translator immediately shared his words in English for all to understand. The Pope looked at Sami. "I can take care of the permits from Gaza and will try my best with the full list I got from our friend Max: Iran, Syria, Jordan, Iraq, Turkey, Ethiopia, Somalia, Sudan and Egypt." Then addressing all of us, he said, "I would like to personally invite the imams and rabbis I've been in touch with for interfaith peace dialogue all these years—so maybe you can leave three slots for me, an imam and a rabbi."

"We sure will," Max assured him "It would also be our privilege to have you invite three main local monotheistic religious leaders to the Old City of Jerusalem on our behalf." Pope Francis gifted me an old *shofar*[7] which used to belong to an Italian Kabbalist from the thirteenth century. To Sami, he gave a rosary which had belonged to St. Francis of Assisi himself. To Max he gifted a copy of the Vatican's history. After a warm blessing and hugs all around, we left the Vatican and hurried to the hotel. Mona had packed my little bag and my guitar

---

[6] *La combinación del fútbol con la paz es algo que me alegra el corazón, y encima en la Santa Jerusalén! Una maravilla*: In Spanish: "The blend of soccer and peace brings joy to my heart. Furthermore, it's in Holy Jerusalem. How wonderful!"

[7] *Shofar*: A Hebrew ceremonial ram's horn. It was used for announcing new moons and holidays. Nowadays it is blown mainly in the Days of Awe as an awakening call for the New Year.

for me. Even so, we barely made it to our flights on time. Sami and the girls were off to Bethlehem, through Amman; Max, to Switzerland for a well-earned vacation with his beloved Laura. Vasilis and Gena would stay working in Rome and meet us later in Portugal.

It was from Portugal that we would witness the launch of the actual caravans on pilgrimage to Jerusalem.

CHAPTER 10

BACK TO PORTUGAL

It was summer. We landed in Lisbon, just in time, then had to drive and arrive before dark to a friend's regenerative forest project in central Portugal. We got there at sunset. There was just one volunteer left, who showed us how to feed the dog, the cats, and the rabbit, and irrigate the gardens, pots, and everything else in need of water. The next morning, she had left us a note saying she was off. She had written some last instructions and told us that Miguel and his family would be coming back in a week. Mona and I were all alone at the river farm. This was the second empty paradise resort granted to us for free, which had to be a good sign. We slept in a big dome, and there was some food in the fridge: veggies, grains, cheese, beers, wine, butter, and bread. Enough for a week for the two of us, anyway.

As soon as the volunteer left the next morning, the first thing we did was dip into the fresh and delightful Pera River. After we came out, Mona looked straight into my eyes, "Please let's not speak about the project." In fact, she insisted we go into full silence for three days and three nights. "I need the quiet," she said with full authority. "Real sacred action has to be rooted in silence and mystery." We had been high from the outside world and now Mona challenged our balance, encouraging us to be high from the inside too. I agreed, because I'd been challenged by my Goddess. As I had learned from experience, when she proposed something seriously, it worked for me too. So we went into silence for three days.

After eating, drinking, washing dishes, and bathing in the river without saying a word for three full days, we found it hard to start talking again at first. As we re-encountered language, we both noticed the rhythm of our thoughts had changed, and our words came out heavily and slowly. It was a recalibration of sorts; we were re-aligning. Mona was disturbed and wanted to explore if this really was her path to follow. She was questioning my "savior-of-the-world syndrome," my messianic tradition, my father's work. At the river, the day before our silent retreat, Mona had asked me some tough questions. "Are you trying to outdo your father? Are you in competition with him?" The morning after, though, she came to me by surprise, giving me a nourishing, present hug and a sweet kiss on my lips. She simply said, "I'm with you all the way. Thank you! My fiery magical fish." As if nothing had happened, she started giggling, put on some funky music, and started dancing, seducing me to dance with her in the morning-wet grassy moss next to the dome.

Our insides had been dealing with turmoil. Now, we opened our laptops to the outside world. US police were arresting Indigenous elders at sacred Mauna Kea in Hawaii, record heat waves were cooking Siberia, and big fires had just hit Sertã, close by in Central Portugal. Nevertheless, it felt inevitable to continue our quest; it seemed like our destiny, especially after the endorsement of the Pope and the Nobel laureates. And yes! We had just gotten news from Ibrahim: Messi was in! Now it was certain: we had no excuse to drop the ball.

Max, in tandem with Clemens, was by now fully engaged in creating the hologram map. They had sent us an urgent message to get all of our communication out of WhatsApp immediately and move to the safer app Signal, as one of the groups they were involved with had been hacked. We didn't want any of those big names to leak to the press without our consent, so we followed their advice, right there and then.

It was time to go south, to Alentejo, close to where we would meet the rest of our crew. Max had arranged for us to stay at an old mill with a little pond full of lotuses, overlooking the valley near a tiny town called Amoreiras Gare. It was the perfect setting. Vasilis and Gena made sure we were equipped with state-of-the-art screens, projectors, and a strong internet signal. And no matter how bad the news— fires, deforestation, species becoming extinct—it felt like we couldn't go back. Even as Greenland, the Arctic, and Antarctica were melting and the Amazonian, Siberian, Indonesian and Congolese forests were burning. This re-membering of the human family, all the nations finally together at one focal point of our Mother Earth at the same time, in Jerusalem, supported by our elders, the animals, the trees, and all beings, praying in pursuit of sacred Life, was cheering us on. Apparently, our quest for the "sacredness" of the human part of the big puzzle had its own melody which was carrying us forward. The Great Hoop, The Wholly One was sending us wild clues as they emerged through the cracks of Mystery.

We were set in our positions, in tune and ready for the first launch from East Africa: a caravan of camels and humans on pilgrimage to Jerusalem. Probably the first since the Queen of Sheba, who ended up marrying Solomon, the Wise King of Peace: a lineage through which several great great great great great great great spiritual grandchildren later begot good old Bob Nesta Marley.

CHAPTER 11

LAUNCH OF THE CARAVANS

"I'M HEARING a signal from Somalia," Vasilis announced. "They are releasing some big storks that will fly to Jerusalem, above the camels. They tell me these birds know the camels well—they grew up together. So now they are on their way: due north!"

The first camel contingent had left from the border between Somalia and Ethiopia towards Sudan and then Egypt, to join the Sinai southern caravan onto Jerusalem. At the same time, Gena received signals of movement on two fronts. The first was from the Uruguayan horse riders, who had begun their journey by ship towards Portugal where they would travel on horseback towards Turkey and eventually join the northern horse caravan. The second signal was from the Pacific Islands warriors, a contingent traveling on an enormous ship with their original boats and canoes on board, to join the western caravan in Crete.

It had begun! There was no stopping now. And yet, in some intimate part of my heart, I was still in search of my quiet, beautiful, clean, river community. Loving friends and neighbors around, healthy food grown locally, and abundant empathy for the tons of refugees which were predicted in later catastrophes.

As we waited for dinner, Max updated us about the map. We had a satellite talk with the kids from Bethlehem, who broke it down for us. Clemens shared the news: in each town where there had been caravan departures—Somalia, Ethiopia, Uruguay, and Vanuatu in the Pacific Islands—they had released the online holographic map. The next day, Mona and I were off to Israel. We would be in touch with Musallem as soon as the camel caravan got to Egypt, a month after crossing Sudan. That would coincide with when the boats sailed out from Crete towards Haifa and the smaller ports. Gena, Vasilis, Max and Laura had set up camp in an elegant and spacious home in Ein Karem. Max had also rented a home in the Armenian quarter, as our center of operations in the Old City of Jerusalem. Another two-story home served as our press and media center, right next to the Sultan's Pool at the crossing between east and west Jerusalem. Mona and I went up north for a couple of weeks and reconnected with Maya and her herd of horses in the Galilee. We got in touch with Sami and started to dream up and plan the actual healing ceremonies in Hebron and Jerusalem.

When the time came for the synchronized launchings almost a month later, everything was ready. The relay went like this:

Horses from the north: The Uruguayan horse riders had left Portugal, heading to Turkey to join the northern caravan from Urfa to Jerusalem.

Camels from the south: The camels from Somalia and Ethiopia had miraculously crossed safely through Sudan and had arrived in Egypt. They had joined the Sinai contingent to form the southern camel caravan to Jerusalem.

Boats from the west: The Pacific Islanders had reached Crete to join the western fleet towards the entry ports of Haifa, Caesarea, Herzliya, and Jaffa.

By the time all the contingents started approaching the holy land by boat, camel, and horse, Mona and I had already moved to Ein Karem. The map was gaining online traction and had also been launched in Turkey, Crete, Rojava, Standing Rock, Taos, Ireland, South Africa, India, Iraq, Cyprus, Iran, and Norway. Wherever there was an official guest of the ceremony on pilgrimage to Jerusalem, their trip was preempted by the launch of our map.

Around this time, our Indigenous leaders and sports, arts, fashion, and peace luminaries began arriving in Jerusalem. Meanwhile, the small contingent of canoes, surfers, and swimmers who had joined the western boat caravan in Cyprus had docked at Jaffa's port. They had synchronized their departure with the horses, who had already arrived in the Galilee, and the camels who had crossed successfully (at least one hundred and fifty of them) into Israel—plus the local ones, who were now stationed at Beer Sheva, resting and waiting for the last part of their trail to Jerusalem. Finally, the walkers from the east, stationed at Bethlehem, were still on hold, waiting for a tiny contingent coming all the way from Basra, Iraq to join them. The Pope, Fridays for Future, the Earth Guardians, Youth for Ganges, March of our Lives, the Indigenous youth, and Women Wage Peace would be walking together to Hebron, and from there onward to Jerusalem. In short: the camels were stationed at Beer Sheva, the horses at Park Shuni, the walkers in Bethlehem, and the bicycles at Latrun Monastery.

The celebratory chain of events was generating a fertile field in resonance with the trusted and beloved wave of people arriving in Jerusalem. The holographic map was taking off and having its effect. The word was out, and the major online and cable news channels were covering the massive movement. It seemed as if a significant representation of human beings were remembering their evolutionary moment on Earth to be initiated into maturity. We humans are the youngest siblings of Creation. As infantile terror-makers and juvenile delinquents, we are the ones who break stuff out of clumsiness and ignorance and get a thrill out of our own inventions without considering the consequences. We're the ones who get carried away by success and glory and commit reckless acts of destruction. We are the last creatures to arrive to this world. Accordingly, we have much less experience than our elders: the animals, the trees, the mountains, the rivers.

Nevertheless, as the Benjamins, the last born in the family, we are usually cherished and indulged, loved and giggled with. The moment when human beings tenderly create a piece of art, sing, recite a poem, tell a story, or cry and laugh in beauty, angels rejoice—and clouds, baobabs, and wallabies too. It seems that even hummingbirds and zebras like to listen to our songs. When we are aligned with Life, our elder beings appreciate our contribution to the Hoop of Life. It appears that we humans also have a role as "sacred agents" in the poly-concert of beings within the body of Nature. According to Hebrew legend, that's why when confronted by the Divine, the Angel of Peace defended the creation of Human, while the Angel of Truth argued it would be a disaster and tried to convince God not to go ahead with it. Fortunately for us, the Angel of Peace won over the Angel of Truth, and human beings were created from and with the Earth.

Travelers, activists, artists, peace pilgrims, and guests were converging in Jerusalem, from the four corners of the Earth. That week, the spirits of Adam, Eve, and even Lilith felt palpable as we, their offspring, hosted a new future. It seemed that our ancestors, the patriarchs and matriarchs of the Semitic family, the children of Shem, son of Noah, became accessible in their shrine. Their precious archetypes felt approachable; they had come back to Life. Somehow, in a nonlinear dreamlike dimension, the Universe knew that the meeting of the offspring of Isaac and Ishmael would ripple out across all realities. Their spirits' encounter would happen at the same sacred location—but this time, by digging into a deeper root level, this encounter would have a very different result, surprising our collective perceptions, agreements, and stereotypes. It would be a sweetening of judgment, a rekindling of primordial love.

In those days, constellations of healthy life were replicating themselves in the *wholly land* more than we had ever expected. Clans came with the explicit mission of sharing their gift of presence to help clean up our collective act. It felt like there was an opening for a happier, healthier, and more beautiful life together in diversity at the "wholly Fertile Crescent."

Finally, it was time. The four caravans converging on Jerusalem had become a powerful meme on social media, in the global news, and on highway billboards throughout the world. It was exhilarating to see everyone arriving: so many boats, surfers, and swimmers arriving into the port of Jaffa, then switching onto bicycles reaching the Latrun Monastery. Hundreds of camels were leaving Beer Sheva and horses were leaving the Galilee, all bound for Jerusalem. A life feast. A celebration of the possible. By now, Mandela's slogan, "It always looks impossible until it's done" had become our mantra.

I kissed Mona with passion, and in that kiss, we felt the rafts of the Polynesians, the Australian swimmers, the camels from Somalia, and the walkers from Jordan and Palestine. We felt the beat of hooves thundering across Rojava, Turkey, the Galilee, Uruguay, and Portugal. It was the global body awakening our Eros, as it should, tantrically. The essential and unmediated blending with our Earth's health. The human nation remembering our sacred role. In the flesh of our lips, in our tongues, in our embrace, in the muscles of our legs and our skin. The Skin of Great Spirit, the Organs of the Goddess, the Bones of Allah, the Sinews of the Great Mystery and the Blood Vessels of Ein Sof. Our primary relationship with the Divine, getting played by our kisses, by our eloquence and stories, by our eyes and ears. The kinesthetic Godly dance of all these creatures, reverberating as the hum of a wholly roar inside our lovemaking. In my testicles, the vital flame of life and in the tremors of Mona's juices, the elixir of Divine immanent breath.

CHAPTER 12

BEYOND GRIEF — CAVE OF MACHPELAH, IBRAHIMI MOSQUE

THE WALK from Bethlehem began at 6 AM. By then, most of the horses from the north, the camels from the south, and the bicycles from the west had parked on the outskirts of Jerusalem and hundreds of thousands of people were setting up camps surrounding the Old City. Nothing of the sort had been seen in Jerusalem since the festival pilgrimages in the times of The Temple. A hundred thousand people were walking in pilgrimage to Hebron with the Pope, his Jewish and Muslim clergy colleagues, and the Nobel laureates we had met at the Vatican. Leading the procession were our brother Sami, an Indigenous Lakota youth leader, Greta Thunberg and Fridays for Future, the Earth Guardians, Emma Gonzales and the March for our Lives, Malala, Youth for the Ganges, and our *Follow the Young*, with Little Julie grinning on her donkey.

As floods and tornadoes hit the Americas, typhoons raged across Japan, forest fire disasters consumed the news cycles from the US to Indonesia and Congo, from Siberia to the Amazon—amidst global pandemics, wars, and endless social unrest—here was a critical mass of humans generating good and surprising news from the most unlikely city on the planet. Probably the last time we heard good news coming directly from Jerusalem *El Quds*[1] was during the reign of King Solomon in his forty years of peace, about 2,800 years ago. His

[1] Al Quds: "The holy" in Arabic.

revolutionary ideas about religious freedom were evident in the different coexisting temples to the local goddesses and the desert God of the freed Hebrew slaves coming from Sinai, who were simultaneously celebrated and worshiped in peace at that time in Jerusalem.

As the media kept reporting on new famous celebrities arriving, the pilgrims marched on, eventually landing at the Cave of the Machpelah, the Ibrahimi Mosque. Amid Byzantine Christian, Mameluque, and Ottoman Muslim architecture and Hebrew, Arabic, and Latin inscriptions, the best of Abraham's family came alive. According to the Biblical story, Abraham had paid Hebron the Hittite four hundred shekels to buy the cave for his family burial grounds. The last letter of the Hebrew alphabet is the "tav," which equals four hundred and represents, among other things, the gate of death according to *gematria*, or Kabbalistic numerology.

Four thousand people, mostly Palestinians and Israelis, were arranged in the outer courtyards of the cave in concentric spiraling circles. Inside, four hundred people, mostly from Hebron and the surrounding area, took their positions in Isaac's Hall. The actual graves of the patriarchs and matriarchs were said to be under the hall. An uncanny breeze impregnated the space with the sweet smell of the primordial Garden, which legend says comes from an actual covered hole in the ground.

The military police had given us the precise borders for our spiral and had set a limit on how many people could enter the cave. We set the outer circle at the cave's border so we could still all form a circle together. Within the inner circle of four hundred, there was yet another circle of forty elders and artists representing Oceania (Aboriginal, Māori and Pacific Islanders), Africa (Morocco, Ethiopia, South Africa, Senegal), Asia (India, China, Indonesia, Iran and the Philippines), Europe (Russia, Germany, Turkey, Greece, Sami, Basque, and Kurdish), Turtle Island (Lakota and Hopi), Mesoamerica (Maya and Huichol), as well as representatives from Amazonia, Mapuche, Aymara and Kogi. Rounding out the circle were the Nobel Laureates Malala, Perez Esquivel, the Dalai Lama, Mary Robinson, the Pope, and local spiritual and religious leaders. A group of fashion models interspersed within the elders, dressed in full regalia representing all the species of creation and guilds of humanity. After the guests of honor were seated, the models meandered through the cave for all to see. They were a resplendent plethora of color: blue, green, red, and black, mothers holding babies, shoemakers, divers, and garbage collectors.

We had created a set of movements and a lexicon of sounds, which we taught inside the cave and through large screens Vasilis had devised for everyone outside. It was also being broadcast through mainstream and social media. We had developed and spread our "flash mob healing language" online via the holographic map app, which was available in publicity campaigns and through the NGOs and social, political, and religious alliances who had endorsed our "Direct Spirit Action."

Our collective choreography ignited the ceremony as everyone took their place. We had three different collective moves and sounds, which set the sonic and emotional field supporting the soloists' singing of their specific trauma and their healed version of it. The language we had was simple and eloquent. The finger snap had come out of our days in Crete diving underwater together as one. Our friend Tiokasin had taught us the collective hum in tandem with the heart hug. The collective clap functioned as the transition and cue to begin our song. These three actions all had different cues signaled by "sound guides" who were spread throughout the spiral, making sure everyone was on time. Together they created a deep presence, a fertile ceremonial ground and safe space for the soloists to voice their painful litanies and healing prayers.

The ceremony at the Double Cave would be a micro dose of the Jerusalem ceremony. The ceremony in the cave was *below* ground, under the mainstream version of patriarchal his-tory, and the other, in Jerusalem, was at the *heart of the matter*.

First came the finger snap as people settled in their spot, giving them a moment to center, attune their intention, and check out who was to their left and who was to their right. Even the Pope and Malala were finger-snapping in the second concentric circle together with the Dalai Lama. By the time the powerful collective hum began, overwhelming chills and tremors were traveling along my spine. The kinetic and vocal sequence traveled in a spiral from the innermost circle in the cave to the outermost circle in the city of Hebron and back! Mona was so excited she kept squishing my hand. As the hum reverberated inside the cave, those in the inner circle each said their names and their peoples of origin in their own languages. As the hum continued, the three main local religious leaders at the cave offered short blessings in Arabic, Latin and Hebrew. Then the first Palestinian soloist from the innermost circle around the grave of Abraham started singing a litany over the collective hum: an eyewitness depiction of the twenty-nine people massacred by Rabbi Baruch Goldstein in that same cave in February 1994.

A torrent of collective tears gushed forth, born of our shared grief at the cave in the Old City of El Halil. At that crucial moment, I suddenly had to pee urgently. It wasn't easy to disentangle from the circle and leave without breaking the energy, but I was glad I made it out for a moment. There were concentric circles of people as far as I could see. At the gate of the cave, Ronaldinho and Karim Abdul Jabbar were holding guard like cherubs with flaming swords guarding the entrance of Eden, and through them, all the sports lovers in the world were with us. We felt protected.

As I was coming out of the cave and trying to get through the crowd, Gena pulled me aside. She had just enough time to tell me that the word had gone out globally. There were by now at least one million people gathered around Jerusalem, and hundreds more flights and buses full of people were arriving in Jerusalem for the big ceremony. As I managed my way back into the cave, the sound guides were playing the crowd, and our gigantic spiral was relaying the three moves and sounds all the way from its origin to its tail. After this was the next collective trauma-holder, this time from the Jewish Israeli side—someone who'd had his whole family massacred in Hebron in 1929. While the soloist sang and everyone kept humming, each one of us raised our right hand and placed it on our heart. Then we placed our left hand behind the heart of the person to our left. We were holding our own and each other's hearts. The multitudes of participants were becoming one organism going through an initiatory ancestral soul surgery.

As the soloist ended with a clear reference to the healed image of the traumatic story he had just sung, we kept the collective humming alive. From there, we joined in a clapping call and response, then sang a song that everyone had learned to sing that day, led by Baaba Maal and a Pakistani Qawwali master who was accompanying the chorus with his harmonium. Of course, Mona and I joined in:

Remember us for Life Great Mystery of Life
Inscribe us into Life Majestic Breath of Life
For You my Love for You my Life
Are Everywhere in Everyone
Everywhere in Everyone!

It was time for the concluding children's prayer at the gate of the Garden of Eden. Little Julie and a couple of Palestinian and Jewish Israeli children bowed down and reached with their noses to smell together, under Isaac's grave, the sweet fragrance of the Garden from below. Kneeling, they invoked their prayer for Life. Everyone ended up yet again in our signature heart hug, our spiral connected from an unknown mysterious origin to an endless end.

CHAPTER 13

AS BELOW, SO ABOVE

AFTER THE groundbreaking two-hour ceremony, everyone seemed radically shaken as Ronaldinho and Kareem Abdul Jabbar entered the cave to announce the all-star soccer match in Jerusalem. Teddy Stadium was packed and ready for it. At the Sultan's Pool, everything was in place for the procession after the game as the celebrities and the rainbow brigades took their positions holding guard at each of the eight gates of the Old City.

It was almost noon when we left the cave. Max, Clemens, Vasilis and "the hologram kids" had outdone themselves with memes of all colors careening through the sky. An ultra-organic light show had taken over the heavens, offering spatial beauty outbursts of orange and purple inscribed with the words *"Organize at the speed of trust."* Messages of deep peace, fierce justice, and joy emanated from the clouds on gigantic kites: *"Justice is what love looks like in public"*[1] and *"La fiesta de la siesta"*—a new version of de-growth, a massive outburst of rest and replenishment, a transformation from human "doings" to human "beings" as I had heard Tiokasin say countless times. These enormous bubbles of inspiration perforated the daily worry of passersby looking up. Solar hot air balloons fertilized the skies of El Quds with colorful messages. *"Surprise reality until it changes."* An intricate hologram of heavenly and earthly Jerusalem, inspired by our friend Daniel from the Old City, glistened and dangled in mid-air as white doves were being released into freedom from its eight gates. As

[1] "Justice is what love looks like in public": quote from Cornel West.

below in the cave, so above in the astonishingly new-born friendly skies of Jerusalem.

The Old City had been closed off for all public and private transportation. No comings or goings, no cars, buses or taxis. Only pedestrians were allowed in, and only hospital staff, ambulances, firefighters, and security officers were on duty in the city.

Camels, horses, and bicycles were parked and standing still. It felt nourishing and grounding to meet on the way with my old buddies Tiokasin and Sami in the midst of the excitement within the masses.

"Habibi! Wow!" Sami said. "Enjoying this? It's all happening."

"So good to see you," I replied, thrilled. "Thanks for everything."

"Are the birds enjoying this?" Tiokasin asked. "Are the trees and the winds into this?" We all three seemed to agree as we smiled widely to each other, then parted company, each one to his place in the plot. Earth was with us.

As the Pope, Ronaldinho, and Messi landed with a transparent solar helicopter on the stadium's turf, all the other players—amongst them Zanetti, our dear Ibrahim, Ronaldo, Zidane, Salah, Higuita, and Di Maria—were ready to start the game. It lasted forty minutes: fifteen minutes for each half and a ten-minute break in the middle. After the fantastic, upbeat catwalk led by octogenarians Catherine Deneuve and Jane Fonda at halftime, we got breathtaking news during the game's second half: more than half of the police in charge of security, encouraged by Emma Gonzales's March for our Lives, had pledged not to wear their firearms at the ceremonial event. They had heard the call to act as an example for humanity, practice nonviolence, and become a "please force" (as I heard Bernie Glassman say) instead. Israeli and Palestinian authorities, and the *waqf*[2] responsible for the

---

[2] *Waqf*: The Jerusalem Islamic Waqf is an Islamic religious trust (sometimes called an "Islamic Religious Endowments" organization) best known for controlling and managing the current Islamic edifices on and around the Temple Mount in the Old City of Jerusalem, including the Al-Aqsa Mosque and the Dome of the Rock. Some form or another of the waqf has governed access to Haram al-Sharif since the Muslim reconquest of the Kingdom of Jerusalem in 1187, with the latest version instituted by the Hashemite Kingdom of Jordan after its conquest and occupation of the West Bank and East Jerusalem during the 1948 war. Accordingly, the King of Jordan currently supplies all the funding needed to operate the waqf, which is in effect the civil administration for the holy site.

area, concurred in a decision to open the holy "Haram al-Sharif" for all, surprising the world.

Youth grassroots groups, the Nap Ministry, and child brigades began performing mass *siesta* events, resting celebrations, and slowing down happenings around our beautiful planet. They declared the massive launching of a global de-growth campaign, undermining at its root the fallacy of the GDP as the measurement of thriving life for all creatures and human happiness. With uncanny synchronicity, we heard that an alliance of mayors from major metropolises around the world had announced the "re-wilding" of their cities. The first big news came from New York. Central Park would be expanded tenfold for massive edible forest and vegetable gardens from which the population could eat for free. Rainwater retention spaces and the cleaning of the water sources had already begun. Wild animals were expected to return.

Meanwhile, in Jerusalem, the surprising, unannounced messages raining from the heavens seemed to be working as thousands of people were looking up and breaking down in tears of joy right there in the streets. The peaceful sky parade for global systemic change was disrupting reality and igniting our future ancient story.

As the game ended, a big message lit up the sky right above the stadium. It began gliding through the clouds just as the first ones made their way towards the Old City, passing through the Sultan's Pools. It twinkled phosphorescent, a blend of watery fire:

Peacemaking doesn't mean passivity. It is the act of interrupting injustice without mirroring injustice, the act of disarming evil without crushing the evildoer, the act of finding a third way that is neither fight nor flight, but the careful, arduous pursuit of reconciliation and justice. It is about a revolution of Love that is big enough to set both the oppressed and the oppressors free.[3]

---

[3] Quote by Shane Claiborne, from *Common Prayer: A Liturgy for Ordinary Radicals*.

CHAPTER 14

THE HEART OF THE MATTER

THE NUMBER of people who had shown up in Jerusalem was astronomical. By the time the main procession reached the gates of the Old City of Jerusalem, the modest police calculations had surpassed one million people. Children were still savoring the message-balloons that had fallen from the skies, which tasted like passionfruit and vanilla.

The event was being transmitted live and simultaneously by nearly all international media, online channels, mainstream TV, and radio stations. At each gate of the Old City, a celebrity stood guard in tandem with a human guild representative—making it safe, visible, and accessible for paparazzi from around the world to capture the moment. Brigades of breastfeeding mothers, lawyers, actors, fashion models, sports people, musicians, astronauts, chefs, scientists, poets, movie makers, shoemakers, and garbage collectors joined forces to create a field of peace and splendor in Jerusalem, magically disrupting business as usual. This was a moment to behold: a critical mass focusing on spirit, body, emotional and cultural healing, applying synchronized acupuncture on Jerusalem, together.

As the spirit guards remained firm at the eight gates of Jerusalem, the spiral of humans began forming once again, now around the walls of the Old City, inside and around the three holy sites, filling one square kilometer including Haram al-Sharif, the Wailing Wall, and The Holy Sepulcher Church. Māori Haka warriors and Hawaiian hula dancers ignited the ceremony into trance, and the dances began to impregnate and re-wild Jerusalem. This was the cue for the Nobel laureates, the Original Peoples Elders, the representatives of the three local religions, and six new soloists— two Palestinian, two Israeli, and two children—to begin. The sound and choreography guides and the guild brigades spread across these million people. This time, tens of thousands in the inner concentric circles already knew the drill. They had learned the basic movements, sounds, and the heart hug.

More than a million spiraled humans snapped their fingers at once.

It was as if, with their sound, they were breaking through the cracks of a six-thousand-year-old spell. They clapped the song without words, finally humming together as cross-pollinators of collective trauma, composting it into a culture of regenerative spontaneity. The whole spiral supported the soloists as we held each other's hearts, all the way from the temple mount to the last of the bystanders on the outskirts of the old city of Jerusalem.

At the Holy Sepulcher, a stork showed up. Remember the ones who came with the camels, all the way from Somalia? It kidnapped the skullcap from the Pope's head, making everyone laugh, and dropped it with its beak to land smack in the hands of the Amazonian chief. Pope Francis kneeled in front of the chief, surprising everyone including me, Tiokasin, and our dear Lakota elder friends. Then, in an uncanny move, while down on his knees in front of the Indigenous chiefs, he asked for fire. The Imam next to him provided him with a lighter. The Pope materialized an ancient parchment from his pocket robe, read its title out loud—and burnt to ashes the original document of the *Doctrine of Discovery*.

In tears, he recalled the crusades and the inquisition, declared them abominable, and ecstatically pronounced the official end of missionary Christianity. Finally, prostrating on the grave of Jesus, he apologized in the name of the Church and Western monotheistic civilization, and proclaimed 90 percent of all the lands owned by the Vatican to return to the stewardship of the Indigenous people. The elders and youth of the Lakota and the Mapuche, the Hopi and the Huichol, the Maya, the Australian Aboriginal, the Sami, the Maori, the San from South

Africa, the Inohuetes, and the Pacific Islanders helped the Pope stand up and surrounded him from all sides, forming a circle.

Rejoicing, they led the Pope and the dance procession through the narrow streets of ancient and sacred Jerusalem. West African dances, Lakota dances, Taoist dances, Mapuche dances, Hopi dances, Sami dances, all accompanied him to the center of Haram al-Sharif. There, the Israeli rabbi and Palestinian imam joined hands with the Pope and Amazonian chief. The chief offered a coconut from the Amazon rainforest for them to drink from, inviting them to Amazonia as his guests to co-create a similar kind of ceremony in support of Life on this planet.

Then it began to rain! Jerusalem smelled like the Queen of Sheba's hair after a ceremonial bath. Sweet and fresh aromas—a blend of cedar, palo santo, baobab, sage, frankincense, myrrh, sandalwood, vanilla, and cinnamon—impregnated the wind. The rabbi, imam, pope, and chief drank from the same cup, fertilized by raindrops. They raised the chalice in a toast together and declared, "From the four corners of the Earth, we have come to witness, heal, and celebrate Jerusalem!" The youth ended with a prayer song, and everyone joined in for the chorus:

Love and Truth Met
Justice and Peace Kissed.

Then Little Julie proclaimed: "Jerusalem shall be called, from now on, 'The Inheritance of Peace and Wholeness': a global peace sanctuary for all peoples to remind human beings that a new way of living in peace with Earth and all her creatures is possible." After she finished, the Dalai Lama, Amma Ji, and Malala planted a baby tree that had grown from one of Musallem's Sinai seeds in the center of the Temple Mount as custodians for this ancient, renewed, and re-sacralized Life sanctuary. The Amazonian chief poured the last remaining coconut water on the tree as Jerusalem, the rain, and the Great Hoop of Life celebrated. *Shofarot*, horns, conchs, *zurnas, shenais* and trumpets sounded off in wild splendor! The drumbeats, dancing, and rejoicing reigned throughout the hills of Jerusalem. Myriads of choreographies and ancient chants and prayers, as different as the cultures of people gathering in the Old City, sparkled as diverse as Oneness. The gigantic screens were streaming to social, local and international media, showing images from the past weeks and days: horses from the north, camels from the south, boats from the west, and walkers from the east. Snippets and videoclips of the "beyond grief ceremony" went viral, first on screens in Jerusalem, then on the news and social media. The shadow was being seen. Pain had been given a space, and healing was pouring into the crack.

Had human beauty and eloquence impressed the Gods, the Divine Mother, the Angels, the Ancestors, the Earth? Was it enough? Was this the last human poem, our last attempt in trying to remember our role in the Sacred Whole?

Whatever the answer was, the vital prophetic buzz had spread worldwide.

We spent the next couple of days in the apartment at Ein Karem, excited and exhausted. The whole crew was together for the last time in that constellation, downloading and uploading press, memes, laughter, and documentation from around the world. Stories began to emerge about the "Sacred Agents" from all peoples and all directions who'd arrived in Jerusalem, risking it all in joy for an act of beauty, for a love affair with Life, with the Earth.

Would the melody of the miracle be exquisite enough? Was our piercing action authentic? Would it be effective enough to divert and divest from all conditioned responses, entrenched in the robust defense mechanisms of Reality? Could fierce beauty, wild love and radical humor shift the morphic field? Could it ripple and reverberate strong enough to dismantle the rules and agreements that held our universe together in unjust illusion and separation throughout most of our world for the past seven thousand years?

It sounds like a ton of time, but considering we've already been here for hundreds of thousands of years…it might just be possible.

EPILOGUE

THE OLD story is crumbling and the new one hasn't yet clearly emerged. Grounded in uncertainty, the border closures, the pandemics, the global unrest, the wars, the heavy weight of daily life, the loneliness.

Back down from the mountain, from scouting with the Global Clans in new alliances, dancing to the dawn of a renewed ancient family. Where to go?

Still, with a Message
Too Young to Pronounce
and too Sacred to Forget.

Two indispensable roles to embody during the current waves of collapse and rebirth: hospice caregivers for our dying story and midwives of the new story.

Embracing the paradox.

Geographical doubts. Where to park my life? Community questions.

Too early to answer.

As natural and human-made disasters pop up these days with millions of victims all over our beautiful Earth, the "war culture" continues to crawl inside us every time we go back to our scary shenanigans, antique addictions, passé emotional elbows, and take our "selfie" drama too seriously. The body feels out of tune and aches in many different ways and places we thought we'd never meet.

So, where is our heart news, our creations, our new songs, our play, our new recipes, our lullabies, our lovers? Beyond the buzzwords of "systemic shift" and "regenerative culture," what do we see?

Yearning for the poetry of the miracle, for the overtones of mainstream reality to pierce our shells, right into the original will and instructions of our solar plexus. Where the lion roars drunk, in love with life, and friendship shines like a salad of a million emeralds, rubies, and malachite.

Hook your pupils to the elevator inside the passenger next to you and conspire. Invoking hunter-gatherers of the wind, shepherds of the clouds, like giraffes galloping in slow motion along your metatarsals.

The chant of the solar hot air balloon, the healing of re-ligion (re-linking) and science, the re-union of masculine and feminine, the human and the humus. The celebration of the Great Mystery and simplicity with all creatures. A sacred life shield made out of honey.

The secret for sustaining the circle-becoming-a spiral is free. The organization must be decentralized, loose, so loose that it holds. Just support and deliver the precise signal to the untidy spirit warrior at their weakest moment. The alliance will catch. It's sacred timing which will drum you closer to breath and the wholly playfulness of these letters being read by you.

SONGS FROM THE BOOK

 "One Being This"

 "Liminal Grace"

 "Shalom"

 "Skin of God"

 "Veahavta"

 "Rei - I'm a Mirror to You and You Are a Mirror Unto Me"

 "Wholly One"

 "Human" Bonus track—the dream about Bob Marley, Mother Teresa, and Nusrat Fateh Ali Khan and the vision of a *spirit security council* in Jerusalem was one of the main seeds for this book.

GABRIEL MEYER is a "radical flexitarian minstrel," musician, poet, and spiritual activist, born in Cordoba and raised in Buenos Aires, Argentina. The son of human rights champion and seminal disciple of A.J Heschel and Martin Buber, the late Rabbi Marshall T. Meyer and Naomi Meyer, co-creator of the Argentinian Jewish youth summer camp where Gabriel was born.

Upon his arrival to Israel/Palestine, Gabriel co-created the ritual theater collective "Metatron" (1994–2001) and initiated the Hebrew Holiday Gatherings (1997–2001) for the renewal of Hebrew wisdom and ritual, attended by over 1,500 participants.

At the outset of the second Intifada, he co-founded the Sulha Peace Project (2001) with the late Elias Jabbour and was its co-director until 2009. These gatherings and reconciliation programs for Palestinians, Israelis and internationals, adults, youth and children were attended by over 15000 participants.

Gabriel co-created the collaborative music albums *Merkavah* (2001) and *Hateva: Skin of God* (2008) with Amir Paiss, and Spiritisreal (2006). Gabriel has also released a solo album, *The Human Project* (2013). In 2021 he released the singles: "Liminal Grace" and "Rei Shirat Hael" (Mirror of the Divine Song).

His two self-published books of poetry in Spanish are entitled: *Cincuenta D'estos Para Empezar* (1990) "Fifty of These to Start With" and *Tribus de Pura Temperatura* (1995) "Tribes of Pure Temperature."

Gabriel was initiated into the "Order of Disorder" by the late Zen Roshi Bernie Glassman, and was ordained "a true representative of the Jewish People" by the late Rabbi Zalman Schachter Shalomi, Through his peace work he had the honor of the support, and a private audience with HH Dalai Lama. He is an active core member of the global alliance of spiritual activists "Defend the Sacred", which was inspired by Standing Rock and is currently based in NYC, caring for his dear mom.

www.ingramcontent.com/pod-product-compliance
Lightning Source LLC
Chambersburg PA
CBHW031139160426
43193CB00008B/194